BEYOND THE WAGE

Ordinary Work in Diverse Economies

Edited by
William Monteith, Dora-Olivia Vicol
and Philippa Williams

BRISTOL
UNIVERSITY
PRESS

First published in Great Britain in 2021 by

Bristol University Press
University of Bristol
1-9 Old Park Hill
Bristol
BS2 8BB
UK
t: +44 (0)117 954 5940
e: bup-info@bristol.ac.uk

Details of international sales and distribution partners are available at
bristoluniversitypress.co.uk

© Bristol University Press 2021

British Library Cataloguing in Publication Data
A catalogue record for this book is available from the British Library

ISBN 978-1-5292-0893-1 hardcover
ISBN 978-1-5292-0895-5 ePub
ISBN 978-1-5292-0894-8 ePdf

The right of William Monteith, Dora-Olivia Vicol and Philippa Williams to be identified as
editors of this work has been asserted by them in accordance with the Copyright, Designs and
Patents Act 1988.

Bristol University Press works to counter discrimination on grounds of gender,
race, disability, age and sexuality.

Cover design: Gareth Davies at Cube
Front cover image: GettyImages-180202370
Bristol University Press uses environmentally responsible print partners.
Printed and bound in Great Britain by CPI Group (UK) Ltd, Croydon, CR0 4YY

In dedication to David Graeber
(1961–2020) and all those he has
inspired to make the world differently

Contents

Part III Struggles

Part IV Possibilities

Acknowledgements

This book is the product of the type of generative conversations and exchanges that take place when academia is at its best. These conversations began on a sunny afternoon at Queen Mary University of London in the summer of 2018 before moving into pubs and pizza restaurants, digital forums and email chains. They took place among a group of interdisciplinary friends and colleagues committed to asking different types of questions about 'work', including Claudia Strauss, Tatiana Thieme, Mechthild von Vacano, Patrick Bottazzi, Sabin Bieri, Louise Waite, Nithya Natarajan, Andrea Weiss, Marco Di Nunzio, Asiya Islam, Kavita Ramakrishnan, Harry Pettit, Sam Strong, Liz Fouksman, Emil Dauncey, Michele Lancione, Annemiek Prins, Francisco Calafate-Faria, Smita Yadav, Vinzenz Bäumer Escobar, Lizzie Richardson, Al James, Frederick Harry Pitts, Illana Gershon, Kate Hardy, Kavita Datta, Lorena Lombardozzi, Vincent Guermond and Theo Barry-Born. Some contributed a chapter to the book, while others contributed through their feedback, scholarship and support. Our thanks to you all.

We are grateful to the Institute for the Humanities and Social Sciences at QMUL for funding the workshop that inspired the book. Finally, we would like to thank the anonymous reviewers and the team at Bristol University Press for their generous support. We couldn't have hoped for a better home for the project.

Notes on Contributors

Vinzenz Bäumer Escobar obtained his PhD from Utrecht University, the Netherlands on the everyday construction of alternative economic formations in Catalonia. His research lies at the crossroads of political and economic anthropology, with a particular focus on (the future of) work, sovereignty, the performativity of the economy, and the commons. Vinzenz is currently employed as a postdoctoral researcher at University of Oslo, Norway in the ERC project PORTS, which examines the shifting nature of the global economy through labour transformations and capital accumulation in port cities.

Katherine Brickell is Professor of Human Geography at Royal Holloway, University of London, UK. She is editor of the journal *Gender, Place and Culture* and is former Chair of the RGS–IBG Gender and Feminist Geographies Research Group. Katherine's feminist-oriented research cross-cuts social, political, development and legal geography, with a long-standing focus on the domestic sphere as a precarious space of contemporary everyday life. Katherine has published multiple co-edited collections which speak to her connected interests in home (un)making, displacement and (im)mobilities, including *Translocal Geographies* (2011 with Ayona Datta), *Geographies of Forced Eviction* (2017 with Melissa Fernández Arrigoitia and Alex Vasudevan) and *The Handbook of Displacement* (2021 with RHUL colleagues). Katherine's monograph *Home SOS: Gender, Violence and Survival in Crisis Ordinary Cambodia* (Wiley RGS–IBG Book Series, 2020) focuses on the survival work of living with, and on from, domestic violence and forced eviction.

Hannah J. Dawson is a Postdoctoral Research Fellow at the Society, Work and Politics Institute (SWOP), University of the Witwatersrand, Johannesburg, South Africa. Her research interests focus on youth marginality and unemployment, the future of work, and more expansive forms of social protection, with a special focus on South Africa. She recently published an article entitled 'Labour, laziness and distribution: work imaginaries among the South African unemployed' (co-authored with E. Fouksman) in *Africa* (2020). Hannah is currently working on a manuscript provisionally entitled 'Beyond the job: emerging forms of work and life in urban South Africa', which explores young men's everyday experiences of unemployment, and the ways in which unemployment is shaping economic, social and political life in contemporary South Africa.

E. Fouksman is Lecturer at the Centre for Public Policy Research at King's College London, UK and a Research Associate at the Society, Work and Politics Institute (SWOP) at the University of the Witwatersrand Johannesburg, South Africa. Liz's research interests revolve around perceptions of work, deservingness and the redistribution of wealth, particularly in southern Africa, as well as the politics and theory of post-work and universal basic income. Recent publications include 'The Moral Economy of Work' in *Economy and Society* (2020), and, with Hannah Dawson, 'Labour, Laziness and Distribution' in *Africa* (2020).

Asiya Islam is the Joyce Lambert Research Fellow at Newnham College, University of Cambridge, UK. She is a sociologist and ethnographer interested in gender, class and labour. Her research explores the lives of young women in urban India in the context of contemporary socio-economic change. Her PhD (2019) from the University of Cambridge focused on the experiences of young lower middle class women working between cafes, call centres, malls and offices in the service economy of New Delhi.

William Monteith is Lecturer in the School of Geography at Queen Mary University of London, UK. He obtained his PhD at the School of International Development at the University of East Anglia, UK in 2016 based on an ethnographic study of socio-economic life in a central marketplace in Kampala, Uganda. Will is interested in the question of what it means to work in contexts in which people's labour is not valued by the state or capitalist economy. His research documents experiences of work – or 'make do' – at the margins of formal economies; the politics and places produced by these experiences; and the ways in which they challenge theories of work and economy based on the historical experiences of advanced capitalist societies in the global North.

Nithya Natarajan is Lecturer in International Development at King's College, London, UK. Her work explores processes of rural–urban transition, shifting relations of labour, and the impacts of, and resistance to, ongoing climate and environmental change in India and Cambodia. She is currently Co-Investigator of a GCRF-funded project exploring microfinance and nutrition through a gendered lens in Cambodia and South India. Nithya's latest publications include 'Diffuse Drivers of Modern Slavery: From Microfinance to Unfree Labour in Cambodia's Brick Kilns' (*Development and Change*, 2020) and a forthcoming co-edited volume, *Climate in the Global Workplace: Labour, Adaptation and Resistance*, published with Routledge.

Mara Nogueira is Lecturer in Urban Geography at Birkbeck, University of London, UK. She is an urban geographer with a PhD in Human Geography and Urban Studies from the LSE, UK. Her research focuses on socio-spatial inequality and the urban politics of urban space production in Brazil. Mara's current work looks at the relationships between the popular economy and urban space, exploring the multiscalar geographies and socio-political repercussions of the labour crisis. Her work has been published by journals such as *Urban Studies* (2020) and the *International Journal of Urban and Regional Research* (2019).

Laurie Parsons is Lecturer in Human Geography at Royal Holloway, University of London, UK. His work examines the contested politics of climate change on socio-economic inequalities, patterns of work and mobilities. Strongly committed to policy engagement, Laurie has conducted large-scale projects examining inequalities in Cambodia's economic development for Transparency International, Plan International, Save the Children, CARE International, ActionAid, the IDRC and the Royal University of Phnom Penh, among others. His first book, *Going Nowhere Fast: Mobile Inequality in the Age of Translocality* was published by Oxford University Press in 2020.

Annemiek Prins is Postdoctoral Researcher with the Department of Anthropology and Development Studies at the Radboud University of Nijmegen in the Netherlands. She completed her PhD with the University of Aberdeen, UK focusing on cycle-rickshaw drivers in Dhaka, Bangladesh. Her doctoral dissertation, 'Unfixing the City: Rickshaw Mobilities, Modernities and Urban Change in Dhaka', explores different aspects of contemporary urbanism, including mobility, informal labour, peripheral urbanization and urban modernity. Annemiek is currently developing a new research project that looks at the construction of the Padma Bridge in Bangladesh and focuses on the intersections between urbanization, infrastructure and climate change within a riverine context.

Claudia Strauss is Professor of Anthropology at Pitzer College, Claremont, California, USA. Her research includes culture theory (*A Cognitive Theory of Cultural Meaning*, co-authored with Naomi Quinn, Cambridge University Press, 1997) and cultural models of public policy in the United States (*Making Sense of Public Opinion: American Discourses about Immigration and Social Programs*, Cambridge University Press, 2012). She is currently completing a book about unemployed Americans' work meanings (*Beyond the Puritan Work Ethic: Diverse Meanings of Not Working in America*).

Samuel Strong is Junior Research Fellow at Homerton College, University of Cambridge, UK. His research lies at the intersection of urban, cultural and political geography, with a specific interest in contemporary poverty and inequality in the UK. Samuel has been published in a range of popular and academic forums, including the journals *Transactions of the Institute of British Geographers*, *Political Geography* and *Geoforum*.

Tatiana Thieme is an urban ethnographer and Associate Professor in Human Geography at University College London, UK. With field sites in Nairobi, Paris, Berlin and London, the thread running across Tatiana's research is a preoccupation with the geographies of work within, alongside and outside the insecure wage, and the everyday coping strategies of individuals cut off from formal institutional support in precarious urban environments. Recent articles related to this book chapter feature in *Progress in Human Geography* (on 'the hustle economy', 2018), *Social and Cultural Geography* (on 'planning working futures' outside of prison, 2018), and the *Journal of the British Academy* (on 'refugees as new Europeans', 2020).

Dora-Olivia Vicol is an anthropologist with a long-standing interest in justice and mobility. She co-founded the employment rights charity the Work Rights Centre in 2016, while still a doctoral candidate at the University of Oxford, UK. Straddling the worlds of academia and third sector work ever since, Olivia's research documents Eastern European migrants' encounters with bureaucracy, employers and the migration industry.

Mechthild von Vacano is Doctoral Researcher at the Institute of Social and Cultural Anthropology, Freie Universität Berlin, Germany. Her doctoral research is a 17-month ethnographic study on the subjective experience of work in a South Jakartan neighbourhood in Indonesia. Her previous involvement in an Indonesian-German research project on the 2008 Bantul earthquake and post-disaster coping resulted in the co-edited volume *Cultural Psychology of Coping with Disasters* (Springer, 2014).

Philippa Williams is Reader in Human Geography at Queen Mary University of London, UK. Her research intersects political, digital and development geography, with a focus on everyday digital-political life in India and its transnational community. Her publications have examined how the state is experienced, how citizenship is articulated and how marginality, particularly in the context of violence/nonviolence, is lived and increasingly mediated by 'the digital'. Philippa's monograph *Everyday Peace?: Politics, Citizenship and Muslim Lives in India* (Wiley RGS-IBG Book Series, 2015) examines practices of peace and the political through the everyday work lives of weavers and traders in the silk sari industry in Varanasi, India.

Introduction: Work Beyond the Wage

William Monteith, Dora-Olivia Vicol and Philippa Williams

> We need to be careful with how we use the term *work* –
> since its definition affects how we imagine future worlds.
> Shaw and Waterstone (2020, 108)

When we hear of 'work', it is usually of the type particular to industrial capitalism. Governments rarely speak of the work of hustling, child-rearing or subsistence farming, or single out the 'hard work' of hustlers, parents or smallholders. Instead, work generally is referred to in the narrowly economistic and legalistic sense; as 'non-domestic, paid, legally codified, institutionalised and socially safeguarded employment' (Komlosy, 2018, 8). Many of the concepts we have to describe work – 'informal', 'precarious', 'decent' – are constructed against this ideal type.

Yet this model of work is a historical and geographical exception. Recent developments in the social and spatial organization of production have facilitated the decline of wage employment in many regions of the world (Beck, 2000; Standing, 2011; Breman and van der Linden, 2014). Historical forms of precarious work have been accompanied by more recent waves of casualization, leaving a growing proportion of the workforce flexible, poor and devoid of the protections associated with the standard employment relationship. At the same time, digital technologies have facilitated the emergence of new forms of precarious (self-) employment in the burgeoning 'gig economy' (Wood et al, 2018). The resultant proliferation of 'wageless life' (Denning,

2010) poses a number of challenges to the ways in which citizens, researchers and governments think about 'work'.

Reflecting on these challenges, Franco Barchiesi argues there is a growing 'mismatch between the official imagination of work' and 'its ordinary material experiences' (2011, 21). This mismatch is evident, for example, when governments cite low unemployment rates as evidence of economic prosperity. However, it is also evident when researchers and activists seek to 'formalize' diverse livelihood activities across different regions of the world. Such 'wage work-related melancholia' (Barchiesi, 2011, 246) limits opportunities for critical self-reflection and forecloses alternative futures in which work, identity and security might be woven together differently. By clinging on to the 'phantom limb' of wage employment (Gorz, 1999, 58), we are left only with a politics of cruel optimism (Berlant, 2011).

This collection proposes to revitalize debates on (the future of) work by de-centring theories of wage employment in order to examine the multitude of ways in which work is imagined and practised in different regions of the world. It brings together an interdisciplinary group of researchers committed to thinking through the question of work from multiple 'elsewheres' – from Bangladeshi garages to Brazilian markets; Cambodian brick kilns to Catalonian cooperatives. How is 'work' imagined and practised within wage-scarce economies? What types of aspirations and demands do the people carrying out this work articulate? How might these aspirations unsettle taken-for-granted ideas in the literature on work, and what alternative projects might they bring to the fore? We came together at Queen Mary University of London in the summer of 2018 to explore these questions, united by James Ferguson and Tania Li's call for a 'profound analytical decentering' of wage employment as a 'presumed norm' (2018, 1).

Provincializing the wage

Feminist and postcolonial theorists have demonstrated the ways in which dominant discourses – such as 'commodification' (Gibson-Graham, 1996) and the 'Third World' (Escobar, 1995) – reproduce regimes of truth that position certain populations at the forefront of 'development' and 'progress' and confine others to the 'waiting room of history' (Chakrabarty, 2000, 8). We contend that the discourse of wage employment imposes a similarly restrictive order on debates on work, foreclosing alternative experiences and possibilities. There is thus an urgent need to provincialize the wage by tracing the ways in which contemporary conceptualizations of work 'bear the burden of European thought and history' (Chakrabarty, 2000, 4).

Wage employment is a relatively recent invention that dates back to the attempts of European states to establish markets for labour during the Industrial Revolution (or 'great transformation') of the eighteenth and nineteenth centuries (Polanyi, 1944). The creation of 'employment' as a legal artefact legitimated the process through which a person ('employee') could sell their labour power to a consumer ('employer'); normalizing subservience through the 'fiction' of an equitable exchange between two consenting parties (Polanyi, 1944). Employment was subsequently elevated above all other forms of work to assume the mythical status it now occupies in our politics and imagination (Shaw and Waterstone, 2020, 110). Rather than being performed by a family in the field, workshop or household, 'work' was now understood to be carried out almost exclusively by waged men in factories, creating the myth of the able-bodied male 'breadwinner' (Ferguson, 2015). The discourse of wage employment thus created a site of struggle through which groups of predominantly white, male workers in Western Europe and North America were able to obtain a minimum wage, paid leave, and the right to rest and retirement. However, it also served to eject other value-generating activities from the formal economic sphere, relegating them to the status of the 'domestic', the 'informal' and/or the 'subsistent'.

This new understanding of work as wage employment was exported to other regions of the world through the project of European colonialism. Achille Mbembe writes of the ways in which European colonial powers used wage labour as a tool to discipline indigenous populations 'with the aim of making better use of them' (2001, 113). The salary was a resource with which the colonial state sought to 'buy obedience and gratitude' in the context of systematic dispossession (2001, 45). It came to symbolize an enduring opposition between those included in and those excluded from the fruits of the colonial economy (Fanon, 1963). For the vast majority of those subjected to colonial rule, wage employment stood for 'alienation, disintegration of communities, violation of personhood, and the ultimate denial of meaningful activity' (Barchiesi, 2011, 250). Understood this way, the refusal of the wage in much of the postcolonial world forms part of a longer history of anti-colonial resistance.

By the turn of the twentieth century, wage employment had been embedded into state administrations, legal codes and 'the political imagination of the labour movement itself' (Komlosy, 2018, 3). When labour organizations called for full employment, they reinforced a singular understanding of work as wage labour. When women's movements called for full inclusion into the labour force, they also contributed to the consolidation of this idea. Furthermore, when national liberation parties attempted to indigenize the labour force, they adopted this notion of work from their colonial oppressors (Komlosy, 2018, 16). No matter their political differences, politicians were united in their celebration of wage earning (Barchiesi, 2011, 250).

Yet this model of work remained accessible only to a global minority. Even at the apex of the Industrial Revolution in Western Europe, people's lives continued to be shaped by a broad range of socio-economic activities, including crafting, householding and subsistence agriculture (Komlosy, 2018). Meanwhile, working life in the majority world continued to be characterized by subsistence agriculture, forced labour and slavery, generating the supply of cheap raw materials necessary to sustain the new labour markets in Europe (Bhattacharyya, 2018; Pettinger, 2019). One of the contemporary legacies of the piecemeal project of capitalist modernization in the postcolonial world is a so-called 'surplus population' that has been expelled from agricultural systems of production but not incorporated into the waged workforce (Li, 2010; Ferguson, 2015).

Today, a global majority (61 per cent) make a living outside of formal wage employment in the 'informal economy' (ILO, 2020). However, the discourse of employment continues to characterize this majority through notions of deviance; as informal workers, 'dangerous classes' (Standing, 2011) and 'wasted lives' (Bauman, 2003). Two implications emerge here. First, the diversity of actually existing forms of work in the world is homogenized and the value produced by this work obscured. Second, people making a living outside of wage employment – disproportionately women of colour in the global South – are excluded from debates on the future of work except in dystopian scenarios to be avoided (see, for example, Gorz, 1999; Beck, 2000).

The discourse of wage employment thus stops us from asking important questions about the forms of value produced by people subsisting outside of wage employment, impoverishing debates on (the future of) work. As Ian Shaw and Marv Waterstone (2020, 70) argue:

> The repertoires and improvisations that make everyday life possible for those outside of waged work might provide key insight for new forms of production, reproduction and social

relations to replace the present (but rapidly disappearing) arrangements – even if these alternate forms are now often produced in brutal and exigent circumstances.

There is therefore an urgent need to rethink 'work' from the perspective of the global majority for whom wage employment is not the norm. This collection represents the start of such a project. Following Williams (2007, 3), we adopt a 'kaleidoscopic view' in which there are no universal logics but instead many fragments moving in different directions which serve to open up – rather than tie down – debates on the future of work. Individually, the chapters trace the historical constitution of these activities within their particular social and political contexts, while paying attention to the gendered, classed and racialized ways in which they are experienced by the people who perform them. Collectively, these chapters challenge singular conceptualizations of 'work' and 'working life' and open up new possibilities for how work, identity and security might be co-constituted.

Conceptualizing work: three approaches

The task of provincializing the wage also requires us to historicize conventional understandings of work. In the following subsections, we provide an outline of three dominant ways of conceptualizing work and demonstrate the ways in which all three are constructed against a discourse of wage employment. We then make the case for an alternative conceptualization of 'ordinary work'.

Commodified work

A significant historical tradition conceptualizes work in terms of its relationship to capital. This tradition dates back to Karl Marx's observations of the working conditions of factory workers in Manchester in the nineteenth century. For Marx, the employment exchange is fundamentally exploitative insofar as it commoditizes labour in order to create more value for the employer (or capitalist). In other words, an employee is not permitted to control or keep the surplus value created by their own labour power ('the aggregate of mental and physical capabilities ... a human being sets in motion whenever they produce a use-value of any kind') ([1867] 1977, 270). The fundamental experience of employment is thus one of alienation, reducing relations among people to the status of relations among things.

This process of commodification ends only with the overthrow of capitalism by an organized movement of the workers.

Contemporary debates on the commodification of work have transcended the factory floor to focus on forms of domestic and forced labour inspired by works of Marxist feminism (Federici, 1975; Mies, 1986) and racial capitalism (Robinson, 1983; Bhattacharyya, 2018). This scholarship has done much to diversify our understandings of work beyond wage employment, based on the understanding that the history of work under capitalism is not one of universal proletarianization but of gendered and racialized differentiation, inspiring political movements including the Wages for Housework campaign and Black Panther Party. Nevertheless, there remains a productivist tendency within heterodox Marxism to reduce work to the use value of capitalism, foreclosing alternative experiences and imaginations (Gibson-Graham, 1996; Gidwani, 2008). As Jodi Melamed argues, 'the desire to have a materialist form of appearance ("value") for social forces as a whole everywhere motivates much of the rationalism, Eurocentrism, reductive materialism, and developmentalism, which limits Marxism's usefulness for decolonizing and anti-racist activism' (2015, 82). A singular emphasis on commodification thus stops us from asking important questions about the values, relations and subjectivities produced by non-commodified and partly-commodified forms of work in different regions of the world (Millar 2018, 8).

An alternative commodification thesis is provided by Karl Polanyi (1944). Drawing upon the contributions of a number of anthropological studies of non-Western cultures in the early twentieth century (Malinowski, 1922; Mauss, 1970 [1925]), Polanyi argued that the commodification of labour was a recent and historically rare phenomenon. Prior to the Industrial Revolution, the 'work' of human societies was structured around three interrelated activities: *householding*, *reciprocity* and *redistribution*. The market reforms of the eighteenth and nineteenth centuries caused significant disruption to these activities, however the reforms did not succeed in eradicating or disembedding them in the ways suggested by orthodox Marxism. Instead, for Polanyi, economic activity remained embedded in a broad range of institutions, including families, communities and congregations of faith. As market reforms pushed commodification, these institutions pushed back, forming a 'double movement' that produced different forms of work and organisation in different places. While retaining a Eurocentric distinction between 'economy' and 'society', Polanyi's intervention is helpful for pluralizing our understandings of work and the institutions that regulate it, inspiring broader approaches such as

J.K. Gibson-Graham's (2008) 'diverse economies'. The diverse economies framework understands all economies to be composed of *market, alternative market* and *non-market* transactions; of *waged, alternative paid* and *unpaid labour*. While feminist scholars have drawn attention to the significant contribution of unpaid labour – between 30 and 50 per cent of all economic activity in the world (Gibson-Graham, 2008) – less attention has been paid to the increasing significance of alternative paid work, including work in the so-called 'informal economy'.

Informal work

A second approach conceptualizes work in terms of its relationship to the state. In the early 1970s, the anthropologist Keith Hart (1973) coined the concept of the 'informal sector' (now broadened to the 'informal economy') to describe the livelihood activities of the thousands of people arriving in Ghanaian towns and cities in search of an income. The sector comprised all forms of work outside of the boundaries of state regulation, including 'legitimate' activities, such as petty commerce, personal services and home-based production, and 'illegitimate' activities, such as prostitution, pickpocketing and scavenging (Hart, 1973). In other words, forms of work that have a very long history. At the time of Hart's intervention, much of the development industry – including the World Bank and the International Labour Organization (ILO) – understood the informal sector as a 'backward' or 'traditional' realm of the economy in need of modernization. Informal work was portrayed as a problem insofar as it was illegible to the state, evading government accounting and quantification. The dominant policy prescription was thus to formalize the sector through the extension of regulation and taxation, accompanied by a shift to more capital-intensive forms of production capable of generating mythical wage employment.

Dualist conceptions of the informal sector have since come under substantial critique for invoking a marginal or traditional set of activities separate from the formal capitalist sector of the economy (Potts, 2008). For example, Tania Li has argued that the concept of 'informal work' is dangerous insofar as it feeds the 'transition narrative' through which it is assumed that those arriving in towns and cities will eventually be absorbed into the formal waged workforce (2017, 1250). An alternative, structuralist perspective instead conceives of 'informalisation' as a process through which employers in the formal sector seek to reduce wage costs and enhance flexibility by making use of unprotected workers (Meagher, 1995, 259). However, missing in both accounts is an acknowledgement of the historical origins of many of the types of work now described under the banner of the 'informal economy'. Indeed, the concept may be said to constitute an 'inverted mirror of others' reality' (Esteva, 2010, 2), which renders deviant entire sectors of economic activity that have long constituted the basis of the 'real' economy in much of the global South (MacGaffey, 1991; Simone and Pieterse, 2017). While the concept of informal work foregrounds the relationship between workers and the state – invoking an ideal model of legally codified, institutionalized and socially safeguarded employment – it obscures the role of older institutions, including kinship and religion, in the regulation of working life.

Precarious work

A third and related approach conceptualizes work in terms of socio-economic security. The concept of 'precarity' came into currency as a term to describe the emergence of a class of underemployed and socially excluded workers in Europe and North America. The term was invoked to capture the proliferation of 'McJobs' in France in the 1990s (Bourdieu, 1998) and the May Day protests of casual workers in Milan in 2004 (Breman, 2013). More recently, it has been developed in the work of Guy Standing (2011), who conceives of the 'precariat' as a global class of workers who have been pushed out of stable wage employment as a result of the attempts of governments and corporations to increase labour flexibility (akin to the 'informalisation' thesis outlined earlier). For Standing, the precariat constitutes 'a new dangerous class' that combines blue- and white-collar workers on temporary contracts with zero-hours workers in the gig economy – a class that is less secure and more reliant on diverse livelihood activities and support channels than the conventional working class. The ILO (2011) has since taken up the idea of 'precarious work' – defined as 'non-standard employment, which is poorly paid, insecure, unprotected and cannot support a household' – as a way around the dualism implicit in the concept of 'informal work'. Its 'decent work agenda' promotes an oppositional idea of work as '*employment* in conditions of freedom, equity, human security and dignity', based on a set of universal criteria that include working hours, job tenure, healthcare provisions and union coverage.

The opposing concepts of 'precarious' and 'decent work' have been critiqued for reproducing a singular idea of work based on the historical experiences of industrial workers in Western Europe (Munck, 2013; Scully, 2016). Simplistic assumptions of convergence – of the emergence of a 'global precariat' – obscure the diverse histories and experiences of wage employment in different locations in the world. For example, as Franco Barchiesi has argued, South Africa did not have to wait for the 2007 financial crisis to see precarity emerge as a way of life (2012, cited Munck, 2013, 758). Furthermore, the decent work agenda draws unfortunate parallels with the historical attempts of European colonial powers to use wage work as a tool to discipline indigenous populations based on a moral discourse that associated work with 'decency' (Mbembe, 2001). Indeed, facilitating entry into wage employment continues to be presented as a kind of 'civilisational quest' in contemporary development discourse (Bhattacharyya, 2018, 52). In reality, as many of the chapters in this collection demonstrate, people's decision to work 'non-standard' jobs is motivated by a range of factors which often include a desire to avoid the degrading and isolating aspects of wage labour (Millar, 2014, 38).

So what is the common story emerging from these three conceptualizations of work (commodified, informal and precarious)? Colin Williams argues that all three are the product of looking in particular places at particular periods in time and 'universalizing the trends identified' (2007, 2–3). In the first step, most, if not all, economic life is marshalled into 'one side or the other of a dichotomy' (for example commodified/uncommodified; formal/informal; decent/precarious). The two sides of the dichotomy are then ordered into a temporal sequence – a vision of the future of work – in which 'one side is seen as universally replacing the other' (for example 'commodification'; 'formalisation'; 'precariarisation') (2007, 2–3). Rather than contesting these processes, critical perspectives have tended simply to reverse their sequence; for example, through narratives of '*de*commodification' and '*in*formalisation', inverting their normative implications (see Breman and van der Linden, 2014). In both scenarios, the diverse futures that workers are building for themselves in different regions of the world are 'swamped and overwhelmed' by the future divined by the author (Chakrabarty, 2000, 87) and 'a gross injustice is done to the complex and multiple directions of change that are occurring in lived experience' (Williams, 2007, 3). In place of universal visions, this collection seeks to foreground these complex and multiple directions of change through the framework of 'ordinary work'.

Ordinary work: towards an alternative framework

The heart of the problem and the stakes in the central conflict can be summed up in the following alternative: either

> work can be integrated into a multi-active life as one of its
> components, or multi-activity can be integrated into 'work'
> as one of its forms. (Gorz, 1999, 73)

Once we recognize that wage employment constitutes only one form of work, the question arises of where to draw the line between work and non-work (Glucksmann, 1995, 64). The challenge is thus to rescue work from the confines of wage employment without dissolving it altogether. In his treatise on 'reclaiming work', André Gorz presents us with two options: either we retain a narrow conception of work as wage labour and subordinate this activity to other socio-economic activities in our lives, or we expand our conception of work to include these other socio-economic activities. This book takes the latter approach, following two generations of feminist activists and researchers in recognizing the political power of 'work' as a concept around which to organize and stake claims (for example Federici, 1975; Weeks, 2011; McDowell, 2014). We understand work broadly as the act of *provisioning for material wants and needs*, based on a substantivist reading of the economy that is attentive to the diverse range of social and institutional forms through which provisioning is organized and understood (Polanyi, 1944; Peck, 2013). This understanding situates work 'back in the context of the social whole' (Block and Somers, 1984, 63), foregrounding the ways in which the act of making a living is dependent upon broader systems of social reproduction *as well as* contingent forms of entrepreneurship and self-employment. We thus consider wage employment as one of multiple forms of work, alongside forced labour, hustling, cooperative living and digital platform tasking, to name but a few. Rather than seeking to categorize these activities through the familiar binaries of formal/informal, precarious/decent or capitalist/non-capitalist, we propose to understand them as examples of *ordinary work* in order to advance debates on (the future of) work in three distinct ways.

First, we deploy the concept of *ordinary* in order to broaden the socio-economic imaginary of work, dislocating the figure of the wage labourer as the 'paragon of meaningful work and social dignity' (Shaw and Waterstone, 2020, 44). For too long, theorists of work have restricted their epistemological gaze to the industrialized regions of the global North, making reference to 'Brazilianisation' (Beck, 2000) or 'South Africanisation' (Gorz, 1989) only as examples to be avoided. The notion of *ordinary* (as opposed to 'informal' or 'precarious') work is adopted here in order to cut across the long-standing division between Northern (formal/developed) and Southern (informal/

developing) economies, while repopulating the world of work as a 'proliferative space of difference' (Gibson-Graham, 2008, 615). Within this framework, the future of work is plural and open ended; rather than the invention of particular groups of people in advanced capitalist economies, it is the product of 'the inventiveness of people ... everywhere' (Robinson, 2006, 1). We pursue this approach while retaining an ambivalence about the potential of different forms of work to contribute to emancipation and self-actualization. Any project of expanding the imaginary of work must engage with the wide variety of socio-economic practices present in the world; we can neither romanticize, not blindly judge such activities, but rather see them as 'part of the landscape from which a project of becoming can emerge' (Roelvink et al, 2015, 10). The project of ordinary work is thus likely to return as many dysfunctional alternatives and 'real dystopias' as it does functional alternatives and 'real utopias' (Peck, 2013).

Secondly, we deploy the concept of *ordinary* in order to rethink work through the realm of the everyday. Work is part and parcel of everyday life, shaped by the day-to-day variability of socio-economic relations, values and practices; 'always hybrid and always in a state of becoming' (Lee, 2006, 413). Attending to work as *ordinary* necessitates an engagement with the ways in which it is experienced and understood in everyday life; its entanglement with other activities, relations and projects. Furthermore, it requires an attention to the norms and values against which these experiences and understandings are rendered meaningful; the ways in which work is seen as 'a key site of struggle in everyday efforts to construct the good ... in the sense of what is valued, desired and aimed for in the living out of life' (Millar, 2018, 12). *Ordinary work* thus necessitates an ethnographic sensibility capable of carving out spaces in which people are able to define their working lives according to their own culturally defined values and aspirations. It is in this realm of the everyday – the quotidian, the routine and the mundane – that alternative possibilities come into view, along with the tactics and strategies necessary to transfer them into the future (de Certeau, 1984).

Thirdly, we deploy the concept of *ordinary* in order to compare lived experiences of work across taken-for-granted conceptual and geographical boundaries. In place of linear and teleological analyses, *ordinary work* presents a licence for relational geographies of 'variegated economic transformation', animated by 'crisis and contradiction' as well as a variety of different practices, strategies and imaginations (Peck, 2013, 1600). It thus entails a commitment to 'weak' or 'minor theory' by describing emergent activities in ways that generate new theoretical openings; prioritizing experimentation and engagement over 'masterful knowing' (Katz, 1996; Sedgewick, 2003). Rather than 'positing unfolding logics and structures that limit politics', the aim is to bring things together 'from different domains to spawn something new' (Spinosa et al, 1997, 4; cited Gibson-Graham, 2008, 625); for example by seeking to understand the activities of an unemployed 'jobseeker' in the Welsh Valleys through the 'hustle' of Kenyan sanitation workers (Strong's chapter); or the decision of Catalonian activists to quit their waged jobs through the rhythms of Brazilian waste pickers (Bäumer Escobar's chapter). The analytical challenge is to theorize work across 'spatially differentiated, heterogenous economies'; from Dhaka to Catalonia; Jakarta to London; Johannesburg to Blaenau Gwent (Peck, 2013, 1600).

Structure of the book

This book is the product of a conversation that started at Queen Mary University of London in the summer of 2018. The conversation brought together a group of 30 friends and colleagues – predominantly early-career researchers – asking questions about work and working lives in all corners of the globe. We have tried as far as possible to structure the book in a way that reflects the flow of this conversation; beginning with the question of the decline of wage employment in post-industrial regions of Western Europe and North America, before thinking about imaginations and practices of work in regions of the world in which such employment has never been the norm (Africa, South and Southeast Asia, and Latin America); the struggles through which people have attempted to generate dignity and meaning outside of the wage, and the possibilities these provide for re-describing 'work' and reimagining the future.

Ruptures

What forms of work are emerging as the tide of wage employment continues to recede in the post-industrial regions of Western Europe and North America? What are the key points of rupture? How do people experience these forms of work, and to what extent are their experiences marked by 'post-Fordist affect' (Muehlebach and Shoshan, 2012) or 'wage work-related melancholia' (Barchiesi, 2011)? In economies offering only 'shit wages', Tatiana Thieme invites us to rethink work through the lens of the side hustle. She demonstrates how a hustler in Nairobi, a prison leaver in London and a refugee in Berlin engage in forms of low-end wage employment in order to conform to institutional narratives of the 'good citizen' while engaging in various side hustles in order to boost their income and provide for their dependants. Rather than conforming to the either/or categorizations in the conventional literature on work (formal/informal, waged/unwaged, licit/illicit), she argues that working lives at the margins of urban economies are increasingly dependent on straddling these divides while investing in social relationships of various kinds in order to transcend a life of mere 'existence'.

Samuel Strong also deploys the concept of the hustle to shed light on the 'work of looking for work' in the Welsh Valleys. He dismantles the divisive 'workers' and 'shirkers' rhetoric of the Conservative-Liberal Democrat Coalition Government of 2010–15 in order to lay bare the cruel optimism of a workfare system that promises forms of employment that have long ceased to exist. Through a personal engagement with the working life of Jeff, Strong demonstrates the various forms of hustling, gifting and volunteering that are required to sustain life in 'wage-scarce space' and calls for an end to the social contract which positions wage employment as the locus of social citizenship. In a similar fashion, Claudia Strauss invites us to think about possibilities for social attachment outside of the 'proper job' in the US (Ferguson and Li, 2018). Her chapter sheds light on contemporary ruptures in the US labour market through an analysis of the experiences of external workers, including misclassified 1099 contractors. She argues that workers often prioritized social relationships and belonging over contractual conditions, encouraging us to diversify our understandings of work beyond the material in order to understand the appeal of 'nonstandard' work.

Resignations

How might we resist 'shit wages' in order to pursue more rewarding life projects? What does it mean to quit wage employment in contexts in which it is scarce? To what extent is the act of resignation a harbinger of a more fulfilling working life or simply a bridge to a different form of exploitation? This section plays with the double meaning of 'resignation' as both an agentive act of exit and a submissive state of acceptance in wage-scarce economies. In the first chapter on 'wilful resignations', Asiya Islam follows the travails of three young lower middle class women in India's 'new economy'. She argues that their decision to resign from low-end service jobs represents an expression of dignity in a workplace in which their prospects are severely limited by gender and class constraints. Rather than subscribing to an employment/unemployment binary, the women see wage employment on a continuum alongside a number of life-sustaining activities, including domestic labour, status-protection work and education.

In 'Be Your Own Boss', Hannah Dawson asks why so many young men in South Africa express a preference for self-employment in the informal economy. Drawing upon the life histories of Thatho and Hloni, she demonstrates the ways in which wage work in South Africa's racialized economy disrupts the rhythms of life in places such as Zandspruit, disembedding people from the relationships that are essential to achieving socio-economic prosperity. In this context, resignation represents both a rejection of low-end wage employment and a statement of autonomy made on the promise of a better future. Vinzenz Bäumer Escobar reveals a similar disposition among men and women aspiring to escape the 'hamster's cage' of capitalist employment in Catalonia. Instead of informal self-employment, these men and women seek to find fulfilment in a cooperative that collapses the distinction between work and life through the concept of the 'life project' (*projecte de vida*). Through their experiences, Escobar argues that the work of creating 'a life worth living' is simultaneously materially challenging, emotionally draining and socially rewarding.

In the final chapter in this section, Nithya Natarajan, Katherine Brickell and Laurie Parsons caution against romantic accounts of unwaged work. Through the testimonies of brick kiln workers in Cambodia, they reveal the ways in which workers are resigned to becoming 'unfree' by entering into debt bondage arrangements with kiln owners. Here indebtedness, rather than the wage, is the defining feature of work at the margins. Their findings illustrate the importance of situating workers within broader structural processes – including those of land enclosure and capital accumulation – in order to better understand their (in)capacity to exit.

Struggles

How do workers organize to improve their working conditions outside of the formal labour struggle? What opportunities exist for political action in wage-scarce economies? How do workers navigate these opportunities at the urban scale, in cities undergoing market reforms of various kinds? In this section we examine the evolving relationship between workers and the state in diverse urban economies. In the first chapter, Annemiek Prins examines the politics of work-related vulnerabilities from the vantage point of Dhaka's rickshaw garages, where drivers access flexible forms of work and 'instant cash' in times of economic and ecological crisis. She argues that the analytical association between wageless work and precarity averts attention away from the role of politics and policy in reproducing the vulnerability of transport workers, using the example of a neighbourhood licensing scheme to demonstrate the ways in which municipal regulations have rendered rickshaw drivers vulnerable to debt and displacement.

In her chapter on competing visions of work in Jakarta's transport industry, Mechthild von Vacano argues that the arrival of platform capitalism in Indonesia has exerted a similar pressure on conventional *ojek* taxi drivers. Encouraged by a favourable regulatory environment, ride-hailing platforms have disrupted the informal *pangkolan* system of *ojek* riding – and associated forms of social security and redistribution – placing drivers' livelihoods at risk. However, von Vacano shows how drivers have responded by successfully combining historical forms of territorial organization with digital communication and affiliations with formal labour unions in order to obtain better working conditions as drivers on the digital platform.

Mara Nogueira begins the final chapter in this section by asking why street vendors in Belo Horizonte have withdrawn their support for the Workers' Party (*Partido dos Trabalhadores*) in Brazil. She shows how the party – and broader trade union movement – was founded on the idea of the able-bodied male wage worker, popularized in the metal factories of the 1970s. The movement thus excluded all those earning a living outside of formal wage employment, who were left to fend for themselves amid the privatization initiatives of the early 2000s. Nogueira argues that it is only by paying attention to the subjectivities of street vendors – the rhythms they rely upon and the 'forms of living' they enable (Millar, 2018) – that we might arrive at a more inclusive politics that is able to overcome the global crisis of labour.

Possibilities

What possibilities might the global decline of wage employment provide for re-describing work and reimagining the future? What alternative possibilities are obscured by the veil of 'wage work-related melancholia' (Barchiesi, 2011)? And how might this veil be lifted? In this final section, we reflect on the constrained possibilities of wageless life in the present and future. In the first chapter, Dora-Olivia Vicol demonstrates the possibilities afforded by the work of charity in light of the global COVID-19 pandemic. Necessitated by government neglect, Vicol conceptualizes charity work as the work of negotiating between a wage-centric state and a wage-scarce economy, connecting workers in London's migrant economy to limited protections and entitlements. Here, charity renders visible valuable forms of work outside of the wage relation – including personalized forms of service and care – rebuilding the fabric of society in spite of precarity.

In the final chapter, E. Fouksman asks why governments have yet to provide citizens with a universal basic income. She argues that it is not only politicians, economic elites or even the middle classes who are attached to the idea of wage employment. Counterintuitively, it is often those who are excluded from the formal wage economy that demonstrate the strongest forms of wage attachment. Through fieldwork with long-term unemployed populations in Namibia, Fouksman shows that people retain moral, psychological and social attachments to wage employment in the absence of more compelling imaginations of moral deservingness. In order to realize a new politics of distribution, she encourages us to engage in the political work of reclaiming livelihood, identity and community from the confines of the wage.

References

Barchiesi, F. (2011) *Precarious Liberation: Workers, the State, and Contested Social Citizenship in Postapartheid South Africa*, Scottsville: University of KwaZulu-Natal Press.

Bauman, Z. (2003) *Wasted Lives: Modernity and its Outcasts*, Cambridge: Polity.

Beck, U. (2000) *The Brave New World of Work*, Cambridge: Polity.

Berlant, L. (2011) *Cruel Optimism*, Durham, NC: Duke University Press.

Bhattacharyya, G. (2018) *Rethinking Racial Capitalism: Questions of Reproduction and Survival*, London: Rowman & Littlefield.

Block F. and Somers M.R. (1984) 'Beyond the economistic fallacy: the holistic social science of Karl Polanyi', in T. Skocpol (ed) *Vision and Method in Historical Sociology*, Cambridge: Cambridge University Press, pp 47–84.

Bourdieu, P. (1998) 'La précarité est aujourd'hui partout' ['Precariousness is everywhere nowadays'], in *Contre-feux*, Paris: Raisons d'agir, pp 96–102.

Breman, J. (2013) 'A bogus concept?' *New Left Review*, 84 (Nov–Dec): 130–138.

Breman, J. and van der Linden, M. (2014) 'Informalizing the economy: The return of the social question at a global level', *Development and Change*, 45(5): 920–940.

Chakrabarty, D. (2000) *Provincializing Europe: Postcolonial Thought and Historical Difference*, Princeton, NJ: Princeton University Press.

Comaroff, C. and Comaroff, J. (2012) *Theory from the South: Or, How Euro-America is Evolving Toward Africa*, London: Routledge.

de Certeau, M. (1984) *The Practice of Everyday Life*, trans. Steven Rendall, Berkeley, CA: University of California Press.

Denning, M. (2010) 'Wageless life', *New Left Review*, 66: 79–97.

Escobar, A. (1995) *Encountering Development: The Making and Unmaking of the Third World*, Princeton, NJ: Princeton University Press.

Esteva, G. (2010) 'Development' in W. Sachs (ed) *The Development Dictionary*, London: Zed Books, 1–23.

Fanon, F. (1963) *The Wretched of the Earth*, New York, NY: Grove Press.

Federici, S. (1975) *Wages Against Housework*, Bristol: Power of Women Collective and Falling Wall Press.

Ferguson, J. (1999) *Expectations of Modernity: Myths and Meanings of Urban life on the Zambian Copperbelt*, Berkeley, CA: University of California Press.

Ferguson, J. (2015) *Give a Man a Fish: Reflections on the New Politics of Entitlement*, Durham, NC: Duke University Press.

Ferguson, J. and Li, T. (2018) 'Beyond the "proper job": Political-economic analysis after the century of labouring man', Working Paper 51. PLAAS, UWC: Cape Town.

Gibson-Graham J.K. (1996) *The End of Capitalism (As We Knew It): A Feminist Critique of Political Economy*, Oxford: Blackwell.

Gibson-Graham, J.K. (2006) *A Postcapitalist Politics*, Minneapolis, MN: University of Minnesota Press.

Gibson-Graham, J.K. (2008) 'Diverse economies: Performative practices for "other worlds"', *Progress in Human Geography*, 32(5): 613–632.

Gidwani, V. (2008) *Capital, Interrupted: Agrarian Development and the Politics of Work in India*, Minneapolis, MN: University of Minnesota Press.

Glucksmann, M. (1995) 'Why "work"? Gender and the "total social organization of labour"', *Gender, Work & Organization*, 2(2): 63–75.

Gorz, A. (1989) *Critique of Economic Reason*, London and New York: Verso.

Gorz, A. (1999) *Reclaiming Work: Beyond the Wage-Based Society*, London: Polity.

Hart, K. (1973) 'Informal income opportunities and urban employment in Ghana', *The Journal of Modern African Studies*, 11(1): 61–89.

ILO (2011) Symposium on Precarious Work, 4–7 October (http://www.ilo.org/actrav/what/ events/ WCMS_153972/lang–en/index.htm, accessed 11 November 2019).

ILO (2020) *Transition to Formality and Structural Transformation: Challenges and Policy Options*, Geneva: ILO.

Katz, C. (1996) 'Towards minor theory', *Environment and Planning D: Society and Space*, 14(4): 487–499.

Komlosy, A. (2018) *Work: The Last 1,000 Years*, London: Verso.

Lee, R. (2006) 'The ordinary economy: Tangled up in values and geography', *Transactions of the Institute of British Geographers*, 31(4): 413–432.

Li, T. (2010) 'To make live or let die? Rural dispossession and the protection of surplus populations', *Antipode*, 41: 66–93.

Li, T. (2017) 'After development: Surplus populations and the politics of entitlement', *Development and Change*, 48(6): 1247–1261.

MacGaffey, J. (1991). *The Real Economy of Zaire: The Contribution of Smuggling and Other Unofficial Activities to National Wealth*, London: James Currey.

Mauss, M. (1970). *The Gift: Forms and Functions of Exchange in Archaic Societies*, London: Cohen & West.

McDowell (2014) 'Gender, work, employment and society: Feminist reflections on continuity and change', *Work, Employment and Society*, 28(5): 825–837.

Malinowski, B. (1922) *Argonauts of the Western Pacific: An Account of Native Enterprise and Adventure in the Archipelagoes of Melanesian New Guinea*, London: Routledge & Sons.

Marx, K. ([1867] 1976) *Capital: A Critique of Political Economy*, Vol 1, London: Penguin.

Mbembe, A. (2001) *On the Postcolony*, Berkeley, CA: University of California Press.

Meagher, K. (1995) 'Crisis, informalization and the urban informal sector in sub-Saharan Africa', *Development and Change*, 26(2): 259–284.

Melamed, J. (2015) 'Racial capitalism', *Critical Ethnic Studies* 1(1): 76–85.

Mies, M. (1986) *Patriarchy and Accumulation on a World Scale*, London: Zed.

Millar, K. (2014) 'The precarious present: Wageless labor and disrupted life in Rio de Janeiro, Brazil', *Cultural Anthropology*, 29(1): 32–53.

Millar, K. (2018) *Reclaiming the Discarded: Life and Labour on Rio's Garbage Dump*, Durham, NC: Duke University Press.

Monteith, W. and Giesbert, L. (2017) ' "When the stomach is full we look for respect": Perceptions of "good work" in the urban informal sectors of three developing countries', *Work, Employment and Society*, 31(5): 816–833.

Muehlebach, A. and Shoshan, N. (2012) 'Post-Fordist affect: Introduction', *Anthropological Quarterly*, 85(2): 317–343.

Munck, R. (2013) 'The precariat: A view from the South', *Third World Quarterly*, 34(5): 747–762.

Peck, J. (2013) 'For Polanyian economic geographies', *Environment and Planning A*, 45(7): 1545–1568.

Pettinger, L. (2019) *What's Wrong With Work?*, Bristol: Bristol University Press.

Polanyi, K. (1944) *The Great Transformation*, Boston, MA: Beacon Press.

Potts, D. (2008) 'The urban informal sector in sub-Saharan Africa: From bad to good (and back again?)', *Development Southern Africa*, 25(2): 151–167.

Robinson, C. (1983) *Black Marxism: The Making of the Black Radical Tradition* (1st edn), London: Zed Books.

Robinson, J. (2006) *Ordinary Cities: Between Modernity and Development*, London: Routledge.

Roelvink, G., St. Martin, K. and Gibson-Graham, J.K. (2015) *Making Other Worlds Possible: Performing Diverse Economies*, Minneapolis, MN: University of Minnesota Press.

Scully, B. (2016) 'Precarity North and South: A southern critique of Guy Standing', *Global Labour Journal*, 7(2): 160–173.

Sedgwick, E. (2003) *Touching, Feeling: Affect, Pedagogy, Performativity*, Durham, NC: Duke University Press.

Shaw, I. and Waterstone, M. (2020) *Wageless Life: A Manifesto for a Future Beyond Capitalism*, Minneapolis, MN: University of Minnesota Press.

Simone, A.M. and Pieterse, E. (2017) *New Urban Worlds: Inhabiting Dissonant Times*, Cambridge: Polity.

Spinosa, C., Flores, F. and Dreyfus, H.L. (1997) *Disclosing New Worlds: Entrepreneurship, Democratic Action and the Cultivation of Solidarity*, Cambridge, MA: MIT Press.

Standing, G. (2011) *The Precariat: The New Dangerous Class*, London: Bloomsbury.

Weeks, K. (2011) *The Problem With Work: Feminism, Marxism, Antiwork Politics and Postwork Imaginaries*, Durham, NC: Duke University Press.

Williams, C. (2007) *Rethinking the Future of Work: Directions and Vision*, Basingstoke: Palgrave Macmillan.

Wood, A., Graham, M., Lehdonvirta, V. and Hjorth, I. (2018) 'Good gig, bad big: Autonomy and algorithmic control in the global gig economy, *Work, Employment and Society*, (Online First): 1–20.

PART I

Ruptures

1

"Shit Wages" and Side Hustles: Ordinary Working Lives in Nairobi, London and Berlin

Tatiana Thieme

As we enter the third decade of the twenty-first century, a different set of optics is required to grasp the ways in which *work* is practised and understood in wage-scarce economies across the world. The urgency of this exercise is exacerbated by the overlapping crises that have marked this young century. In 2009, a year after the global financial crisis of 2008, Keith Hart and colleagues published an edited volume entitled *The Human Economy* in response to a growing interdisciplinary thirst for other ways of thinking and doing the economy. They argued that a human economy requires four key elements: a relevance to everyday life; an application to diverse situations; a recognition of plural needs and interests (beyond income and consumption); and an expansive commitment to addressing 'humanity as a whole' (Hart et al, 2010a, 5). Before embarking on the intellectual exercise of imagining what the post-crisis *human* economy could look like, the authors urge us to pay attention to what already exists: 'The human economy is already everywhere. People always insert themselves practically into economic life on their own account. What they do there is often obscured, marginalised or repressed by dominant economic institutions and ideologies' (Hart et al, 2010a, 5). More than a decade later, the signs of a post-crisis 'human economy' remain elusive. Instead, protracted uncertainty and austerity have become the norm as the world grapples with the confluence of global financial crises and global health pandemics.

This chapter examines how people *make a living* in conditions of protracted uncertainty, and the ways in which the labour involved in doing so comprises a diversity of 'cultural logics' (Gidwani, 2008) and social and economic forms that are too often overlooked (Hart et al, 2010a). The chapter responds to recent invitations to 'rethink work' and broaden debates beyond what constitutes formal or informal labour, by encouraging 'openness to plurality of form' itself (Hart, 2009, 158). The aim here is to offer ethnographically informed reflections that might deepen our understanding of how diverse economic activities are organized and narrated through ordinary individual working lives in different regions of the world.

The popular idiom of the 'proper job' dominated conceptions of industrial labour throughout the twentieth century; a relic of Fordist labour arrangements that associated secure labour with particular temporalities and spaces of work legitimized through the wage (Ferguson and Li, 2018). The wage was thus directly linked to the visible organization of productive labour, demarcating social–economic relations along spatial and temporal boundaries and rendering labour 'legible' to the state (Scott, 1999) in contexts where the state was a central 'unit of organisation' (Amin, 2011, 2). Such conceptions of the 'proper job' also have shaped gendered representations of productive labour, positioning the 'male bread-winner' as the main household provider, in spite of the fact that unpaid reproductive and care work and 'non-market transactions' make up 30–50 per cent of economic activity across the globe (Gibson-Graham, 2008, 615). As the 1970s cleared the ground for a new phase of capitalist development often referred to as 'post-Fordism' (Amin, 2011), sites of industrial production splintered across space and time through processes of offshoring and automation. And yet, mainstream conceptions of work retained a normative attachment to the wage as the primary channel through which productivity and recognition could be obtained.

At the margins of wage work, however, it has become difficult to render 'legible' the relationship between labour, resources and time, and on whose terms work is made and unmade. One of the dominant ways of conceptualizing non-waged work since the 1970s has been through the concept of the 'informal economy', coined by anthropologist Keith Hart (Hart, 1973) in recognition of the diverse livelihood activities lying outside the purview of the state that had been until then disregarded by development economists (Myers, 2011). More recent scholarship, including by Hart himself, has been critical of the term's static and pejorative connotations, calling for a more differentiated understanding of the social and economic forms that comprise so-called informal economies (Roitman, 1990; Hart, 2009, 4–6).

Over the past decade, a new set of social and economic forms have proliferated through digitally mediated platforms. These have been celebrated by some scholars and practitioners who hail the 'market efficiencies' of digitally mediated 'peer to peer capitalism', which was seen as an opportune antidote to the economic downturn spawned by the aftermath of the global financial crisis of 2008 (Sundararajan, 2016). Such platforms have become synonymous with flexible but insecure forms of 'gig' work, situated within the context of continued de-industrialized economies in the global North. Sharing features with the 'informal economies' often contextually associated with the global South, the 'gig' economy reflected changes in industrialized and post-industrial economies and, as such, operates within (and arguably perpetuates) an increasingly precarious labour market which normalizes protracted austerity and the continued erosion of welfare services employment (Waite, 2009; Standing, 2011; Meagher, 2018). This raises questions about the extent to which 'learning to labour' has been decoupled from class and formal education (Willis, 1981), and tied to the particular structures of opportunity that are made and performed in particular urban environments (Saitta et al, 2013; Richardson, 2015).

As postcolonial and post-industrial labour markets move synchronously away from wage employment, the future of work is increasingly and globally uncertain, especially for young people (Barford and Coombe, 2019). However, therein lies a paradox: livelihood activities continue to be understood in relation to the normative ideal of formal wage employment (or the 'proper job'). Notably, while the International Labour Organization (ILO) has moved beyond the familiar rubric of 'informality', it continues to categorize a broad range of livelihood activities as 'non-standard forms of employment', including all work that is not continuous, full time and involving a clear relationship between an employer and an employee (ILO, 2018). And yet, it is clear that in the absence of a wage, or in the case of an insecure one, forms of 'getting by' will continue to proliferate even (and especially) in conditions of austerity, adversity, and resource scarcity (Saitta et al, 2013; Mckenzie, 2015; Barford and Coombe, 2019).

How might we then re-describe modes of work that fall outside of the confines of 'standard' employment because they are neither continuous nor full time, nor involve a clear contract with an employer? Modes of work that may escape state regulation, but which reflect economic forms that have existed for millennia? Perhaps rather than seeking to classify these diverse income-generating strategies as either 'informal' or 'gig work', we might return to an older expression – 'Système D' – used in North and West Africa to connote systems of 'débrouillardise' (to find a way) (MacGaffey, 1991; Neuwirth, 2012). We might also turn to the work of feminist geographers including Gibson-Graham (2008), who deploy the concept of 'diverse economies' in order to draw attention to the multitude of economic forms that make up 'real economies' in practice (MacGaffey, 1991). These scholars call for an expansion of 'the space of the ethical and political' (Laclau and Mouffe, 1985 cited in Gibson-Graham, 2008, 615), inviting us to bring an ethnographic sensibility to the norms and values that inform particular 'cultural logics' of work (Gidwani, 2008). These logics may involve 'having multiple things on the go' if economic and social terrains are persistently uncertain (Cooper and Pratten, 2015; Simone and Pieterse, 2017), including potentially engaging with forms of work that might be regarded by mainstream institutions as demeaning, hazardous or 'illegitimate' (Hart, 1973; Saitta et al, 2013). For example, as Millar (2018) shows in her ethnography of *catadores* (waste pickers) in Brazil, working 'on the dump' may be regarded as a last-resort livelihood strategy for the downtrodden, but it is also agentive work that provides forms of flexibility and 'relational autonomy' that are valued by those whose everyday lives are mired in emergencies and uncertainty that need tending to and who cannot afford to be constrained by inflexible waged employment. Her research thus provides an example of how suspending normative classifications of work might expand existing fields of possibility and a way of *seeing* a range of 'other economies' (Hart et al, 2010a, 9).

Thus, in order to reflect on the transition away from formal wage employment, we need to reconsider the relationship between people and work, and return to the foundational question of how people 'devise their own means of survival and sometimes of prosperity' in diverse economies (Hart, 2010, 152). Now more than ever, we need to move beyond binary classifications of work as either formal or informal, licit or illicit, waged or self-employed in order to better understand the complex realities of contemporary working lives, especially at the urban margins (Lancione, 2016). As labour uncertainty and in-work poverty expand across diverse geographies, the 'side hustle' becomes a pragmatic response to increased economic disenfranchisement. I argue here that side hustles operate as flexible 'top-ups' to insecure wages or insufficient 'main' streams of income. They are simultaneously creative and ambiguous in form, often operating outside the scrutiny and legibility of institutional association.

Side hustles

What might a Kenyan woman whose place of work and belonging is known locally as an urban 'ghetto' have in common with a London-based prison leaver transitioning back into life and work after prison, and a Syrian refugee making his way in Berlin as a 'new European'? In this chapter, I explore the interconnections between three ordinary 'working lives' at the urban margins of very different cities (McDowell, 2013). I show that in each case, the art of making a living involves the pursuit of multiple sources of income and diverse and often paradoxical forms of institutional recognition. It entails forms of unlikely accumulation and spontaneous loss; efforts to *make* work when 'proper jobs' are not obtainable. My aim is not to present 'simplistic assumptions of convergence' (see the Introduction to this volume) but rather to think across field sites and working lives that are, as Linda McDowell (2013) would say, 'ordinary but remarkable' in ways that trouble the presumed division between working lives in the global North and global South.

Against a global backdrop of labour uncertainty, an increasing number of working lives are characterized by occupational straddling, side hustles and back-up plans. The experiences of my three interlocutors shed light on the ways in which the practice of making a living at the urban margins is often contingent on combining low-end wage work with various forms of 'hustling'. I refer to hustling here as an urban practice that lies outside normative social institutions, involving a constellation of deals, opportunism and unlikely accumulation in conditions of scarcity, marginality and adversity (Thieme, 2018). It is thus a form of work that emerges amid the erosion of wage employment. For example, Ned Polsky (1967) encourages us to think about the gambling practices of low-wage workers in the underworld of American pool halls as a crucial composite of their livelihood activities. Polsky (1967, 92) refers to the hustler's search for a job that would permit him to 'drop into the poolroom', a kind of 'moonlighting' that supplements the meagre wage with an 'extra bit on the side' and also allows the hustler to 'grab whatever action might present itself'.

As the stories of my interlocutors demonstrate, this '*side* hustle' or 'extra bit on the side' provides a crucial mechanism of support beyond the precarious waged job or workfare subsidy. Hustling constitutes a response to circumstances in which individuals are cut off from formal institutional support in a context of labour insecurity, and experience stigma associated with their social, economic and/or legal status. It reflects an ontological uncertainty: hustling is at once reflective of particular forms of dispossession and injustice and suggestive of openings for new ways to reimagine and remake work and livelihood. It is this paradox that positions hustling as a condition of urban life that works with, but also confronts, existing economic, political and social structures and (dis)orders.

In their work on Kinshasa, De Boeck and Baloji (2016, 16) describe the forms of 'closure, junction and seam' that urban inhabitants harness in order to turn otherwise 'impossible circumstances of living' in the city into a possibility. The metaphor of 'suturing' connotes a continuous process of sealing and stitching. Like hustling, suturing represents an attempt to imagine alternative futures while contending with the constant (re)opening of wounds. Suturing thus compels us to pay closer attention to the ways in which work 'is imagined and lived' in cities around the world (De Boeck and Baloji, 2016, 17). It points us to the diffuse forms of knowledge, barriers and dreamscapes that animate the everyday lives and imaginaries of individuals at the urban margins. In their life worlds, particular forms of 'social navigation' (Vigh, 2010, 420) take place where, 'people invest a great deal of time in making sense of and predicting the movement of their social environment, in clarifying how they are able to adapt to and move in relation to oncoming change'.

The chapter challenges normative understandings of 'productive labour' in an effort to 're-describe' actually existing practices of work in diverse urban economies (Gibson-Graham, 2008; Simone and Pieterse, 2017). It foregrounds the experimental and ordinary undertakings that 'make' work in potentially subversive ways in contexts where wage employment is absent, insufficient or degrading. I present the vignettes of three ordinary working lives in Nairobi, London and Berlin in order to make three key points. First, I demonstrate the entanglement of multiple economic practices and social navigation that make up a working life; practices that often *combine* formal waged labour and ad hoc hustle, challenging binary conceptualizations that reduce work to an 'either/or' category (formal/informal; waged/precarious). Second, I shed light on the ways in which people labouring on the margins of the urban wage economy encounter and articulate their precarious economic practices through a cultural language and 'logic of work' (Gidwani, 2008) that reveals agentive struggles to navigate uncertain terrains with dignity. Third, I show how these different practices and logics produce specific social and economic forms and functions (Hart, 2009); namely, accumulation, redistribution and performance.

In the next section I introduce three interlocutors, Eliza, Damien and Nafea, through vignettes of their ordinary working lives in Nairobi, London and Berlin, respectively. I present these vignettes in order to illuminate a question posed in my recent writings on the 'hustle economy' (Thieme, 2018): to what extent does hustling reinforce pre-existing forms of exploitation and dispossession in 'impossible' urban economies (De Boeck and Baloji, 2016), and/or to what extent does it constitute a generative form of work in its own right?

Hustling as place making in Nairobi

Eliza was born and raised in one of the largest and oldest informal settlements in Nairobi. When I met her in 2009, she was 24 years old. Elsewhere (Thieme, 2016), I have written about her experiences as a young working single mother navigating the largely male-dominated informal waste economy in Nairobi. Waste work was her primary source of income for many years. During the early 2000s, development actors seeking to engage the growing youth demographic in urban 'slums' noticed that neighbourhood-based informal waste collectors operated in groups and occupied particular territorial zones. Like many of her generation who grew up during the rise of 'NGOisation' in Nairobi, Eliza became a savvy navigator of the development and social business sectors seeking to harness the entrepreneurial skills of youth groups across these largely underserved urban neighbourhoods. By 2016, Eliza's portfolio of income-generating activities included a 'day job' with a sanitation social enterprise, where she worked as a 'field officer'. Here she was paid a wage and given a uniform; two markers of professionalism and formal employment in Nairobi. But through my conversations with Eliza that year, I understood that her working identity was not tied to her 'day job'. Instead, she self-identified as a 'hustler', where survival and recognition were understood to be contingent upon a combination of improvised income-generating activities, unpaid social activism work, and an active presence on social media (Facebook especially), where she would often proudly sign off with the hashtag #ghettoGal. A key manoeuvre in Eliza's everyday 'social navigation' was a concerted effort to 'be seen' in her neighbourhood when it mattered. Eliza's hustle thus combined low-end wage employment with ad hoc self-provisioning in the neighbourhood economy and various forms of social activism and reciprocation that fed her street credibility – activities that provided a 'back-up' or safety net in the context of economic uncertainty.

Work that takes place outside of formal professional categories and qualifications is often characterized as 'low skilled'. However, the work of hustling in Nairobi requires a broad range of skills and forms of tacit knowledge. Young people born and raised in Nairobi's 'slums' create their own cartographies of the city, translating between different vernaculars and institutional spaces; calling themselves 'entrepreneurs' when it resonates with social enterprise investors, while self-identifying as 'hustlers' back on the stoop in order to foster a solidarity grounded in the shared experience of joblessness, opportunism and hope. In a context where opportunities are contingent on being in the right place at the right time and where 'people are infrastructure' (Simone, 2004), young people are at once always on the move, and yet can be found standing in place at particular times of the day, when it makes sense to be seen at the 'baze' (base).

Eliza's commitment to hustling was born out of a recognition that social enterprise gigs come and go in Nairobi. Despite periodical accolades and pay raises, Eliza expressed a dislike for the lack of input she had in operational decisions. She explained:

> 'You see I used to be field officer around my baze in Huruma and Mathare, where I know people and they know me. Then they said, Eliza you go to Mukuru. But you see that is a place where I am not known and it is more difficult to feel safe and get people to listen to you, you get? But me I know as long as I'm field officer, I have to go where they say I need to go, and I have targets I need to make. I have ideas, but the decisions they're made by the sonko (boss).'[1]

Eliza took her job and her perception of the organizational hierarchy very seriously. She also knew having a wage was unique for people living in her neighbourhood. But she increasingly expressed cynicism for the stalled and perhaps overly predictable trajectory of this job, where she would at best remain a foot soldier within the organization – that is, as long as she met the 'targets'. At the same time, Eliza's scepticism about her day job enabled her to hold on to a narrative of *hustling*, which in contemporary Nairobi meant finding a way to make a living but also being sly about your politics and your moral modes. As a woman, she also knew that talking about your hustle could be usefully ambiguous, and even a form of security, as she explained at her flat in Huruma one evening in 2017: "You see, when I see those boys who snatch [steal belongings] at night, I walk alongside them and

I say, '*Hey maboyz, mnafanya hustle? Mimi pia ninafanya hustle*' ['Hey my boys, are you guys hustling tonight?']. Me too I'm hustling."

Eliza explained to me that in this moment, the 'boyz' thought she meant that her hustle was sex work, a common form of 'night hustle' among some women who are still out after dark. Identifying as a fellow 'night hustler' was a form of 'bluffing' (Newell, 2012) that afforded her an ephemeral sense of safety through performed camaraderie and shared struggle. It was in recounting this story to me that I also sensed in Eliza's storytelling that this bluff was more than mere deceit: it was a way of forging a connection and affinity with the "bag snatching boys" in the after-hours, because as she put it, "you know it's a real struggle right now, and when the day hustle goes down, the night hustle goes up." Her story also underlined the moral codes of the night time economy, where nocturnal hustlers operate side by side, respecting each other's craft. And it was not until later that I realized her story refrained from judgemental remarks on the economic form that is sex work or even bag snatching. These were understood as viable modes of getting by under the circumstances. "Even *matatus* let sex workers take a ride for free, because they know she is at work so they give her a break."

By day, Eliza straddled these different life worlds, her uniformed self hopping on a *matatu* to 'go to work' but knowing that the duration of the job was always uncertain. But Eliza also recognized the 'social thickness' (Ferguson, 2006, 198) of the hustle as a double-edged sword. One the one hand, she explained, "For us youth, opportunity is [the place] where you stay … you can hustle in a place where you stamp your authority." Here, place-based recognition – or street credibility – was key to being able to 'make things happen' through hustling. On the other hand, Eliza invoked a kind of success penalty when someone is perceived to be 'doing too well', explaining that people are expected to redistribute what they make to others whose hustle "is down". Eliza thus managed her income very carefully; paying for her children's school fees, starting small businesses on the side, upgrading her living situation one moment, but being ready to downgrade as soon as money was tight. As she put it, "It is best that people don't know where I stay exactly." In 2017 Eliza was staying on the top floor of an eight-storey tenement walk–up in one of Nairobi's densest low-income neighbourhoods. She joked that it was the "penthouse", with perks including anonymity and no one's wet laundry dripping on hers. However, hers was always the first floor to run out of water.

Today, Eliza's hustle continues in different forms: she lost the waged job in 2019 because targets were not met that year. But through the connections she made with various NGOs and social enterprises in the last few years, she has been able to get contract work for shorter periods. She has also moved out of the "penthouse" and now resides in a flat on the ground floor of one of Huruma's tenement buildings, able to point out the perks of living "near the action" of the street. All the while, on Facebook, Eliza uploads selfies of prosaic moments "at work" in all its different iterations – from the office to the street – still signing off as 'Ghetto Gal'.

Side hustling in London

Damien[2] is a prison leaver whom I met in London in 2016 while conducting fieldwork on the journeys of prisoners nearing the end of their sentences (Richardson and Thieme, 2020). Over 60 per cent of prisoners in the UK are under the age of 40 (Sturge, 2019, 9). Like many other young male prison leavers in London, Damien took up a job in the construction industry. As another prison-leaver once explained to me: "Construction companies don't care what your past is. As long as you can graft, they'll give you a chance." At first I was pleased to hear that Damien had found a job so soon after his release. But upon meeting Damien for the first time outside of prison in 2018, I learned that this job was contracted through a temp agency which took 40 per cent of his wages. Damien was initially housed in temporary hostel accommodation; a post-release 'get back on your feet' housing scheme that typically lasts six weeks. However, he subsequently struggled to find a stable place to live and did not qualify for council housing as an 'able bodied adult male' in the eyes of the austere state (Dowling and Harvie, 2014; Mckenzie, 2015). Paradoxically, he was told by his probation officer that the only way he would qualify for subsidized housing was if he gave up his job, which Damien was not prepared to do. Instead, he told me of his plans to earn additional money 'on the side' of the construction job. All of his ideas for how to 'top up' his meagre earnings to cope with the financial demands of life in London and provide for his dependants transcended conventional normative and legal boundaries, reproducing a cycle of reconviction. At the time of his release, Damien's dependents included a one-year-old son and his 'baby mama', a 12-year-old son from a previous partnership, and his current girlfriend.

Tatiana: Do you know of anyone who did time, got out and struggled like you now to find decent paying work, and eventually [went] 'straight'?

Damien: Yes, but they didn't go straight the whole time.

Tatiana: So you mean you get out, realize you can't get make enough money with the shit job, get back into some crime to get a bit of extra cash or whatever, and then you go back 'straight'?

Damien: Exactly. And you make sure that the bit where you went back into criminality, you just don't get caught.

Tatiana: Are there any programmes that help guys like you who are business minded and could use support for starting a business or whatever?

Damien: Yeah, but they only target 19–25 year olds. If you're older like me (30), no one gives a shit. You're on your own.

Damien was caught in a grey zone. He did not qualify for any support for housing or entrepreneurship. So he decided to go it alone.

When I met Damien six months later, he was still in construction. He had been promoted, but he said he was still making 'shit money' that barely exceeded minimum wage (£7.50 per hour). He then introduced his 'side hustle': "You see this is the thing. I work over 65 hours a week in construction. It's a legit job, right? But I work my ass off to basically just survive and exist. And I'm not interested in just existing. I want to live too. So I do other stuff on the side ..." Damien explained that he had started to rent out the council flat of a friend who was still in prison and who would stand to lose the flat if he defaulted on payment. Damien paid the landlord directly and sent his friend an extra £100 each month. In the meantime, he received a daily rental fee from a self-employed sex worker from Eastern Europe,[3] Zofia, who ran her business out of the flat. Damien explained that because this was a one-person business operating out of a private flat, it was not considered a brothel. He thus did not consider his role to be that of a pimp. He collected four times as much rent as he paid to the landlord. Meanwhile, Zofia covered the daily rent through a single hour of sex work and retained the rest of her earnings. She went back to her home country every month, where her income helped to support her family. Damien explained: "These [Eastern European] girls choose to come 'cause they know they can make good money here. They come and work for a few weeks at a time, then go back. They don't have pimps, they look for safe places to rent a room or a flat, asking around who they can trust ..." He noted that while hotels were exposed and risky, private rental flats provided a safer and potentially lucrative environment for all parties. If all went to plan, Damien emphasized, everyone made money. The landlord received a 'bit extra' on top of their standard rent, the middleman (Damien) extracted a surplus rent, which enabled him to send his friend £100 and still have a nice sum left, and Zofia made a profit after her first hour of work.

As I listened to Damien's story, I tried to suspend my own preconceived ideas about the kinds of transactions he was describing. I wanted to understand the moral and economic logics that underpinned the claim that his side hustle was fair because everyone was able to make their share, and thus retain a sense of agency within a broader context of austerity and insecurity. In the absence of Zofia's testimony, it is difficult to make any assertions about her agency in this arrangement. And certainly, this example could be portrayed as a straightforward story of exploitation in the unregulated economy involving a shady landlord, a male British prison leaver, and a precarious migrant sex worker. But it is worth noting that like Eliza, Damien made no judgement of Zofia's line of work; rather, he expressed concern for sex workers operating 'without protection' and at the mercy of trafficking rings or exposed to the risk of street violence. His account thus sheds light on the forms of 'social thickness' (Ferguson, 2006) and mutual understanding born out of shared experiences of in-work poverty that have consigned people such as Damien to merely 'existing'. His account revealed that money was accrued by each participant at each stage of this 'value chain' without necessarily dispossessing another. It was all legally and normatively questionable, and yet the logic that transpired was one of reciprocity and 'shared self-provisioning' (Kinder, 2016, 11).

Much like Polsky's (1967) description of moonlighting, Damien's 'hustle' served as a form of self-provisioning that 'topped up' his income from low-end wage labour and provided him with a safeguard against in-work poverty. At the same time, there was clearly some value in continuing his 'day job' insofar as it sustained the narrative of 'going straight' propagated by the criminal justice system, and thus reduced his chances of going back to prison. Despite the increasing difficulty of securing a 'proper' wage-earning job, the UK criminal justice system continues to associate the wage with a commitment to 'staying straight', thus ironically compelling prison leavers like Damien to 'top up' their low wages with other (illicit) activities.

Damien spent much of his 20s in and out of prison. During one of our conversations, he remarked, "I don't mind prison. I know how to do prison. But it's just a fucking waste of time." Well versed in how prison 'works' and convinced that it was 'a waste of time', he was determined to stay out this time, albeit on his own terms. Navigating the criminal justice system in the tenuous post-release period meant a double performance of sorts. He adhered to a particular institutional performance of 'going straight', which (as for so many prison leavers) involved engaging in low-end wage work that limits one's 'existence', in Damien's words, to mere 'survival'. In the meantime, the side hustle became a crucial form of self-provision and affirmation, rooted in the familiar terrain of what he called 'doing road', which had become his life world since the age of 12 when he left school. 'Road life' is an emic term deployed by Black British youth in inner cities which refers to particular forms of 'street culture'. It is an amalgam of social and cultural repertoires as well as various 'underground economies' in the absence of mainstream economic opportunities (Venkatesh, 2008). 'Road life' is associated with youth living on council estates, where they might be both perpetrators and victims of crime, often in response to structural forms of exclusion and precarity in relation to mainstream education, housing and employment (Bakkali, 2019; White, 2020). Navigating 'road life' and 'straight life' for Damien involved a constant calculated performance to different audiences and at different moments in his life. During the week, from 7am to 7pm, he had to appear a serious 'grafter'. On the street, he pretended he was broke to avoid excessive attention, especially from police who are known to over-police young Black men on probation. In the clubs on Saturday night, he wanted to look good and make sure the right people (potential customers) knew where to find him. But he was also a man in his early 30s who just wanted to enjoy the urban night life and the ephemeral, performative conspicuous consumption that went along with it (Newell, 2012); the freedom of moving around the city after conventionally marked 'working hours' after years in prison where all night hours were unequivocally bounded to the cell.

Hustling for papers in Berlin

Nafea arrived in Berlin in 2011 as a 28-year-old Syrian political refugee. When we first met in June 2018, he explained the graft involved in navigating the 'integration system' for refugees in Berlin. Like other refugees making their way to Europe during the Syrian conflict, experiencing borders took on several temporal and spatial registers (Darling, 2017), from the challenges of moving from the 'camps' where refugees wait in 'protracted displacement', to navigating the city where getting by combines moments and dispositions of waiting, imagining futures, and 'urban negotiations' of various kinds (Darling, 2017). He recalled making use of the refugee camps on the outskirts of Berlin during the first few months following arrival. Though carceral in several ways, the camps provided a source of basic security and sustenance in addition to introducing him to "so many different people". He explained: "I had nice relations with all, I wanted to understand them." But there were no livelihood opportunities in the camp, and Nafea could not stand "being there without action". He came to see the weekly *Taschengelt* (pocket money) provided by the German government as a trap that rendered life in the camp a kind of Sartrian 'No Exit'. This weekly allowance – a kind of state-sponsored subsidy that required recipients to return to the camp every three days – was not sufficient to cover the costs of living independently in Berlin and thus consigned refugees to a state of suspended dependency.

Nafea explained how he sought to acquire economic independence by moving between the camp and what he called Berlin's "black employment market", finding work first as a cleaner, then as a cook. Through these jobs, Nafea began to build up his 'Vitamin B'; a colloquial expression referring to the various ways in which individuals can benefit from mutual cooperation, contacts and support (*Beziehungen*). The forms of income and social connection provided by the jobs enabled him to gradually detach himself from the camp and the *Taschengelt* it provided. He cycled between different jobs and temporary accommodation, and soon became entangled in Germany's 'workfare system', which requires refugees to take part in a series of labour arrangements with local municipalities and companies who offer '*Ausbildung* (apprenticeship) schemes' in exchange for the right to stay.

Professional training has long been central to the celebrated *Ausbildung* model in Germany, but a combination of increased numbers and austerity measures since 2015 have conspired to create the *semblance* of work, while often compelling refugees to participate in unwaged and/or part-time, low-skilled work, similar to that experienced by Damien in London. Some of these casualized forms of work were cynically referred to as 'mini jobs' that paid as little as €1 an hour, often for no more than five hours per week. These mini jobs were allowed to persist because government subsidies effectively incentivized unliveable wages. As one social worker put it, it became a form of 'structural demotivation' for many refugees, who expected or hoped for eventual waged work. For Nafea, the *Ausbildung* programme was important not for its provision of decent work, but for its promise of legal rights and social welfare. Indeed, the contract that underpins recent integration policies in Germany requires refugees to demonstrate economic independence through participation in the labour market in exchange for welfare benefits that eventually might lead to legal rights, what Nafea referred to as 'papers'. As such, 'new Berliners' must somehow demonstrate that they can be aspiring wage-earning subjects, rendering them economically 'productive' and 'legible' vis-à-vis the state.

Nafea moved between black market jobs and mini jobs every few weeks, but the 'work' that was most meaningful to him was a combination of his music and the social work he did with at-risk refugee youth. He became a member of a band that included four Syrian friends who had all studied in the music conservatoire in Syria, whom Nafea helped settle in Berlin. The labour involved in busking, chasing gigs and finding space to rehearse is familiar to any musician living in a creative and bohemian city – for most this labour also involves 'extra bits on the side', to subsidize one's musical vocation. Nafea combined this with social work, mentoring Syrian and other immigrant youth who moved between school, petty street crime, and special 'camp flats' where they lived with over-worked social workers. As Nafea put it:

> 'They are not afraid of police, because the police is less strict than their family culture back home. But here they don't have the family culture – where your neighbourhood all know your family and everyone knows you and your father. It keeps you in line. Here they don't have that. So because I passed all their problems when I first arrived here in Germany, one by one, I know. So I sometimes use that family culture, but mostly I try to put them in a winner situation.'

By 'winner situation' Nafea meant that he taught these youth how to 'play with the rules' of the German bureaucratic system. The 'job centre', for example, offered a form of housing, work and family subsidy, but navigating 'the system' was cryptic if you did not speak German, if you did not understand the legal requirements and/or if you did not know how to find out what forms of support you were eligible for. Once you were in the system, the paper work, the queues, the forms ... "they are shitty but it's better than the street."

Thus, for Nafea, *hustling* involved keeping one foot in the *job centre* (and the exploitative mini-jobs it promoted) and one foot in the informal employment market, all the while seeking out opportunities for more meaningful work that mobilized his musical passion and social activism. For Nafea, music was one among multiple other means to connect with people, to help them find their way as 'new Berliners', to defy the tropes of the refugee label and blend in with other musical artists in a creative makeshift city. Nafea's life in Berlin thus required the simultaneous navigation of welfare subsidies, *Ausbildung* opportunities, and meaningful (though not always remunerated) forms of creative work.

Conclusion

The labour required to make a living in 'impossible' urban landscapes (De Boeck and Baloji, 2016) poses a challenge to dominant normative and institutional understandings of work, existing at the interstices between mainstream and marginal forms of labour, legality and legitimacy. Here, diverse forms of labour coexist, associated with the making of urban life when returns are highly uncertain, and when the nature of work can involve forms of unlikely accumulation, spontaneous loss, efforts to keep trying, and the hunt to find 'extra bits on the side'. The three vignettes presented here shed light on the 'productive potentials of uncertainty' (Cooper and Pratten, 2015, 1) and associated economic experiments across three ethnographic contexts.

Moonlighting has long been an essential strategy of the entrepreneurial poor in their attempts to supplement the meagre income provided by low-end wage employment (Polsky, 1967). But how are we to make sense of cases in which moonlighting becomes more secure and more meaningful than the wage (or subsidy) itself? Hustling in all of the three cases described earlier involved moonlighting as a form of self-provisioning alongside the semblance of a wage. At the same time, each of my interlocutors saw some value in persisting with the 'day job' insofar as this job afforded them a certain legibility and legitimacy vis-à-vis the probation officer, the social enterprise or the asylum system, conferring access to particular resources and rights. Rather than replacing the wage, the hustle operates strategically alongside it, to the extent that the two become relationally contingent. In a world of 'shit wages', the side hustle has become a key strategy for staving off destitution and helplessness, enabling a kind of precarious endurance. However, rather than challenging racialised, classed and gendered inequalities and vulnerabilities, it may serve to deepen them, as Tressie McMillan Cottom (2020) has recently cautioned in the case of the tech industry.

The experiences of Eliza, Damien and Nafea point to particular subjectivities and social relations that position the side hustle as a subversive response to persistent legacies of uneven development and socio-economic injustice. Read together, these portraits explore the hustle as an economy in action and a mode of social life that reach across contexts of postcolonial and austerity urbanism (Simone, 2004;

Tonkiss, 2013; Vasudevan, 2014) where social and economic relations are continuously reconfigured. For all three of my interlocutors, the posture and practice of hustling justifies both constantly being on the move, while assuming a certain discretion about *where* one is moving. Each of their side hustles is difficult to pin down, even by friends and close peers (let alone the elder, the probation officer, the job centre or the prefecture). And while plans can be made, and futures imagined, plans are expected to be altered at best, and broken most of the time, so in practice what 'gets done' is never *what was planned* but rather what was *put in place* given the structures of opportunity at hand.

I wish to end by outlining three ways in which the experiences of Eliza, Damien and Nafea might contribute to recent debates on (the future of) work. First, in spite of the global decline of formal wage employment and proliferation of 'shit wages', mainstream institutions including governments persist in positioning wage labour as an essential vehicle of citizenship, inclusion and recognition. The experiences of my three interlocutors demonstrate how particular welfare conditionalities on the one hand and 'targets' on the other seek to turn informal workers, refugees and prison leavers into disciplined, 'economically productive' wage-earning subjects. And yet, the types of wage employment that these policies valorize are in sharp decline, replaced instead with a constellation of precarious low-end jobs with 'shit' or 'mini' wages. In this context, the continued valorization of wage employment serves to perpetuate a mirage of the 'proper job' (Ferguson and Li, 2018), conferring a sort of 'cruel optimism' (Berlant, 2011).

Second, the three vignettes presented here challenge the presumption that those consigned to 'shit wages' might resign themselves to in-work poverty. Confounding legalistic and economistic approaches which seek to classify work through the binaries of formal/informal, waged/unwaged, licit/illicit, the experiences of Eliza, Damien and Nafea demonstrate the ways in which ordinary working lives at the urban margins are increasingly dependent on straddling these divides, creatively combining different forms of work and suspending their legal, moral and economic parameters. Rather than an *alternative* to wage labour then, the side hustle might be read as an essential composite in the face of declining wages and increasing austerity.

Third, this chapter contributes to the collective retheorization of work by re-centring the form of work that takes place 'on the side', and its entanglement with 'social thickness', which differs from that of the unionized wage earner so often centred in the literature on work. Rather than professional skills and formal qualifications, the working lives of my three interlocutors are propelled forward by social relationships – or 'vitamin B'. It is through a focus on these relationships – and the various forms of support and reciprocation and moments of micro-exploitation they entail – that we might move towards a different understanding of ordinary working life. This approach draws parallels with Ferguson's (2015, 94) argument that for an increasing number of people around the world, the work of 'surviving' is 'less about producing goods and services than it is about securing distributive outcomes'. However, as Damien reminds us, and Eliza and Nafea show, these relationships also open up possibilities – however fleeting – to aspire to a life beyond mere survival.

Acknowledgements

I am grateful to the funders of the three research projects from which this chapter draws: the ESRC and the BIEA, who funded my research in Nairobi, Kenya; a Cambridge Humanities grant, which funded the project *Making Work outside of Prison*; and the British Academy, who funded the project *Temporary migrants or new European citizens*. I would like to thank the editors of this book for inviting me to take part in this meaningful collection on the back of several memorable workshops over the past few years, focused on rethinking work in the post-wage economy. Their editorial comments and encouragement on draft versions of this chapter were much appreciated and helped me sharpen my overall argument. Most of all, my deepest gratitude goes to my three interlocutors featured here for sharing their time and stories, shedding light on the thorny and creative economic arrangements that make up a living when formal systems of support fail. I hope I have shown that their economic knowledge and expertise merits greater attention and respect.

Notes

[1] Informal conversation, April 2017, Huruma.
[2] A pseudonym is used here to protect his identity.
[3] Again, to protect her identity, I avoid specifying which Eastern European country.

References

Amin, A. (ed) (2011) *Post-Fordism: A Reader* (1st edn), Oxford: Wiley-Blackwell.

Bakkali, Y. (2019) 'Dying to live: Youth violence and the munpain', *The Sociological Review*, 67(6): 1317–1332.

Barford, A. and Coombe, R. (2019) 'Getting By: Young People's Working Lives', University of Cambridge. Available at: https://www.geog.cam.ac.uk/research/ projects/decentwork/gettingby.pdf.

Berlant, L. (2011) *Cruel Optimism*, Durham, NC: Duke University Press.

Brun, C. (2015) 'Active waiting and changing hopes: Toward a time perspective on protracted displacement', *Social Analysis*, 59: 19–37.

Cooper, E. and Pratten, D. (eds) (2015) *Ethnographies of Uncertainty in Africa, Anthropology, Change, and Development*, Basingstoke: Palgrave Macmillan.

Cottom, T. C. (2020) 'The hustle economy', *Dissent Magazine*, special issue on Technology and Crisis of Work. Available at: https://www.dissentmagazine.org/article/the-hustle-economy

Darling, J. (2017) 'Forced migration and the city: Irregularity, informality, and the politics of presence', *Progress in Human Geography*, 41(2): 178–198.

De Boeck, F. and Baloji, S. (2016) *Suturing the City: Living Together in Congo's Urban Worlds*, London: Autograph ABP.

Dowling, E. and Harvie, D. (2014) 'Harnessing the social: State, crisis and (big) society', *Sociology*, 48(5): 869–886.

Ferguson, J. (2006) *Global Shadows: Africa in the Neoliberal World Order, A Nice Book, Minimal Shelf Wear*, Durham, NC: Duke University Press.

Ferguson, J. (2015) *Give a Man a Fish*, Durham, NC: Duke University Press.

Ferguson, J. and Li, T.M. (2018) 'Beyond the "proper job": Political-economic analysis after the century of labouring man', Working Paper 51. PLAAS, UWC: Cape Town, 26.

Fredericks, R. (2014) '"The Old Man is Dead": Hip hop and the arts of citizenship of Senegalese youth', *Antipode*, 46(1): 130–148.

Gibson-Graham, J.K. (2008) 'Diverse economies: Performative practices for "other worlds"', *Progress in Human Geography*, 32(5): 613–632.

Gidwani, V. (2008) *Capital, Interrupted: Agrarian Development and the Politics of Work in India*, Minneapolis, MN: University of Minnesota Press.

Hart, K. (1973) 'Informal income opportunities and urban employment in Ghana', *Journal of Modern African Studies*, 11(1): 61–89.

Hart, K. (2009) 'On the informal economy: The political history of an ethnographic concept', Centre Emile Bernheim CEB Working Paper No. 09/042, 22.

Hart, K. (2010) 'Informal economy', in Hart, K., Laville, J.-L. and Cattani, A. (eds) *The Human Economy*, Cambridge: Polity, 142–153.

Hart, K., Laville, J.-L. and Cattani, A. (2010a) 'Building the human economy together', in *The Human Economy*, Cambridge: Polity, 1–17.

Hart, K., Laville, J.-L. and Cattani, A.D. (2010b) *The Human Economy*, Cambridge: Polity.

Holston, J. (2009) 'Insurgent citizenship in an era of global urban peripheries', *City and Society*, 21(2): 245–267.

ILO (2018) 'Informality and non-standard forms of employment'. Available at: https://www.ilo.org/wcmsp5/groups/public/—dgreports/—inst/documents/publication/wcms_646040.pdf

Kinder, K. (2016) *DIY Detroit: Making Do in a City without Services*, Minneapolis, MN: University of Minnesota Press.

Lancione, M. (ed) (2016) *Rethinking Life at the Margins* (1st edn), London: Routledge.

MacGaffey, J. (1991) *The Real Economy of Zaire: The Contribution of Smuggling and Other Unofficial Activities to National Wealth*, Philadelphia, PA: University of Pennsylvania Press.

McDowell, L. (2013) *Working Lives: Gender, Migration and Employment in Britain, 1945–2007*, Chichester: Wiley-Blackwell.

Mckenzie, L. (2015) *Getting By: Estates, Class and Culture in Austerity Britain* (1st edn), Bristol: Policy Press.

Meagher, K. (2018) 'Cannibalizing the informal economy: Frugal innovation and economic inclusion in Africa', *European Journal of Development Research*, 30: 17–33.

Millar, K.M. (2018) *Reclaiming the Discarded*, Durham, NC: Duke University Press.

Myers, G. (2011) *African Cities: Alternative Visions of Urban Theory and Practice* (1st edn), London; New York, NY: Zed Books.

Neuwirth, R. (2012) *Stealth of Nations* (reprint edn), New York, NY: Anchor Books.

Newell, S. (2012) *The Modernity Bluff: Crime, Consumption, and Citizenship in Côte d'Ivoire*, Chicago, IL: University of Chicago Press.

Polsky, N. (1967) *Hustlers, Beats, and Others* (1st edn), New Brunswick, NJ: Aldine Transaction.

Richardson, L. (2015) 'Performing the sharing economy', *Geoforum*, 67: 121–129.

Richardson, L. and Thieme, T.A. (2020) 'Planning working futures: precarious work through carceral space', *Social and Cultural Geography*, 21(1): 25–44.

Roitman, J.L. (1990) 'The politics of informal markets in sub-Saharan Africa'. *Journal of Modern African Studies*, 28(4): 671–696.

Saitta, P., Shapland, J. and Verhage, A. (eds) (2013) *Getting By or Getting Rich?: The Formal, Informal and Criminal Economy in a Globalised World*, The Hague: Eleven International Publishing.

Scott, J. (1999) *Seeing Like a State: How Certain Schemes to Improve the Human Condition Have Failed*, New Haven, CT: Yale University Press.

Simone, A. and Pieterse, E. (2017) *New Urban Worlds: Inhabiting Dissonant Times*, Cambridge: Polity.

Simone, A.M. (2004) 'People as infrastructure: Intersecting fragments in Johannesburg', *Public Culture*, 16(3): 407–429.

Standing, G. (2011) *The Precariat*, London: Bloomsbury Academic.

Sturge, G. (2019) UK Prison Population Statistics (Briefing Paper No. CBP-04334), House of Commons Library.

Sundararajan, A. (2016) *The Sharing Economy: The End of Employment and the Rise of Crowd-Based Capitalism*, Cambridge, MA: MIT Press.

Thieme, T. (2016) '"The ghetto will always be my living room": hustling and belonging in the Nairobi slums', in Michele Lancione (ed) *Rethinking Life at the Margins: The Assemblage of Contexts, Subjects, and Politics*, London: Routledge, 106–121.

Thieme, T.A. (2018) 'The hustle economy: Informality, uncertainty and the geographies of getting by', *Progress in Human Geography*, 42(4): 529–548.

Tonkiss, F. (2013) 'Austerity urbanism and the makeshift city', *City*, 17(3): 312–324.

Vasudevan, A. (2014) 'The makeshift city: Towards a global geography of squatting', *Progress in Human Geography*, 39(3): 338–359.

Venkatesh, S. (2008) *Off the Books: The Underground Economy of the Urban Poor*, Cambridge, MA: Harvard University Press.

Vigh, H. (2010) 'Motion squared: A second look at the concept of social navigation', *Anthropological Theory*, 9(4): 419–438.

Waite, L. (2009) 'A place and space for a critical geography of precarity?' *Geography Compass*, 3(1): 412–433.

White, J. (2020) *Terraformed: Young Black Lives in the Inner City*, London: Repeater Books.

Willis, P. (1981) *Learning to Labor: How Working-Class Kids Get Working-Class Jobs*, New York, NY: Columbia University Press.

2

The Work of Looking for Work: Surviving Without a Wage in Austerity Britain

Samuel Strong

Speaking at the Conservative Party conference in 2012, the then Chancellor of the Exchequer[1] George Osborne sought to reflect upon the moral underpinnings of the 'age of austerity' introduced by his government. Specifically, he attempted to justify a swathe of cuts to social security, welfare payments, the public sector and local government by invoking a moral notion of *work*:

> Where is the fairness, we ask, for the shift-worker, leaving home in the dark hours of the early morning, who looks up at the closed blinds of their next-door neighbour sleeping off a life on benefits? When we say we're all in this together, we speak for that worker. We speak for all those who want to work hard and get on. This is the mission of the modern Conservative Party. (Osborne, 2012)

For Osborne and his government, it is work that qualifies a person as a citizen of a nation 'working together to get on'. The figure of the 'worker' is variously depicted as 'the owner of the corner shop staying open until midnight to support their family', 'the teacher prepared to defy her union and stay late to take the after-school club', and 'the commuter who leaves home before their children are up, and comes back long after they have gone to bed'. In each iteration, it is the self-sacrifice of the worker that distinguishes them from the abject Other 'sleeping off a life on benefits'. This opposition is central to the cultural political economy of austerity (Jensen and Tyler, 2015), through which the population is divided into 'workers and shirkers' and 'strivers and skivers' (Valentine and Harris, 2014). Such an account not only conflates 'worklessness'[2] with failure: it also positions work as the primary route to social citizenship at a time of austerity (Barchiesi, 2011; Edminston, 2017).

By foregrounding a particular understanding of work, Osborne simultaneously invokes an idea of non-work as indolence. In the Chancellor's pronouncement, those who receive benefits – those unemployed, sick and disabled, and/or with caring responsibilities – are positioned as static, aimless and confined to private space. They are at once both hyper-visible through their moral failure, but menacingly concealed through the closed blinds of their homes. Conversely, in Osborne's vision, those in employment have forsaken these static behaviours in favour of lengthy commutes and late hours working in public spaces of shops and schools. By virtue of their mobility, those who work exercise the necessary self-sacrifice fetishized at a time of austerity. Such a discursive positioning of work allowed the architects of austerity in the UK to position themselves as the party of justice, and a party of the people: 'We modern Conservatives represent all those who aspire, all who work, save and hope, all who feel a responsibility to put in, not just take out ... Whoever you are, wherever you come from, if you're working for a better future – we are on your side' (Osborne, 2012).

Underpinning Osborne's vision of fairness is the apparent moral goodness imparted by work – and the abjectness of a life without it. This imaginative geography of work and worklessness interfaces, then, with a Manichaean tale of good and bad that is mobilized in order to justify cuts to provisions for those without access to employment. Within this imagination, welfare payments are framed as a generous (and unwarranted) 'gift' from those who do work to those who do not (Pemberton et al, 2016). Furthermore, welfare is itself presented as *the* cause of moral failure, and as a positive institution reproducing a 'workless' underclass mired in fecklessness and dependency (Kaufman and Nelson, 2012).

The alignment of hard work with notions of deservingness is, of course, nothing new – it follows a long history in the UK of imaginations of a deserving and undeserving poor (Himmelfarb, 1995). By positioning poverty as a matter of personal failure – of a lack of moral fibre, work ethic and so on – work has been positioned as integral to both the *cause* of poverty (driven by the failure and absence of work) and its *solution* (through the prescription of work to those who seemingly do not). Indeed, since the introduction of the so-called 'New Poor Law' in England in 1834, the role of the state has emerged as both a provider of relief and an engineer, refashioning and recasting behaviour through particular ideas of work – ideas that reproduce the political distinction between work and worklessness (Driver, 2004). Osborne's intervention continues this historical tradition by privileging a narrow understanding of work as *formal wage labour*. This conflation of work with formal employment reifies a masculinist, ableist idea of work as employment that takes place outside of the household, erasing the value of feminized acts of care and reproduction (McDowell, 1991; Rose, 1993). Furthermore, it conceals the diverse range of socio-economic activities – be they based around reciprocity, gifting, sharing or otherwise – that proliferate at a time of austerity (Holmes, 2018; Shaw and Waterstone, 2019).

These other forms of labour include 'unpaid domestic work,' 'unpaid voluntary and community work' and 'paid undeclared work' (Williams and Nadin, 2012, 2, quoted in Monteith and Giesbert, 2017, 817). Such examples of work outside of formal wage employment represent a 'mode of practice' (Roy and Alsayaad, 2004), straddling material labours and those grounded in the reproduction of affective, emotional and social relations between different people and places (Gërxhani, 2004; Bremen, 2010; Thieme, 2018). The refusal of politicians such as Osborne to recognize such activities *as work* is thus fundamental to the reproduction of the binary categories of the worker and shirker in austerity Britain.

In this chapter, I attempt to deconstruct these categories by broadening our understanding of work beyond wage labour. What forms of unwaged work proliferate at a time of austerity? Who carries out this work? And how do we study it when there is no clear 'workplace'? I respond to these questions through an engagement with the lived experiences of Jeff, a long-term unemployed man living in one of the UK's most wage-scarce spaces: the Valleys of South Wales. Jeff's testimony enables us to theorize the often intense and desperate works that punctuate his lifeworld. Far from 'sleeping off a life on benefits', I show that Jeff's endeavours include working in and against increasingly coercive welfare bureaucracies and labouring in his local area to reproduce a loose social safety net at a time of austerity.

One of the central ironies revealed by Jeff's story is that the forms of work that emerge at a time of austerity – what I describe as 'the work of looking for work' – in fact make it more difficult for people to access formal wage employment. Indeed, I argue that the forms of coercion and conditionality increasingly placed upon the unwaged at a time of austerity propagate forms of 'cruel optimism' that keep the wageless in a state of permanent impermanence, waiting for wage employment that will likely never be attainable (Berlant, 2011). I start by outlining the changes to welfare and social security presided over by Osborne's government, before introducing the Valleys as a case study of a wage-scarce space. I then present Jeff's story, reflecting specifically on the changing constellations of work at a time of austerity.

Work and welfare at a time of austerity

The election of the Conservative-Liberal Democrat coalition government in 2010 signalled the beginning of a new 'age of austerity' in the UK, subsequently renewed via Conservative election victories in 2015 and 2017. The relationship between work, welfare and citizenship was significantly redrawn in this period. Specifically, as Cain (2016, 489) notes, 'austerity and recovery rhetoric ... combined with pre-austerity neoliberal imperatives to "responsibilise" the workforce and its counterpart, the "workless" population – emphasising entrepreneurship, personal risk management, and other neoliberal values'.

By downplaying the language of rights, and instead emphasizing the *responsibilities* of those receiving benefits, politicians repositioned work as *the* moral obligation of citizenship. They invoked a discourse of 'hard work' – of toil, routine and the denial of pleasure – in order to generate powerful moral responses to notions of fairness, redistribution and the welfare state (Jensen, 2012). As Forkert (2014, 47) has argued, this discourse has 'created a vocabulary of images and symbols which give shape to a sense of anger and resentment that is focused on the ways in which members of out-groups, namely, those without wage employment, apparently take advantage of the hard work and everyday sacrifices of the majority'. In this reading, the unemployed are rendered responsible for their own unemployment, building consent for a range of reforms that have furthered their disenfranchisement. Policies have included the introduction of a spare 'bedroom tax' and switch-over to Universal Credit, a cap on total household benefit receipt, cuts to payments available to the sick and disabled, as well as freezes on child benefit rates (Hamnett, 2014). These changes have inflicted significant damage on the financial outcomes of those who receive income from the welfare state (Strong, 2020a). At the same time, policies have been introduced to reward wage workers by reducing income tax rates – both by the raising of the threshold at which income tax is calculated (the so-called 'personal allowance') and by cutting the top rate of tax for earnings over £150,000 per year from 50 per cent to 45 per cent.

Together, these changes detail a society that increasingly values wage employment both discursively and financially – with a larger redistributive effect channelling wealth increasingly away from those unemployed, and towards those earning (high) wages.[3] Illustratively, a recent report by the Institute for Public Policy Research (2019) found that social security payments have reached their lowest level since the launch of the welfare state – with the £73 standard weekly allowance under Universal Credit (a benefit now claimed by 2.3 million people) equivalent to just 12.5 per cent of median earnings (compared to unemployment benefit, when introduced in 1948, being worth 20 per cent). Such a privileging of 'work over welfare', to use Haskins' (2006) term, 'has been at the heart of welfare reform changes over the past three decades' (Daguerre and Etherington, 2016, 203). Crucially, however, austerity signals a step change from the 'creeping conditionality' that has characterized workfarism since the 1980s (Dwyer, 2004). For MacLeavy (2011), the age of 'welfare austerity' has been preceded by two main components of workfare introduced by New Labour since the mid-1990s: a focus on 'welfare-to-work' and attempts to 'make work pay'. Put another way, New Labour under Tony Blair sought to introduce a carrot (working tax credits, the introduction of the minimum wage) and stick (welfare conditionality) approach to reforming the welfare state (Peck, 2001). Under austerity, the coercive aspects of conditionality have been strengthened – indicative of the changing imbalance between the right (coercive) and left (caring) 'hands' of the state (Bourdieu 1998). Indeed, the last decade has seen the distinctions between these two hands being reduced, as both become more marketized and punitive (Wacquant, 2009).

This trend is most apparent in the 'welfare contractualism' that has intensified at a time of austerity (White, 2000), 'with the language of contracts pervading most areas of welfare' (Daguerre and Etherington, 2014, 73). Enshrined in the Welfare Reform Act of 2012, those seeking out-of-work payments must sign a 'claimant commitment' – 'a record of a claimant's responsibilities in relation to the award of universal credit' (clause 14.1). Included in this commitment is the ability of the state to expect 'all reasonable action … for the purpose of obtaining paid work' (clause 17.1), and to impose a set of activities, requirements and actions on jobseekers in order for them to continue to qualify for benefit payments. This includes a requirement to comply with 35 hours of weekly jobseeking (which must be evidenced by the claimant), to undertake mandatory work placements, to attend compulsory forms of training, improve personal presentation and to accept suggested work experience programmes. In the words of the then Secretary of State for Work and Pensions Iain Duncan Smith (2014):

> Through the 'claimant commitment', which deliberately mirrors a contract of employment, we are making this deal unequivocal. Those in work have obligations to their employer; so too claimants a responsibility to the taxpayer: in return for support, and where they are able, they must do their bit to find work.

By redefining out-of-work benefits as a form of waged employment (Pfannebecker and Smith, 2020), these contractual obligations have increasingly transformed unemployment into a pastiche of a job (Southwood, 2011). Such claimant commitments are enforced through negative financial incentives – or, put in the language of the Welfare Reform Act, the introduction of 'sanctions' that entail the withholding of benefit payments to those deemed to have breached this contract. While the withholding of benefit payments was not a new practice, sanctioning became more severe and widespread under the Coalition Government. The Welfare Reform Act 2012 increased the minimum sanction period from a single week to four weeks, while the maximum was extended from 26 weeks to three years (Daguerre and Etherington, 2016). Accompanying this raised intensity of potential sanctions has been an increased frequency: compared to an average of 2.2 per cent of Jobseeker's Allowance (JSA) claimants being sanctioned each month between 2000 and 2006, the proportion of JSA claimants being sanctioned peaked at over 8 per cent in 2013 (Webster, 2014). Moreover, the gradual switch-over to Universal Credit has introduced a benefit that is again sanctioned more frequently than for any benefit under the previous Labour government, with the monthly overall average of sanctions between August 2015 and February 2018 standing at 6.7 per cent of claimants (Webster, 2018).

As a tool of governance, welfare reform attempts to transform more than the economy. Sanctioning, contractualism and the contraction of welfare payments all aim at changing behaviour – and ultimately producing new working subjects. Considering the impact of these modes of governance – the forms of work they produce and their geographically uneven distribution over different people and places – allows for an interrogation of how austerity comes to 'actually exist' in everyday life (Hitchen, 2016; Hall, 2019; Strong, 2020b). While policy reforms have lowered the financial incomes and public services available to unemployed groups, austerity has also seeped into the lifeworlds of wageless populations in other ways (Strong, 2020c). For those at the sharp end of these reforms, it is clear that 'austerities matter, keenly and painfully, in everyday spaces' (Horton, 2016, 360).

Work provides an important site in which policy reforms and everyday lived realities of austerity meet. How do wageless populations provision for themselves and others in the context of an increasingly conditional and precarious welfare system? What acts of agency and organization do they deploy in their attempts to survive? And how might these acts encourage us to broaden our understandings of 'work'? I seek to respond to these questions through an engagement with the many works of Jeff, a long-term unemployed resident of the Valleys.

The rise and fall of wage employment in the Valleys

To understand Jeff's story, we must trace the geographical and historical coordinates of his predicament. Jeff lives in the Valleys – a region among the most deprived in Western Europe (WIMD, 2014; Eurostat, 2018). The Valleys experienced its own 'great transformation' in the eighteenth and nineteenth centuries, as a landscape marked by mutualism, agricultural labour and communal economies was (often violently) undermined by industrialization and proletarianization (Polanyi, 1944) – a process the novelist Alexander Cordell (1959) describes as the 'rape of the fair country'. While remnants of the pre-industrial era are still visible in the cultural institutions and social practices of the Valleys, wage labour was instituted as *the* model of social organization in this period.

However, this social and economic model has itself since receded with the decline of industrial capitalism. Home to the largest steelworks in Europe as recently as the 1960s (which has now not only closed, but was erased from the landscape in 2002), the area has since felt the sharp effects of deindustrialization. Illustratively, in the town[4] where Jeff resides, there were 8,900 steelworkers and 1,886 miners employed in 1951 – with only 176 people registered as unemployed (Gray-Jones, 1992). Between 1961 and 1971, Jeff's town lost 2,751 jobs – with actual employment reducing from 15,754 in 1961 to 13,003 in 1971 (Alden, 1977). In April 1976, the male[5] unemployment rate in Jeff's town was 10.0 per cent – compared to a UK rate of 6.9 per cent. At the time of writing, in 2015–16, the male unemployment rate in Jeff's area stood at 10.3 per cent – more than double the UK average of 5.1 per cent (NOMIS, 2017).

Such statistics represent the tip of the iceberg insofar as they only account for those people actively seeking work via the institutions of the state. A recent study by the Organisation for Economic Co-operation and Development (OECD) and Centre for Cities (2019, 32) found that 'when accounting for those who are economically inactive for economic reasons [in the UK] ... the share of people who are not in employment but could potentially work would move more than two times higher [at] 13.2%'. Furthermore, in order to be considered 'in work' by the government, an individual only needs to work for a minimum of one hour per week. Consequently, such statistics do not capture the current state of *under*employment, 'zero hours' and flexible contracts, and the so-called 'gig economy', which are becoming increasingly prevalent in the UK today (Heyes et al, 2017). Crucially, national averages conceal the spatial inequalities in the UK economy – with people's experience and access to work varying regionally and by social group. Given that the Valleys has an unemployment rate twice the national average – and that it has one of the highest rates of sick and disability benefit claimants across the UK – then the more than twofold actual rate of unemployment in the UK identified by the OECD and Centre for Cities is likely to be even higher in this region.

These factors illustrate the shortcomings of national employment statistics and the need for more disaggregated approaches that consider particular histories and geographies of work in different regions and localities. For example, despite being situated in a national context with historically low rates of unemployment, it is important to recognize the Valleys as a *wage-scarce space* – where the availability of wage work is at a quantitative low both historically and geographically. In Marxist theory, such spaces are considered surplus, as reservoirs of labour left marooned by the rise and fall of different flows of capital and their spatial fix (in this case, the receding of industrial development) (Harvey, 1981; Smith, 1984).

But in theorizing the very real economic abandonment of such regions, scholars have often elided the withdrawal of wage labour with an apparent loss of other forms of work – and in so doing followed the same conflation of work and wage labour as evidenced by George Osborne in the introduction to this chapter (Denning, 2016). Illustratively, in seeking to theorize the 'collateral damage' of neoliberal austerity in deprived parts of the UK, it is often assumed that wage-scarce spaces are by extension void of sociality and politics (Strong, 2014). Such assumptions not only oversimplify the everyday realities of unemployment: they also treat those who are unemployed as persons devoid of agency, upon which austerity is straightforwardly secured. Indeed, as Thieme (2018) notes, narratives of abandonment, informality and precarity often miss the social, economic and cultural practices that come to function – and even thrive – in these interstitial spaces. Such narratives run the risk of reproducing territorial stigmatization (Wacquant et al, 2014), rendering wage-scarce space – and, by extension, wageless life – as something that is less than human, and less than life itself (Strong, 2019). They tell a uniform story of economic abandonment, without acknowledging the strategies and practices of coping, survival and organization that emerge in and from these spaces, and the alternative forms of work – broadly conceived – that are exercised to fill these gaps. To think about work in this wider sense thus requires a grounded perspective and an appraisal of the seemingly *ordinary* acts, responsibilities and practices that mark everyday life in the Valleys.

Surviving without a wage in austerity Britain

I first met Jeff at our local food bank in 2014. I had recently moved to the Valleys in order to complete my doctoral fieldwork constructing a 'people's geography of poverty' through a multi-sited, 15-month ethnographic study of the area (Strong, 2020d). As a volunteer for the organization, I found that the food bank became an important space for my research – but also a place to socialize and get to know other local people. I began to spend time with Jeff at a weekly job-searching scheme housed at a local library. Without access to a computer or the internet, Jeff relied upon the library service to keep up to date with his compulsory jobseeking.

At 59, Jeff possessed a dry sense of humour, a fondness for practical jokes, and a love for reading. During our stints volunteering together at the food bank, Jeff would frequently regale me with insights gleaned from the writings of his favourite physicist Stephen Hawking. He had moved to the Valleys seven and a half years previously to take up a high-ranking job in the electronics industry. However, he was made redundant six months later. In the period of unemployment that followed, Jeff experienced the sharp end of austerity – including periods of sanctioning, hunger and homelessness.

Electronics is a sector which has all but disappeared both in Jeff's town and in Wales more broadly. Illustratively, employment rates in production industries fell from 123,000 in 2001, to 101,300 in 2015 in West Wales and the Valleys, and from 209,500 to 172,500 over the same time period across all of Wales (StatsWales, 2016). In Jeff's words, "All electronics companies moved out of the area and went off to Poland.

Leaving us, well, as a destitute area for want of a better word. It was one of the up-and-coming industries at the time, and then it suddenly just went overnight." He emphasized, "There's nothing in the Valleys for me" as deindustrialization had left his town "the unemployed centre of the world". Consequently, he felt geographically isolated from the electronics labour market: "The nearest place is Bristol or Swindon. Commuting to Bristol or Swindon when you're unemployed, and you have no transport, is basically impossible." Such a journey would cost Jeff his entire weekly unemployment benefits for one return trip, with no guarantee of employment at the end of it.

Jeff's ability to find work was stifled by the financial realities of living on unemployment benefits. During our time working together, Jeff was transitioned from JSA to Universal Credit, a system that aims to roll six benefit systems into one – and has been plagued by delays for claimants, legal challenges and administrative errors (Institute for Government, 2016). The delays Jeff faced in receiving his new payments compounded the limits of a system of unemployment relief that is already the lowest among comparative OECD economies (TUC, 2015). Indeed, a study by Glassdoor (2016) found that the UK's unemployment benefit system paid by far the lowest across 14 European countries sampled – with the UK's flat rates of €66 (for 16–24 year olds) and €84 (for those aged 25 and over) much lower than the second-lowest, Ireland's flat-rate of €188 per week. Jeff explained the implications of this system:

> 'When you're living on minimum finances, you can only do certain things. And those certain things mean that you're spending half your time looking for work, the other half you spend trying to support yourself enough to eat. Which means, basically, you're cooking the longest and hardest way possible. Which means it's taking you a lot of time and a lot of money, especially in gas and leccy [electricity]. Which eventually means you're out of heating, or out of something.'

Far from 'a life spent sleeping off benefits', to return to Osborne's statement, Jeff's life is instead punctuated by intense, often desperate works to maintain his existence. Jeff's ability to search for work (yet alone gain employment) is hindered by these day-to-day challenges of living on welfare payments. Put another way, living without a wage necessitates *greater work* in order to survive. Everyday acts of social reproduction – cooking, washing, shopping – all become harder in a lifeworld of pre-payment meters, no access to transport and dilemmas over whether to 'heat or eat'. Such activities all form part of the 'work of looking for work' in austerity Britain.

The work of looking for work

In order to continue to receive his out-of-work benefits, Jeff was required to keep to the aforementioned claimant commitment. He had a contractual obligation to the state, enacted by advisers at the Jobcentre, to prove that he was seeking work. Specifically, Jeff was expected to demonstrate 35 hours of jobseeking each week. During the time I worked with Jeff, he was expected to use the government's Universal Jobmatch (UJM – a website that has since been scrapped by the government) to search for jobs, log those he was applying for, and to fill in or track potential openings. The website included dialogue boxes for Jeff to complete, explaining what he had done in each online session.

As well as adding an extra layer of work for Jeff in the tasks necessary to prove his jobseeking, such actions demonstrate the expansion of the disciplinary optics of the state into the lives and activities of the unemployed (Dean, 1995; Wacquant, 2009; Strong, 2019). Navigating such systems successfully was anything but a given. As with many of Jeff's generation who have little previous experience working with ICT, accessing a computer often relied on the availability of facilities and support at local libraries – a service which is itself facing major cutbacks at a time of austerity (Robinson and Sheldon, 2019). It also required a level of computational literacy in order to surf the internet, set up a working email account, and type enough information into UJM to demonstrate that one was actively seeking work. Thus, for Jeff, both his inability to afford a computer and his age compounded the amount of time he spent documenting and legitimating his search for employment.

Alongside these endeavours, Jeff was required to attend the Jobcentre every two weeks to meet with an adviser. The nearest Jobcentre was three and a half miles away from Jeff's home. Without a car, this journey entailed a walk of over an hour over hilly terrain, or a 15-minute walk aided by public transport (a single bus ticket for this journey costing £7.10 or £10.50 for a return [Stagecoach, 2019]). For a man of Jeff's age, a roundtrip of seven miles was testing. As he put it, "when you're my age, forget it. You're just too old."

Upon arriving at the Jobcentre, Jeff encountered a complex bureaucracy. Appointments were arranged at a time of choosing by the institution, usually with different advisers, and were often the cause of much anxiety and stress given the aforementioned powers to sanction welfare claimants. Jeff's experiences of sanctioning are revealing of a callous system:

> 'I was sanctioned for failing to turn up to an interview – an interview I didn't get the letter [for] because my house burned down and they sent the letter to my old address, not my new address. Which they had been given! So as a result, I ended up on a two month sanction for something that was not my fault, for something which I am still trying to get the money back for. I've not seen a penny of it. And you've got to live without any cash of any description.'

This series of events left Jeff homeless. Furthermore, during this period of sanctioning, Jeff was unable to seek employment. Having been made homeless by the fire, his time was instead spent navigating local charities and services to find emergency housing. Even when he was able to find new accommodation, he lacked the ready capital to put credit into his pre-payment gas meter, which further prevented him from resuming his search:

> 'For three weeks I had no bath facilities while I was trying to get the gas sorted out. Now, I would not want to employ me if I went to an interview if I stunk. End of. I wouldn't employ me. And as I used to be in the employment side of things, I can see all the problems I've got that's against me before I even start.'

Within this context, the Jobcentre's enforcement of a documented search for employment was inimical to Jeff's well-being and survival. Specifically, it made considerable demands on his time and resources and constituted an additional burden of work – travelling, logging activity electronically, attending meetings – all of which inhibited Jeff's struggle for social reproduction and survival:

> 'The Jobcentre is the biggest load of crap I've ever known. Because they don't care whether you get a job, because they're just there to sign you, to pay you. That's all they care about. They don't help you in anyway, other than send you to other people to do the work. They don't do the work themselves. Surely the Jobcentre is there to help you *get a job*?! Not to fend you off to other organizations,

like Working Links, A4E, Want2Work, Communities
First ... It's not their responsibility. Surely, it should be the
Jobcentre's responsibility? But, at the moment, it seems
to be "Ah, I do my bit. I sign you so you can have your
cash. That's it. Bye-bye. Bugger off." And that's the attitude
I get and have gotten all the time since I have ever been
on unemployment.'

The 'passing around' of Jeff to different agencies seemed to operate
as a deliberate tactic, intended to keep Jeff 'in a perpetual state of
jobreadiness' in spite of the chronic shortage of wage employment
the Valleys (Peck, 2001, 12). Jeff was thus left suspended in a state of
permanent impermanence and 'protracted liminality' (Thieme, 2013).
He was made to feel as though his unemployment was a temporary
phase, keeping him in a vigil of expectancy despite his advancing years.
This state of waithood had a significant impact on Jeff's well-being: it
is a function of 'cruel optimism' to engender a sense of hope for Jeff,
while the probability of his finding employment in such a wage-scarce
space is razor thin (Berlant, 2011). These feelings of false hope were
not incidental, but key to the disciplinary objective of keeping Jeff in
a state of readiness for a job that would never come:

'They should send me to the right people, not send me on
wild goose chases that get up my hopes like "yeah, I got a
chance, I got a chance", but nothing happens. And that is
time wasting. And for people that haven't got a bus pass[6],
that's going to cost them money to go to places to find out
that you're no better off when you went in through the
door. Well, what's the point? I don't see any point of that
at all. And I've heard many a person complain about that,
that are unemployed.'

The constant raising and dashing of hopes facilitated by workfare thus
required Jeff to perform another form of work – work of an affective
nature. For Hardt (1999), such affective labour may often appear
immaterial, but is vital to the workings of the reproduction of society.
Jeff was required not only to manage his own dashed hopes, but also to
continue the performance of positivity and optimism when engaging
with the Jobcentre and the various actors to which he was signposted.
    Through institutions like the Jobcentre, the austere state pushes an
ethopolitics that seeks to govern the affective life and the 'soul' of citizens
(Foucault, 1985; Rose, 1999). Specifically, by encouraging individuals

outside of wage employment to take responsibility for managing both their unemployment *and* the feelings of despair, hopelessness and failure that come with this position, the austere state works to instil a 'will to improve' over citizens (Li, 2007). Attempting to meet these demands required a great amount of emotional resilience from Jeff. The fruitless work of looking for work tested this resilience to its limits. When I asked Jeff about his future, he responded, "What future?"

While Jeff's general predicament was one of being marooned by the receding wave of industrial capitalism, his day-to-day activities were anything but static. His engagements with different organizations, coupled with trips to the Jobcentre, employment agencies and local libraries, reveal something of the broad and extended lifeworld of those unemployed in the Valleys. Navigating these different enforced actions was not a straightforward task: it required work – both in terms of the emotional energy needed to sustain such cruel optimism, and the time and energy spent keeping to these commitments.

Work without a wage

Despite Jeff's degrading and inhibiting encounters with the austere state, he managed to subsist by provisioning for himself. In doing so, he engaged in practices of what Thieme theorizes as 'hustling'; 'a constant pragmatic search for alternative structures of opportunity outside formal education, employment, and service provision' which 'assumes a continuous management of risk' (Thieme, 2018, 537). While Thieme's account of 'the hustle' is based upon the experiences of urban youth in Nairobi, Kenya, it finds increasing resonance with the experiences of older unemployed populations in deindustrialized spaces of the global North. In the context of precarious labour markets and lifeworlds, these forms of hustling are exercised as a geography of survival (Butler, 2004) – as acts that make living possible for those excluded from the formal employment market. The reproduction of such geographies of survival is not natural or inevitable, but the product of work:

> People in poverty continue to activate their own geographies of survival, to construct pathways of survival through the urban landscape that link together places ... poor people – housed and unhoused – find whatever means they must, legal or illegal, temporary or relatively permanent, to pay their bills, rest their heads, and meet their basic needs. (Mitchell and Heynen, 2009, 613)

In 'working out' his geography of survival, Jeff pursued two activities outside of the realm of the formal wage economy: gift transactions and reciprocity. For example, I asked him how he coped during his two-month sanction:

'Food bank, basically. With no gas, no electricity. It was hard, but you do what you have to do. You bum off friends to have a cup of coffee. You take your coffee around to them, because they can't afford it either because all your friends are basically unemployed. So you supply the materials, they supply you a drink. And that's the best you can do. And that includes meals as well. I've had to do that many a time.'

Jeff's account reveals the value of social relations in a community of people who are all 'feeling the squeeze' (Stenning, 2018). Through forms of sharing and the gifting of food from his local food bank, Jeff drew upon social support grounded in the politics of place. Rather than organic and inevitable, these relationships were the product of forms of work or what Elyachar (2010, 457) refers to as 'phatic labour' – the creation, maintenance and extension of channels through which resources can potentially flow – in the context of state withdrawal.

Such channels also provided Jeff with opportunities to pursue odd jobs. Whether DIY, decorating or gardening, these activities allowed Jeff to supplement (or partially replace) his jobseeker's income with food, drink and ad hoc forms of social support. As with much work located in the informal economy, such labours blur the distinction between production and reproduction, work and life (Saitta et al, 2013; Thieme, 2018). They blend acts of care with material transactions that bypass the cash economy. Jeff's works here were thus not individual, but *relational*. He explained, "People try their very best to help anybody that's literally down and out – which I have been. I've had a lot of help to get myself back on my feet since the fire. Physical help, and mental help too … It's a lovely area in that way." During this period, Jeff participated in another activity that blurred the boundaries between the state and civil society, production and reproduction. As part of his ongoing 'training' and 'preparation for work', Jeff's Jobcentre adviser determined that Jeff should undertake a voluntary work placement as part of the conditions of receiving his benefit payments. Already familiar with the organization, Jeff chose to volunteer at his local food bank.

The mandating of the unemployed into work placements has been critiqued as at best removing the elements of choice available to those out of work, and at worst as a form of servitude and the franchizing of the 'workhouse model' of welfare (Garland, 2015). It is significant, too, that people like Jeff are being pushed into ensuring the workings of organizations that service those who are themselves struggling – such services with which Jeff has himself been intimate (Strong, 2020b, 8). This shift signifies the appropriation of the labour power of those already struggling at the sharp end of the cuts – coercing them into maintaining a charitable safety net that fills in for the porous gaps left by the austere state (Dowling and Harvie, 2014).

Notwithstanding these structural constraints, Jeff grew to love his work at the food bank. His attendance was exemplary in contrast to my own uneven presence. As Jeff put it, "If I can't make it, I'm either dead or dying. Unlike some who are skiving off and then bugger off to university again!" As well as providing Jeff with an opportunity to develop social connections, volunteering offered him a sense of dignity and achievement that had been denied to him by the work of looking for work:

> 'The food bank has given me respect for myself, respect from others. I feel as if I'm achieving something and putting back where the food bank has helped me in the past. When I was down on my luck and I needed food, they supplied it. I'm now trying to put back what I can to help the community in any direction I can.'

Jeff's engagements with hustling, gifting and volunteering reveal a non-linear spatiality that breaks with the employer–employee model of formal wage employment. His works served his own ends while fulfilling the expectations of the community and the austere state. Indeed, we might consider Jeff's work as building a nascent social safety net for himself and others in his local town – a system born out of the precariousness rendered by austerity. In this sense, Jeff appears to occupy a contradictory position in the eyes of the austere state: he is a failure in his inability to find wage labour, and yet is evidence of the forms of resilience and localized responsibility that the ideology of individualized, anti-state neoliberalism valorizes (Newman, 2013). The ambivalence of Jeff's case is therefore stark, raising urgent questions about how we measure the value and quality of different kinds of work in society (Monteith and Giesbert, 2017). As the feelings of respect and 'giving back' demonstrate, it would be remiss to simply reduce the outcomes of work to an income. But at the same time, such forms of work clearly cannot be romanticized (Varley, 2013). They are driven by a lack of choice, and further normalize the idea that those unemployed should be prepared to work without a wage.

The geography of survival for people like Jeff is, therefore, a *dialectic* (Mitchell and Heynen, 2009). Attenuated and closed down by the acts of an increasingly coercive state, Jeff continues to find new strategies for coping – strategies that are makeshift and grounded in the everyday realities of his local place. These strategies inadvertently challenge the privileging of wage labour and imaginations of 'worklessness' that have underpinned austerity policies. And yet, such acts concurrently achieve the ideological parameters of austerity, pushing new forms of work and responsibility onto those at the sharp end of the cuts (Strong, 2020b). In this way, the acts that maintain Jeff's geography of survival must not be romanticized: such strategies 'sometimes directly confront the relations of power that structure everyday life … [but] at other times seek only to make life tolerable within them' (Mitchell and Heynen, 2009, 613–614).

Conclusion

> 'It's all dying. The whole place is dying. There's no money that goes into the economy in any direction. Everything is just going to be shut down … If less people are employed, that's less money going back into the shops. And the cycle starts again. Down we go another step. We can't keep going down. After the mines closed, we went down so bad. And now, when we try and pick ourselves up, what happens? [Jeff lifts his right foot and stomps on the ground] Boot! Stay down! And repeat. That's what we get.'

Jeff's account of the death of his town is inseparable from the demise of *wage labour*. By charting the economic decline of the Valleys, his testimony reveals the everyday effects of deindustrialization for those left marooned by the spatial fix of neoliberal capitalism. Waged industrial jobs in steelworking, mining and manufacturing have been lost and not replaced, leaving the Valleys in a state of protracted liminality – between a waged, industrial past and an as yet undefined future. For those left marooned like Jeff, it is a story of hunger, poverty and lack – experiences made all the more desperate when combined with the heightened pressures instilled by a contractual and conditional welfare system.

But we should not conflate Jeff's account of the death of wage employment with the demise of work more broadly. Returning to the sentiments of George Osborne at the beginning of this chapter, we see that 'wageless life [is] almost always seen as a situation of lack, the space of exclusion' (Denning, 2016, 274). Only by decentring wage employment as a presumed norm is it possible to appreciate that the Valleys remain *alive* with work. The area may be economically deprived but it is nevertheless animated by relational acts of provisioning and subsistence. Far from 'sleeping off a life on benefits', Jeff's lifeworld is marked by works of various kinds which serve to shield him and others from both the economic deprivation of his area and the coercive actions of the austere state.

Work thus persists in the Valleys in the absence of wage employment. But it is realized in forms that are very different from the models of employer–employee seen in wage labour. This chapter has examined two such examples: the work of looking for work, and the work of survival via hustling, gifting and volunteering. As Jeff demonstrates, this work not only blurs production and reproduction, it also functions at a scale beyond his own individual survival alone, being intertwined with that of his community and place. These acts of agency and negotiation thus demonstrate that austerity is not an endpoint or outcome, but rather an enactor of new forms of work that are both highly precarious and unevenly distributed.

The central irony identified in this chapter is that, in continuing to reify a certain model of citizenship tied to wage labour, the austere state is making these forms of work harder to accomplish. Whether it be via sanctions that attenuate one's ability to secure subsistence, or through mandated work placements and welfare contracts that place coercive controls on activities, Jeff's story demonstrates how austerity impinges on his right to survive. Indeed, the language of fairness, responsibility and moral obligation used to underpin cuts to the social security system that Jeff relies upon are entirely out of kilter with the realities of wageless life in wage-scarce space. Moreover, the continued reification of a model of wage work that is masculinist, ableist and reproductive of strict distinctions between public and private spaces continues to appear all the more outdated and obsolete.

These observations raise one final question to be considered in this chapter. If we are witnessing the death of wage labour as an economic compromise between employers and employees – in wage-scarce spaces such as the Valleys, at least – then what might the future of work look like for people like Jeff? We might turn here to heralds of a post-work future (Rifkin, 1995) – or, indeed, of a return to pre-industrial practices of work bound to forms of reciprocity, sharing and autarky (Shaw and Waterstone, 2019). Jeff's lifeworld, as described in this chapter, is punctuated by all three of these activities. To what extent, then, should we consider these activities forms of 'work'?

Here I suggest that we follow Gorz (1999) in shifting our understanding of work away from something we 'have' (to have a job, to have work on, and so on), and towards an understanding of work as something we 'do' – often in very everyday, banal and ordinary ways. Within this tradition, Shaw and Waterstone's (2019, 111) theorization of 'alter-work' allows us to consider Jeff's efforts as 'autonomous world-making activities that support common coexisting'. However, while it is important to recognize the forms of community cohesion and resilience reproduced by and through this work, the broader picture remains bleak. Life without a wage is precarious. Jeff's experiences clearly warn against the dangers of assuming alter-work will naturally assume the privileged place of wage labour in our theory and imagination. This is because a wage represents more than just a financial settlement: wage labour also remains key to models of social citizenship. Classifying Jeff's activities as alter-work does not address his material poverty and experienced anguish. Instead, there remains a need to socially and politically mobilize alternative forms of work so that they may be recognized by the state and supported through unconditional interventions, including – but not limited to – universal basic income (Standing, 2017). Only by severing the link between wage employment, income security and social citizenship will places like the Valleys escape the hangover of industrial capitalism and realize more equitable and dignified socio-economic futures.

Notes

[1] The Chancellor of the Exchequer is responsible for all economic and financial matters in the UK, equivalent to the role of finance minister in other countries.

[2] 'Worklessness' is the official phrase introduced and repeated in policy and discourse at a time of austerity, used to describe those who are not employed in the formal, waged economy.

[3] It is revealing, and perhaps ironic, that such a reification of wage employment is occurring at the same time as full-time wage employment is on the whole declining in the UK – with the fastest-growing mode of employment being part-time self-employment. For more on the supposed 'death' of this model of waged work, see Gorz (1999) and Rifkin (1995).

[4] To preserve confidentiality and anonymity, the specific town and county that Jeff calls home are not revealed here. For the sake of context, it is the largest town within the most deprived county of the Valleys.

[5] It is telling in itself that these historical statistics were gathered and reported as *male* unemployment – signalling the erasure of other, more feminized types of work that were not being accounted for.

6   When people reach the age of 60 in Wales, they can apply for a free bus pass –
     although the Welsh government has announced that the age of eligibility will rise
     to 65 by 2021 over fears of the rising costs (BBC News, 2019).

References

Alden, J. (1977) 'Economic problems facing urban areas in South Wales', *Regional Studies*, 11(5): 285–296.

Barchiesi, F. (2011) *Precarious Liberation: Workers, the State, and Contested Social Citizenship in Postapartheid South Africa*, Albany, NY: SUNY Press.

BBC News (2019) 'Wales' free bus pass age to rise from 60 to state pension age', 25 July 2019, available at https://www.bbc.co.uk/news/uk-wales-politics-49098325

Berlant, L. (2011) *Cruel Optimism*, Durham, NC: Duke University Press.

Bourdieu, P. (1998) *Acts of Resistance: Against the New Myths of Our Time*, Cambridge: Polity.

Breman, J. (2010) *Outcast Labour in Asia: Circulation and Informalization of the Workforce at the Bottom of the Economy*, New Delhi: Oxford University Press.

Butler, J. (2004) *Precarious Life: The Powers of Mourning and Violence*, London: Verso.

Cain, R. (2016) 'Responsibilising recovery: Lone and low-paid parents, Universal Credit and the gendered contradictions of UK welfare reform', *British Politics*, 11(4): 488–507.

Cordell, A. (1959) *The Rape of the Fair Country*, London: Gollancz.

Daguerre, A. and Etherington, D. (2014) 'Workfare in 21st century Britain', available at http://workfare.org.uk/images/uploads/docs/Workfare_in_21st_century_Britain_Version_2.pdf

Daguerre, A. and Etherington, D. (2016) 'Welfare and active labour market policies in the UK: The coalition government approach', in H. Bochel and M. Powell (eds) *The Coalition Government and Social Policy: Restructuring the Welfare State*, Bristol: Policy Press, pp 203–221.

Dean, M. (1995) 'Governing the unemployed self in active society', *Economy and Society*, 24(4): 559–583.

Denning, M. (2016) 'Wageless life', in A. Eckhert (ed) *Global Histories of Work*, Berlin, Germany: De Gruyter Oldenbourg, pp 273–290.

Dowling, E. and Harvie, D. (2014) 'Harnessing the social: State, crisis and (big) society', *Sociology*, 48(5): 869–886.

Driver, F. (2004) *Power and Pauperism: The Workhouse System, 1834–1884*, Cambridge: Cambridge University Press.

Duncan Smith, I. (2014) 'Speech on welfare reform', Centre for Social Justice, London, available at http://blogs.spectator.co.uk/ coffeehouse/ 2014/01/iain-duncan-smiths-speech-on-welfarereform-full-text

Dwyer, P. (2004) 'Creeping conditionality in the UK: From welfare rights to conditional entitlements?' *Canadian Journal of Sociology*, 29(2): 265–287.

Edminston, D. (2017) 'Welfare, austerity and social citizenship in the UK', *Social Policy and Society*, 16(2): 261–270.

Elyachar, J. (2010) 'Phatic labor, infrastructure, and the question of empowerment in Cairo', *American Ethnologist*, 37(3): 452–464.

Eurostat (2018) 'Gross domestic product at current market prices by NUTS 2 regions', available at http://appsso.eurostat.ec.europa.eu/

Forkert, K. (2014) 'The new moralism: Austerity, silencing and debt morality', *Soundings*, 56: 41–53.

Foucault, M. (1985) *The History of Sexuality: Volume Two*, London: Penguin.

Garland, C. (2015) 'Inflicting the structural violence of the market: Workfare and underemployment to discipline the reserve army of labour', *Fast Capitalism*, 12(1): 99–109.

Gërxhani, K. (2004) 'The informal sector in developed and less developed countries: A literature survey', *Public Choice*, 120(3–4): 267–300.

Glassdoor (2016) 'Which countries in Europe offer the fairest paid leave and unemployment benefits?' available at https://www.glassdoor. com/research/app/uploads/sites/2/2016/02/GD_FairestPaidLeave_ Final.pdf

Gorz, A. (1999) *Reclaiming Work: Beyond the Wage-Based Society*, Cambridge: Polity.

Gray-Jones, A. (1992) *A History of Ebbw Vale*, Gwent: Gwent Libraries.

Hall, S.M. (2019) *Everyday Life in Austerity: Family, Friends and Intimate Relations*, London: Palgrave Macmillan.

Hamnett, C. (2014) 'Shrinking the welfare state: The structure, geography and impact of British government benefits cuts', *Transactions of the Institute of British Geographers*, 39(4): 490–503.

Hardt, M. (1999) 'Affective labor', *boundary 2*, 26(2): 89–100.

Harvey, D. (1981) *The Limits to Capital*, London: Verso.

Haskins, R. (2006) *Work over Welfare*, Washington, DC: Brookings Institution Press.

Heyes, J., Tomlinson, M. and Whitworth, A. (2017) 'Underemployment and well-being in the UK before and after the Great Recession', *Work, Employment and Society*, 31(1): 71–89.

Himmelfarb, G. (1995) *The De-moralization of Society: From Victorian Virtues to Modern Values*, London: IEA Health and Welfare Unit.

Hitchen, E. (2016) 'Living and feeling the austere', *new formations*, 87: 102–118.

Holmes, H. (2018) 'New spaces, ordinary practices: Circulating and sharing within diverse economies of provisioning', *Geoforum*, 88: 138–147.

Horton, J. (2016) 'Anticipating service withdrawal: Young people in spaces of neoliberalisation, austerity and economic crisis', *Transactions of the Institute of British Geographers*, 41: 349–362.

Institute for Government (2016) 'Universal credit: From disaster to recovery?' available at https://www.instituteforgovernment.org.uk/sites/default/files/publications/5064%20IFG%20-%20Universal%20Credit%20Publication%20WEB%20AW.pdf

Institute for Public Policy Research (2019) 'Social (in)security: reforming the UK's social safety net', 14 November, available at: https://www.ippr.org/files/2019-11/social-insecurity-november19.pdf

Jensen, T. (2012) 'Tough love in tough times', *Studies in the Maternal*, 4(2): 1–26.

Jensen, T. and Tyler, I. (2015) '"Benefits broods": The cultural and political crafting of anti-welfare commonsense', *Critical Social Policy*, 35(4): 1–22.

Kaufman, E. and Nelson, L. (2012) 'Malthus, gender and the demarcation of "dangerous" bodies in 1996 US welfare reform', *Gender, Place and Culture: A Journal of Feminist Geography*, 19(4): 429–448.

Li, T.M. (2007) *The Will to Improve: Governmentality, Development and the Practice of Politics*, Durham, NC: Duke University Press.

MacLeavy, J. (2011) 'A "new politics" of austerity, workfare and gender? The UK coalition government's welfare reform proposals', *Cambridge Journal of Regions, Economy and Society*, 4: 355–367.

McDowell, L. (1991) 'Life without father and Ford: The new gender order of post-Fordism', *Transactions of the Institute of British Geographers*, 16(4): 400–419.

Mitchell, D. and Heynen, N.(2009) 'The geography of survival and the right to the city: Speculations on surveillance, legal innovation and the criminalization of intervention', *Urban Geography*, 30(6): 611–632.

Montieth, W. and Giesbert, L. (2017) '"When the stomach is full we look for respect": perceptions of "good work" in the urban informal sectors of three developing countries', *Work, Employment and Society*, 31(5): 816–833.

Newman, J. (2013) 'Landscapes of antagonism: Local governance, neoliberalism and austerity', *Urban Studies*, 2013: 1–16.

NOMIS (2017) 'Labour market profile – Blaenau Gwent', available at http://www.nomisweb.co.uk/reports/lmp/la/1946157401

OECD and Centre for Cities (2019) 'Trends in economic inactivity across the OECD: The importance of the local dimension and a spotlight on the United Kingdom', available at https://www.oecd-ilibrary.org/docserver/cd51acab-en.pdf?expires=1573120244&id=id&accname=guest&checksum=1A5118ABEF49555D967FB5FE901D6E85

Osborne, G. (2012) George Osborne's speech to the Conservative conference: full text, available at https://www.newstatesman.com/blogs/politics/2012/10/george-osbornes-speech-conservative-conference-full-text

Peck, J. (2001) *Workfare States*, New York, NY: Guildford Publications.

Pemberton, S., Fahmy, E., Sutton, E. and Bell, K. (2016) 'Navigating the stigmatised identities of poverty in austere times: Resisting and responding to narratives of personal failure', *Critical Social Policy*, 36: 21–37.

Pfannebecker, M. and Smith, J.A. (2020) *Work Want Work: Labour and Desire at the End of Capitalism*, London: Zed Books.

Polanyi, K. (1944) *The Great Transformation*, New York, NY: Farrar and Rinehart.

Rifkin, J. (1995) *The End of Work: The Decline of the Global Labor Force and the Dawn of the Post-Market Era*, New York, NY: G.P. Putnam's.

Robinson, K. and Sheldon, R. (2019) 'Witnessing loss in the everyday: Community buildings in austerity Britain', *The Sociological Review*, 67(1): 111–125.

Rose, G. (1993) *Feminism and Geography: The Limits of Geographical Knowledge*, London: Wiley.

Rose, N. (1999) *Powers of Freedom: Reframing Political Thought*, Cambridge: Cambridge University Press.

Roy, A. and Alsayaad, N. (2004) *Urban Informality: Transnational Perspectives from the Middle East, Latin America, and South Asia*, New York, NY: Lexington Books.

Saitta, P., Shapland, J. and Verhage, A. (2013) *Getting By or Getting Rich? The Formal, Informal and Criminal Economy in a Globalized World*, The Hague: Eleven International Publishing.

Shaw, I. and Waterstone, M. (2019) *Wageless Life: A Manifesto for a Future Beyond Capitalism*, Minneapolis, MN: University of Minnesota Press.

Smith, N. (1984) *Uneven Development: Nature, Capital and the Production of Space*, London: Verso.

Southwood, I. (2011) *Non-stop Inertia*, Winchester: Zero Books.

Stagecoach (2019) Ticket prices, available at: https://stagecoachbus.com/ticket-results

Standing, G. (2017) *Basic Income: How We Can Make It Happen*, London: Pelican.

StatsWales (2016) 'Employment in public and private sectors by Welsh local authority and status', available at https://statswales.gov.wales/Catalogue/Business-Economyand-Labour-Market/People-and-Work/Employment/PersonsEmployed/publicprivatesectoremployment-by-welshlocalauthority-status

Stenning, A. (2018) 'Feeling the squeeze: Towards a psychosocial geography of austerity in low-to-middle income families', *Geoforum*.

Strong, S. (2014) 'Underclass ontologies', *Political Geography*, 42: 117–120.

Strong, S. (2019) 'The vital politics of foodbanking: Hunger, austerity, biopower', *Political Geography*, 75.

Strong, S. (2020a) 'Austere social reproduction and the gendered geographies of debt', in J. Gardiner, M. Gray and K. Möser (eds) *Debt and Austerity*, Cheltenham: Edward Elgar, pp 151–173.

Strong, S. (2020b) 'Food banks, actually existing austerity and the localisation of responsibility', *Geoforum*, 110: 211–219.

Strong, S. (2020c) 'Towards a geographical account of shame: Food banks, austerity and the spaces of austere affective governmentality', *Transactions of the Institute of British Geographers* (early view), 1–14.

Strong, S. (2020d) 'People's geography', in A. Kobayashi (ed) *The International Encyclopedia of Human Geography* (2nd edn, vol. 10), Amsterdam: Elsevier, pp 55–59.

Thieme, T. (2013) 'The "hustle" among youth entrepreneurs in Mathare's informal waste economy', *Journal of Eastern African Studies*, 7(3): 389–412.

Thieme, T.A. (2018) 'The hustle economy: Informality, uncertainty and the geographies of getting by', *Progress in Human Geography*, 42(4): 529–548.

TUC (2015) 'Welfare states: How generous are British benefits compared to other rich nations?' Touchstone Pamphlets, available at https://www.tuc.org.uk/sites/default/files/Welfare_States_Touchstone_Extra_2015_AW_Rev.pdf

Valentine, G. and Harris, C. (2014) 'Strivers vs skivers: Class prejudice and the demonisation of dependency in everyday life', *Geoforum*, 53: 84–92.

Varley, A. (2013) 'Postcolonialising informality?' *Environment and Planning D: Society and Space*, 31(1): 4–22.

Wacquant, L. (2009) *Punishing the Poor: The Neoliberal Government of Social Insecurity*, Durham, NC: Duke University Press.

Wacquant, L., Slater, T. and Pereria, V.B. (2014) 'Territorial stigmatization in action', *Environment and Planning A*, 46(6): 1270–1280.

Webster, D. (2014) Evidence submitted to House of Commons Work and Pensions Committee, available at http://www.publications. parliament.uk/pa/cm201314/cmselect/cmworpen/479/479vw36. html

Webster, D. (2018) 'Benefit sanction statistics: Universal credit, JSA, ESA and income support', available at https://www. mostewartresearch.co.uk/wp-content/uploads/2018/05/18-02-Sanctions-Stats-Briefing.pdf

Welfare Reform Act (2012). The Welfare Reform Act of 2012. Full text available at http://www.legislation.gov.uk/ukpga/2012/5/ enacted

White, S. (2000) 'Review article: Social rights and the social contract – political theory and the new welfare politics', *British Journal of Political Science*, 30(3): 507–532.

Williams, C.C. and Nadin, S. (2012) 'Work beyond employment: Representations of informal economic activities', *Work, Employment and Society*, 26(2): 1–10.

WIMD (2014) Welsh Indices of Multiple Deprivation, available at https://statswales.gov.wales/Catalogue/Community-Safety-and-Social-Inclusion/Welsh-Index-ofMultiple-Deprivation/ WIMD-2014

3

Seeking Attachment in the Fissured Workplace: External Workers in the United States

Claudia Strauss

Andrew Jones has been working at the same personal training studio in a large city in the north-eastern part of the US for over ten years. He is the onsite manager, responsible for hiring new trainers and taking care of the equipment. He works exclusively at this studio, which advertises its individually tailored sessions with highly skilled trainers. Although the trainers are central to the studio's mission, they are not considered employees of the gym and do not receive a fixed wage; instead, they are classified as self-employed independent contractors. Andrew rents space at the gym and receives a percentage of the fees paid by his clients. As the manager, he also receives a share of the payments collected by the other trainers. Because he has been classified as an independent contractor, there is no withholding from his paycheck for taxes, Social Security (the US federal retirement, disability and survivors income programme), or Medicare (the federal old-age health insurance programme). He is responsible for the paperwork of quarterly estimated tax payments and the financial burden of paying the employer's share as well as his own share of Social Security and Medicare taxes. The gym owner does not provide any health insurance, paid vacations, paid sick days or retirement benefits. Since he is classified as self-employed, Andrew is not subject to minimum wage laws, overtime pay laws, unemployment insurance if he loses his job, or workers' compensation if he sustains an injury on the job. He would not be permitted to join a union[1] – a moot point, since to date no personal trainers in the US are unionized (Club Industry, 2017). Yet, although the fitness studio has absolved itself of legal responsibility for the trainers it depends upon, Andrew remains dedicated to it. When I asked whether he would consider taking another job that provided health insurance and other employee benefits, Andrew replied, "I believe in my brand very much and believe in the environment I've helped create for clients and trainers. Believe strongly." Paradoxically, he expressed loyalty to an organization that seemed to lack loyalty to him.

Misclassifying employees as independent contractors is one of several ways in which companies have been divesting themselves of the costs and other responsibilities of direct employment (Weil, 2014). In this chapter, I explore how workers such as Andrew forge meaning and connection in the face of alienating employment practices in the contemporary US. I show that for many workers, the nature of their employment contract was either irrelevant or a secondary concern. Rather, they wanted to feel pride in their organization, valued and cared for by it, and work closely with co-workers and form social ties to them – connections which, to my surprise, they could find in non-standard employment. These findings encourage us to diversify our understandings of work beyond the material and the contractual in order to consider the appeal of work arrangements outside of standard wage employment.

The rise of the external worker

In *The Fissured Workplace*, David Weil (2014) argues that there were two key shifts in the structure of firms over the twentieth century. Early in the century, businesses grew when they lowered costs by eliminating middlemen, internalizing many of their functions. Employees of these large corporations, especially those with unions, tended to have higher wages and better benefits than workers in smaller businesses (Weil, 2014, 39). However, beginning in the 1980s, investors and global competition pressured corporations to increase revenues, cut costs and respond to sudden fluctuations in demand. New information and communication technologies made it easier to coordinate scattered operations. Public, private and non-profit employers alike began to reduce standard employment, in which workers are on the payroll with an expectation of continuing employment and covered by laws protecting employees, in favour of limited-term or indirect 'arms-length' employment contracts, which depart from the standard employment relationship (Weil, 2014, 8). This trend has been called 'externalization', and workers hired with such non-standard contracts are 'external workers' to indicate that they have been pushed outside the boundaries of the organization (Davis-Blake and Uzzi, 1993).

For example, at one time, the workers who loaded and unloaded trucks for Walmart were employed by Walmart. However, at present, they are likely to work for a third-party logistics firm that faces considerable competition and pressures to cut costs. If that logistics firm fails to pay overtime or forces employees to work in unsafe conditions, Walmart will disclaim responsibility (Weil, 2014, 2, 3, 8, 9).

There are multiple forms of external employment. One common arrangement is for employers to use temporary agency workers or contractors from staffing firms. Although both are temporary positions, in common US parlance 'temps' usually occupy lower-paid positions than 'contractors', as one staffing firm explains (Foxhire team, 2016). Or, like those who load and unload Walmart trucks but work for a third-party logistics firm, they may be employed by a subcontractor that provides services (for example, customer service, warehouse operations, landscaping, cleaning, food services, information technology, payroll) for another organization. Temps, contractors, and subcontract firm employees are in a joint or 'triangular' employment arrangement between the staffing firm or subcontractor that employs them and the client organization for whom they work (Kalleberg, 2000). As employees of the staffing firm or third-party subcontracting firm, they have some guaranteed protections, but they are rarely afforded all the benefits of employees in a standard employment relationship. For example, they are less likely to have employer-provided health insurance (Bureau of Labor Statistics, 2018).

These triangular employment arrangements differ from another kind of external employment: direct-hire temporary workers. At one California computer company, temporary workers hired directly by the company received no fringe benefits, but they were symbolically included: they wore the same coloured badge as permanent workers and could attend social events for employees. By contrast, temporary agency employees at the same company were given badges of a different colour and excluded from company social events (Smith, 1998, 420; see also Chambel and Castanheira, 2006). In US academia, adjunct faculty are direct-hire temporary employees, and colleges have their own rituals of inclusion and exclusion to mark their ambiguous status.

Finally, like Andrew Jones, external workers can be hired by the organization where they work as 'independent contractors', as opposed to employees, on an open-ended arrangement. Taxicab drivers who lease their cab instead of owning a permit are usually classified as independent contractors (Dubal, 2017), as are many construction workers, short-haul and long-haul truck drivers, in-home care workers, hairdressers and loan officers (MortgageOrb Contributors, 2006; Covert, 2015; Leberstein and Ruckelshaus 2016; Appel and Zabin, 2019). By making their employees independent contractors, employers can save about 30 per cent of their labour costs (National Conference of State Legislatures, 2020). Some independent contractors, like Andrew, continue working in this status at the same workplace for many years. Although they control their hours, they do not have a separate business of their own or set their own pay rates; instead, they have all the responsibilities of employees and they are required to follow standards set by the enterprise but lack the legal benefits and protections of employees.

In the US, employees receive a W2 form (for employee income), unlike independent contractors, who receive a 1099 form (for non-employee income). The independent contractors I interviewed often referred to their employment arrangement using the names of those forms ("I was 1099, so I was an independent contractor," "I was 1099," but "[X Company] made us a W2 employee"). When I emailed Andrew Jones to request an interview, he replied, "I would be happy to talk with you about the 1099/private contractor world." To distinguish the externalized independent contractors from those who are truly self-employed, I refer to the former as misclassified 1099 independent contractors. 'Misclassified' is the legal term for those whose work conditions should entitle them to employee protection, but who have been categorized as independent contractors (Weil, 2014).[2] However, it is not a term that workers used in my interviews.

All types of external work are examples of 'non-standard' employment, understood as 'forms of employment that diverge along at least one dimension from year-round, full-time wage employment with a single employer, at the employer's worksite and with the expectation of durable attachment' (Carr, 2015, 386). External workers are an anomaly from the International Labour Organization's perspective because they have jobs in the formal sector of the economy, that is, in entities that are incorporated and state regulated (ILO, 2018, 10), yet they lack many of the protections and benefits of employees in standard employment. In this way, external workers unsettle many of the conventional categories that researchers use to describe work.

It is difficult to pinpoint the incidence of these arms-length arrangements in the US. In May 2017, 10 per cent of the US workforce worked in 'alternative arrangements' as their main job, whether as independent contractors, on-call workers (for example, substitute teachers), temporary help agency workers, or workers provided by contract firms (Bureau of Labor Statistics, 2018).[3] However, the government's category of 'independent contractor' includes those who are genuinely self-employed as well as misclassified independent contractors. Those situations are different, and statistics that conflate them are not useful. Weil (2019) argues that workers are often unaware that their actual employer was not the organization they thought they were working for, or they respond to surveys classifying themselves as employees when they are independent contractors, making it difficult to state the true extent of external employment (Weil, 2019).

External employment is likely to grow. A survey of leading global companies found that almost half expected to externalize more functions to contractors by 2022 (World Economic Forum, 2018, Table 6, 16). Gig workers whose pay and work conditions are determined by the company providing the digital platform (for example, ride hail drivers) are an increasingly prevalent type of misclassified 1099 independent contractor. Weil stresses the harms to workers from fissuring, which 'creates downward pressure on wages and benefits, murkiness about who bears responsibility for work conditions, and increased likelihood that basic labor standards will be violated' (Weil, 2014, 8). Despite all of this, Andrew Jones values his 1099 job at the fitness studio, which raises the question of how other external workers experience their working arrangements, and whether their experiences challenge assumptions in the literature on work.

Affective commitments of external workers

Accounts like Weil's (2014) take a 'rights-based' approach to evaluating employment. However, as Monteith and Giesbert (2017) explain, in judging jobs by a narrow, universal set of criteria, such approaches often fail to consider workers' own values and the full breadth of their conceptions of a good job. This is not to say that fair pay, fringe benefits and safe working conditions do not matter to workers; they do. However, those aspects of work are rarely all that matter (MOW International Research Team, 1987).

One non-economic benefit of work is that it can provide feelings of belonging and connection. Does it make sense for workers to form such workplace attachments amid widespread casualization and externalization? Managers worry that their external workers may be too psychologically detached to do their jobs well, and organizational psychologists have studied such workers' 'organisational commitment', understood as loyalty, belonging and emotional attachment to the organization (Galais and Moser, 2009, 592). Much of the organizational commitment research studies temporarily employed workers. Various theories predicted that because organizations invest little in their temporary workers, they would receive little commitment from them in return, but the findings have been inconclusive. Some studies have confirmed the lower organizational commitment of temporary workers, but other studies have found lower commitment among permanent workers than among temporary workers, or that it depends on the kind of temporary employment (direct-hire temporary workers tend to have higher commitment than temporary agency workers), or no significant difference among any of these categories of workers (De Cuyper et al, 2008, 28–29, 31–32).

One possible explanation for findings that permanent workers do not necessarily have greater affective commitment to their organization is that amid flexibilization and externalization, so-called permanent hires are aware their jobs may not be any more secure than the jobs of the temporary employees (De Cuyper et al, 2008, 39). Indeed, the high-tech workers in Dallas, Texas interviewed by Carrie Lane (2011) were scornful of loyal company men, ' "suckers" and "victims" who perceive job security as a possibility, let alone a right' (2011, 46). Her (mostly male) interviewees advocated thinking of themselves as self-employed contractors, regardless of the formalities of their employment contract.

Emotional detachment from the job seems to be what is recommended by some critical theorists who are concerned that post-industrial jobs require that workers not only labour, but do so with enthusiasm. They consider affective commitment to be a more intensive form of exploitation (Weeks, 2011, 69–70). Thus, ironically, the organizational detachment of the highly skilled workers who advocate self-reliance is consistent with the suspicion of theorists who criticize such neoliberal ideologies.

Other theorists argue that belonging still matters to workers but only as a futile post-Fordist affect, a yearning for a past that has vanished or only ever existed in workers' imaginations (Muehlebach and Shoshan, 2012). Richard Sennett (1998) claims, 'One of the unintended consequences of modern capitalism is that it has strengthened the value of place, aroused a longing for community', but at the contemporary workplace, community is no longer possible (1998, 138). Kunda et al (2002) describe skilled employees who left their firms to take well-paid temporary contracts. Like Lane's interviewees, these contractors reasoned, "If the company is not loyal to me, why should I be loyal to it?" They felt their managers took them for granted, and they disliked the interpersonal office politics needed to get ahead. However, once they began moving from organization to organization on limited contracts, they felt 'antagonism from permanent employees' and a 'sense of isolation, exclusion, [and] estrangement' at their temporary workplaces (2002, 237).

My research among both external workers and those with standard employment contracts has led me to a different finding. Many of those with whom we spoke valued work attachments, and some were able to form them. The attachments they desired and found were not predictable from a general distinction between the external workers and those with standard employment. Instead, we need to untangle the varying kinds of attachments workers want and the distinctive situations of different kinds of external workers. For example, despite their proliferation in the US economy, there is currently a lack of research on the workplace attachments of misclassified 1099 independent contractors. Their situation is not the same as that of temporary workers, who have been the focus of research on organizational commitment.[4]

Researching workplace attachments

This chapter draws upon interviews with unemployed and underemployed workers in southern California. Out of the 64 participants, at least 44 had been, or were currently, external workers as temps, contractors, subcontract firm employees, or misclassified 1099 independent contractors. Participants had a wide variety of occupations, from manual labour and clerical work, to skilled trades, to managerial and professional positions.[5] I interviewed 53 of the participants. In the initial wave of interviews, between the autumn of 2011 and the summer of 2012, I met with each participant twice. I remained in touch with many of the participants, and, two years later, I re-interviewed 41 of them. A native Spanish speaker, Claudia Castañeda, interviewed 11 unemployed or underemployed immigrants from Latin America. Among those I interviewed there were six first-generation immigrants from Latin America, Southeast Asia and Europe. I interviewed one additional participant – Andrew Jones – in 2020, specifically for this chapter. There were 36 women and 28 men in total, with a racial/ethnic mix typical of southern California (25 self-identify as non-Hispanic white, 22 as Latino/a or mixed, 12 as Black/African American, and five as Asian American). The median age of my participants was 54, which meant that many had experienced the shift in the economy from standard to externalized employment. All names have been anonymized.

The interviews explored the meanings of work for the participants. We began by asking them to tell us about their lives leading up to the present, thereby obtaining a complete work history. Other topics relevant to this chapter include the kind of job they wanted, the ways they coped with precarious income, feelings about their job prospects, and their hopes for and fears about the future. The semi-structured interviews permitted interviewees to bring up topics we had not anticipated. Because the focus of my study was not external work, I could see whether my participants highlighted their employment arrangements (external or not) without prompting. In analysing the interviews, I also particularly noted expressions of strong positive and negative emotions. These are clues to work experiences that deviated from the participant's expectations, either because the job was much better than they had come to take as the norm, or much worse.

Seeking connection in the fissured workplace

No one who participated in my study used the term 'external work' or described themselves as an 'external worker'. Instead, they described their experiences with specific kinds of external work, including what they liked or not about those jobs.

Before returning to Andrew Jones, let us consider someone who illustrates the diverse forms of workplace connection desired by my participants.

Terrance West was unusual among my participants in his strong attachment to one of the many companies for which he had worked. In 2006 Terrance took a job as a temporary clerk in the shipping and receiving department of 'H Company', a well-known snack manufacturer. However, Terrance was not working directly for H Company; he worked for 'G Logistics', a subcontracting firm that runs the shipping and receiving departments for businesses like H Company. In other words, Terrance began two steps removed from H Company: as a temp in a triangular employment arrangement. Terrance was eventually hired on, so he was no longer a temp, but he was still at a contractual arm's length from H Company as an employee of G Logistics.

Yet, although G Logistics was Terrance's employer, he never talked about them. I only found out they were his employer over a year after we first met when we reviewed my notes on his work history. Instead, he raved about H Company:

'The [H Company] was *wonderful*. They gave us all kinds
of bonuses. They would throw barbecues for us. We had
wonderful company picnics. I mean, I paid 15 dollars a
month for my [healthcare] coverage, and that covered me
and my kids. ... I was cross-trained, so I worked in more
than one department sometimes. Sometimes I would go and
help out the accountant upstairs because of my accounting
background, and sometimes I would work out at the gate
because I had a security background and they had security
officers at the gate. I was the one that would get called at
two in the morning, "How do you reset this?", "How do
you do this?" I was asked to train new employees. I was
asked to be like an ambassador to all the new temporary
employees that would come in. So every time a new batch
of employees would come, I would be the first face that
they would get to know at [H Company], and I would be
the one to show 'em around, tell 'em about the company,
because [H Company] believed in you knowing everything
about the company.'

Terrance said he would tell the new employees about the founder's
charitable work and that by buying their food products "you're helping
a lot of people in a lot of places ... in South America where the
coconuts are grown, in Hawaii where the macadamia nut plantation
is ..." He summarized his feeling about his job at the H Company, "I
really loved that place. I mean, I would get up in the morning happy
to go to work." He was devastated when H Company moved their
operations out of state three years after he began working there.

After H Company moved out of state, Terrance became a shipping
and receiving clerk at a new warehouse for 'R Company', another
well-known food company. Again, he was in a triangular employment
arrangement as an employee of 'K Logistics', a different subcontract
firm. In this part of his life story, he mentioned both the food company
where he worked and the logistics firm that was his employer: "It
was a third-party logistics company that was running the operation.
There's a company called K Logistics, and they were actually taking
care of the distribution and warehousing for R Company on the west
coast." Terrance said he "liked" that job, but he criticized K Logistics'
management: "I came into basically chaos. They didn't know what they
were doing." When workers complained, they were told, "If you don't
like it here, you don't have to be here. We can make arrangements for

you not to be here." Furthermore, as a gay Black man, Terrance was subject to racial and sexual orientation harassment from co-workers, and his supervisors were "nasty" as well. He did not quietly accept the verbal abuse, and he thinks he was fired because his new supervisor was afraid of him. He was told that he was fired because he had violated work policies, for example by working through his lunch hour when he was legally required to take a break.

Terrance West's experiences illustrate multiple forms of workplace connection: taking pride in one's organization, being included and valued, feeling cared for through fringe benefits, working for a common goal, and forming social relationships.

Taking pride in one's organization

Terrance was proud of working for H Company. H Company is well known; most Americans are familiar with their snack foods. The prestige of a firm has been shown to increase employees' identification with it (George and Chattopadhyay, 2005); perhaps working for them provided him with 'status by association' (Smith, 1998). That may partly explain why Terrance highlighted his connection to H Company, never mentioning his actual employer, G Logistics, which is unknown to the public. I found the same pattern with another participant who was employed by an obscure subcontractor to work in customer service for a well-known company.

However, the R Company, where Terrance worked next, is also a household name. Nonetheless, Terrance did not tell me he was proud to work there, and in giving his work history, Terrance mentioned not only the well-known R Company, but also the little-known K Logistics firm that was his actual employer. A company's public profile, therefore, is not sufficient to explain a worker's pride in working for them. Terrance was proud of the H Company's corporate culture, which stresses social responsibility. Their products (high-calorie snack foods) are arguably not socially responsible; Terrance had nothing to say about the value of the products whose shipments he oversaw. Instead, he stressed the founder's charitable work and responsible sourcing. It was rare for my participants to brag about their organization's corporate culture, products or services; when they brought it up, it was worth mentioning because they considered it unusual. Especially good or bad management also matters. Strong emotions of contempt were clear in Terrance's description of his next shipping and receiving job, for K Logistics, where it was "chaos" and "they didn't know what they were doing." Normal, good-enough management does not evoke pride, but poor management can foster disdain.

However, workers do not always seek status by association with a high-profile organization. Andrew Jones, the personal trainer, had previously worked for a well-known chain of gyms, where he was hired with standard employee protections. He left that job for the tenuous position he holds now with a little-known fitness studio where he has uncertain pay, no benefits, and is responsible for his quarterly self-employment tax, which includes the employer's share of Social Security and Medicare. It was several years before he adjusted to "the 1099/private contractor world", but he was not tempted to return to the kind of job he had before. As I noted at the outset of this chapter, when I asked him why, he replied, "I believe in my brand very much and believe in the environment I've helped create for clients and trainers. Believe strongly." Not only was Andrew proud of his studio, but he also took personal pride in having helped create the environment he appreciates. The mission of his studio aligned with Andrew's own professional goals, allowing him to live up to his standards of excellence in his work.

Being included and valued

Another reason Terrance West felt strong attachment to the H Company is that they symbolically recognized him as belonging and being valued, even though he was not contractually their employee. Some of those symbols of recognition were extended particularly to him. Thus, the H Company chose Terrance to "be like an ambassador" to new temporary employees: to train them, show them around and talk about the company's history and values. In extending that unofficial job to Terrance, the H Company treated him as someone integral to their business.

Andrew Jones has also received recognition from the owner of the fitness studio where he works. Although he is not an employee, the studio owner rewarded Andrew's steadfast, skilled work by making him the onsite manager. Furthermore, the owner has approached Andrew about taking over from him someday. Even though Andrew is a 1099 independent contractor, he has other signs of belonging.

Beyond the recognition extended to Terrance, the H Company makes a point of ceremoniously greeting temporary employees on their first day, giving them a tour and introducing them to the company's history and values. Even subcontracted workers are included in company picnics and barbeques. None of the other external workers we interviewed mentioned such rituals of inclusion. Since we did not ask about them, it is possible that they occurred, but our participants did not find them noteworthy; however, we know from other research that external workers are commonly excluded. Earlier I gave the example of the computer company where temporary agency workers wear different coloured badges and are prohibited from attending employee social events (Smith 1998). Similarly, George and Chattopadhyay (2005) quote a contractor who was surprised and pleased to be invited to company picnics, because that was unusual in their experience (2005, 91–92).

Interestingly, employee social events like the company picnics that were appreciated by Terrance West were resented by a former HR manager I interviewed, who saw these after-hours events as an intrusion on her family time. She believed her decision to skip two such company social events led to her dismissal, after which she had to make do with temporary contract positions. This example illustrates the insightful observation of De Cuyper et al (2008) that organizational commitment may not be interpreted the same way by permanent and temporary workers (2008, 35). Symbols of inclusion may matter more to external workers than to workers with standard employment contracts.

Care through fringe benefits

Terrance West's enthusiastic description of his job at H Company omitted mention of his pay. When I asked about it, I learned he started at US$9.75 an hour as a temporary worker. Temporary agency workers are notoriously poorly paid, which was one reason most of my participants disliked those jobs.

After Terrance was hired on at G Logistics, his hourly pay increased to $11.07, which is still less than a living wage, even in his relatively affordable area of southern California. Pay raises brought him up to $14.95 an hour, which would be a living wage for a single adult with no dependents, but Terrance was supporting his partner and paying child support for two children.[6] However, instead of focusing on his low pay, Terrance chose to highlight the bonuses the company provided for coming to work on time, working without an accident, and increased productivity, and the healthcare benefits he received. He credits H Company for those, but G Logistics was probably responsible.

G Logistics is quite unusual in the extent of the benefits it provided its employees, including the exceptionally inexpensive ($15/month for a family plan), comprehensive health insurance Terrance marvelled at. Andrew Jones purchases his own health insurance for about $300/month for a single-person plan, which he considered unexceptional because it was comparable to his premiums when he was a corporate gym employee. Terrance said he was also eligible for a 401(k)-retirement plan and profit sharing. This highlights disparity among types of external workers: 41 per cent of contract firm employees receive health insurance through their employer, compared to only 13 per cent of temporary agency workers (Bureau of Labor Statistics, 2018). Misclassified independent contractors like Andrew Jones are considered self-employed, hence receive neither fringe benefits nor any other kind of employee protection.

In the US, standard employment lacks many of the guaranteed labour protections found in Europe, yet workers commonly receive key protections, such as health insurance, through their jobs rather than from the state (Carr, 2015). When I began my research in 2011, employees had no legal right to health insurance through their employer, although that was the norm. Since 2016, employers with the equivalent of 50 or more full-time employees must offer a health insurance plan to their full-time employees, but they are required to provide only 'affordable minimum essential coverage that provides minimum value' (Internal Revenue Service, 2019).[7] The plans are partly subsidized by the employer; workers still pay premiums. US employees have no guaranteed right to vacation pay or paid sick leave (US Dept. of Labor, n.d.).[8] An inexpensive, comprehensive health insurance plan, mostly subsidized by the employer, and other fringe benefits are thus optional forms of compensation. As such, they have symbolic value for workers as signs of their employer's caring for them, in addition to their material benefits.

The symbolic value of fringe benefits was clear in one contractor's comments. This engineer, Jagat Bodhi, was forced into short-term contract work when his telecommunications corporation externalized much of their workforce in the late 2000s. He commented on being treated as "just a contractor":

> 'The corporations don't have the same sort of caring as they used to in the past. To them nowadays you're just a number. You are easily replaced. ... Or they only hire you for a certain period of time. No benefits. Nothing. You come to work. Do your work. We don't pay you for your transportation. ... You're just a contractor.'

For Jagat Bodhi, a pay cheque is a contractual requirement: he does his work and in exchange he is paid. Fringe benefits and expense reimbursements go beyond the contractual minimum and thus have affective value. They are signs of caring. Without those signs, he feels relegated to the disposable status of "just a contractor".

Terrance West saw H Company (really G Logistics) as "wonderful" because they provided unusually good health insurance and other fringe benefits, while Jagat Bodhi resented the absence of any fringe benefits. Similarly, Andrew Jones stated that he was "bitter" when he started working at the fitness studio and learned he had to buy his own health insurance. Their strong reactions indicate what they see as deviations, for better or for worse, from typical jobs. By contrast, another telecommunications engineer I interviewed in an earlier project chose the life of a contractor. He knew he would not receive fringe benefits, but he did not mind because he was well paid, his wife had a corporate job that provided health insurance for both of them, and he appreciated contract work for reasons I will explain.

Working for a common goal

Many of my participants, whether standardly employed or external workers, wanted to be part of a group of people working closely and cooperatively toward a common goal. This can be achieved through a participative team-based organizational structure (Smith, 1998), but that formal structure is not needed to create an esprit de corps.

Workers' desires to be part of a cooperative work team were expressed by Krystal Murphy, who had held a standard employment clerical job at a financial institution: "I've always wanted just a normal job where people really enjoy being together. And they work as a unit truly to accomplish whatever it is." She considered that to be "a normal job" because she knew people who had jobs like that and it seemed to her what a job *should* be like, although neither she nor her two sisters, all of them close to retirement, had ever experienced it.

If standard employees do not always experience working together for a shared goal, is it possible for external workers? In some occupations, financial incentives lead external workers to compete instead of cooperating. One of my participants described the "cat fight" among hairdressers who are 1099 independent contractors competing for clients. She missed her last job at a high-end salon where the hairdressers were employees, and "you're able to work as a team on one individual client."

Previous studies report some contractors who were treated as outsiders on work teams because they were there on a short-term assignment. As one technical writer put it, 'As a contractor, I'm temporarily tied to the goals of all these different groups. I have my own personal goals, but less of a sense of, you know, belonging and community.' She contrasted her experience as a contractor with her earlier standard employment where 'there were opportunities for individuals to feel part of something greater' (Kunda et al 2002, 250).

However, Smith (1998) studied a computer company that integrated its many temporary employees into its participative work teams where they felt they were working together for a shared goal, like making up a shortfall in their production quota. At that company, temps were particularly valued because the skills gained from their varied job histories enabled them to pitch in as needed instead of being limited to one kind of task. We saw that with Terrance West, who took pride in helping with security and accounting, in addition to shipping and receiving, and being the one who was called at two in the morning. When I asked him what was the meaning or importance of work for him, he replied, "Well, it gives me a sense of pride that I was able to do something that is beneficial not only to myself, but to a group, to the team."

Similarly, when I asked Celeste Rue, a temporary administrative assistant, what was the meaning or importance of work for her, she replied that the work itself was fun for her because she loved creating complex spreadsheets and formatting documents, but she added that it felt good to know that she was respected by her supervisor and co-workers and had contributed to the success of their projects. She added, "I think we are there, even as an individual, pulling together to get to a common point successfully."

My participants did not appreciate managers using the nice-sounding rhetoric of working together and being a team, while undermining workers' autonomy, playing them off against each other, or laying them off. One non-profit administrator, Lisa Rose, had two previous standard employment jobs where the executives liked to refer to workers as part of their organizational 'family' even as they fired them. She told her boss, "I don't believe you lay off members of your family." While she was looking for another job, she took short-term positions. In one she felt part of a team, but most assignments were too short. She considered continuing her career that way, but it did not appeal to her because she wanted to recreate the experience she had in one standard employment job where "it was just great to feel like you're part of a really smart team of people who really cared." However, standard employment was no guarantee she would find a genuine team spirit, as she had since found.

Forming social relationships

Krystal Murphy, the clerical worker who imagined "a normal job where people really enjoy being together. And they work as a unit truly to accomplish whatever it is", touched on another aspect of work connections desired for their own sake: friendly social interactions with co-workers. For some of the men and women we interviewed, workplaces were the primary places where they socialized.

Some of my external working participants spoke of making friends in their temporary jobs. One young man appreciated his current temporary job because it had introduced him to new friends. Likewise, Celeste Rue commented, "Every job that I've gone to, I've made a new friend – at least one new friend." However, for others, like Lisa Rose, the prospect of uprooting relationships by moving from job to job was unappealing: "I don't have the same mindset as somebody who might go into a career saying, 'I'm gonna work in ten different jobs or fifteen different jobs, and I'm gonna keep moving, and it's about my skillset and what I get to do.'" She added, "I derive a great sense of belonging." Even though she had criticized organizational language of 'being a family' she said, ironically, she really had "made work my family." When I asked what she meant by that, she explained, "Just spending time with people. It's getting to know them. Caring about them."

For workers who want to develop such relationships, the kind of external work matters. Employees of subcontracting firms, like Terrance West, may stay in one workplace for a long time, as may misclassified 1099 independent contractors like Andrew Jones. By contrast, workers on temporary contracts, whether directly hired or working for a staffing firm, either had to settle for shallower interactions or risk losing their 'family' when they moved on, unless they were later hired permanently.

Not all social interactions at work are friendly. At Terrance's job with K Logistics, he was subjected to racial and homophobic slurs. Another Black man I interviewed in a prior project, a telecommunications engineer like Jagat Bodhi, left standard employment to become a contractor because of the discrimination he had experienced. He said, "You do feel like you have to work twice as hard as your white co-worker to receive the recognition that you deserve." Unlike Jagat Bodhi, who did not like being "just a contractor", this engineer sought to minimize his workplace attachments, preferring the life of a contractor where "you go in, you do your job, you get paid, you leave."

Conclusion

It may be surprising that contemporary workers can form work attachments in precarious positions amid ongoing processes of externalization that allow organizations to evade contractual responsibility for their workers. A fine-grained analysis of the kinds of connections external workers prioritize explains why this is possible. For example, some forms of workplace connection appear to be unaffected by their employment arrangement. Pride in one's organization is an example; regardless of their contractual arrangement, workers may feel proud to be connected to a well-known organization or one with values they admire.

Other kinds of connection are more readily available to some categories of external workers than others. Permanent employees of subcontract firms may be symbolically included and valued. Additionally, such employees may receive what they consider to be a good fringe benefits package that shows the organization cares about them, feel they are working together for a common goal, and develop friendly social relationships with peers, depending on the workplace. Misclassified 1099 independent contractors do not receive any employee benefits, and in some professions (for example chair-renting hairdressers) their pay depends on their number of clients, making it hard for them to work cooperatively. Yet, they can be valued, given other signs of inclusion, and because their positions are not temporary, they are able to make friends. Finally, temps and contractors rarely receive fringe benefits and any they do receive are meagre; and it may be harder for them to form close social relationships or feel fully included as members of a team. Of all external workers we talked to, the temps and contractors were most likely to criticize their employment arrangement. However, sometimes they were valued, felt they belonged, and had the satisfying feeling of working with others towards a common goal (see also Smith, 1998).

For many of my participants, their non-standard employment contract was either irrelevant or a secondary concern. Andrew Jones did not like being responsible for his taxes and health insurance as a 1099 independent contractor, but that was much less important to him than being able to do his job the way he felt it should be done. For Terrance West it mattered whether he was a temp or had been hired on, but not that he was working for a subcontracting firm. Lisa Rose did not think she could feel an esprit de corps in contractor positions, but she did not always find it in standard positions either. Krystal Murphy, who "always wanted just a normal job where people really enjoy being together", one where "they work as a unit truly to accomplish whatever it is," had not found that in any of her standard employment jobs. In this chapter I have stressed my surprise that external work arrangements permit more workplace connections than we might have expected, but I could equally well have concluded that standard contractual arrangements often allow for less connection than many workers want.

To be sure, these forms of connection are not all that workers cared about. They often did not like the low pay and uncertain tenure of temp work; some did like the flexible scheduling of 1099 independent contracting. I focused on the value of connections for them because they posed an intriguing puzzle about why such connections form in the seemingly unfavourable environment of a fissured workplace.

External employment is a concern for many researchers and activists insofar as it represents a departure from the protections of standard wage employment. Yet, in the contemporary US with its limited labour protections, the difference between standard and non-standard employment may be overstated. In this environment, the social and psychological characteristics of a job can be as important as its contractual form. Although some workers prefer detachment, others want to feel pride, care, belonging, team spirit, and camaraderie. Some yearned for the imagined or real job relations of the past, but others found the connections they desired in the new forms of work that are taking their place.

Acknowledgements

I am grateful for comments from Matthew Barber and Will Monteith, feedback from 'Andrew Jones' and 'Terrance West' and the stimulation of the 2018 conference organized by this volume's editors, 'Post-Wage Economy: Re-theorising "work" across the global North–South divide'.

Notes

[1] Some independent contractors have organized legally permitted alternative workers' collectives (Esbenshade et al 2019).

[2] Some sources use 'internal contractor' to refer to these employees in all but name only (UpCounsel, 2020). I do not use it here because it would be confusing to talk about 'internal contractors' as a type of 'external worker'. For legal tests of misclassification, see Leberstein and Ruckelshaus (2016) and Murray (2020). In Europe the term 'bogus self-employment' is more common (Eurofound, 2017).

3   The technical note accompanying the release explains that 'main job' means 'the job in which they worked the most hours' (https://www.bls.gov/news.release/conemp.tn.htm).

4   Previous research on misclassified independent contractors in the US, including taxi drivers and truckers, has documented either protests against the misclassification or that workers 'embrace the IC [independent contractor] arrangement for the flexibility and autonomy it provides' (Esbenshade et al, 2019, 83; also Dubal, 2017). Feelings of belonging or connection have not been explored.

5   I found most of my participants at places where unemployed people gathered: job fairs, career counselling sessions, networking meetings, and in small accountability and support groups.

6   See https://livingwage.mit.edu/metros/40140 for a living wage in the Riverside-San Bernardino-Ontario metropolitan area in 2020. In 2010 the living wage for a single parent with two children in that county was $24.85/hour (https://cpehn.org/chart/living-wage-single-mothers-san-bernardino-county-2010).

7   'Affordable' means 'the employee required contribution is no more than 9.5 per cent (as adjusted) of that employee's household income' and 'minimum value' means 'covers at least 60 per cent of the total allowed cost of benefits that are expected to be incurred under the plan and provides substantial coverage of inpatient hospitalization services and physician services' (https://www.irs.gov/affordable-care-act/employers/questions-and-answers-on-employer-shared-responsibility-provisions-under-the-affordable-care-act#Affordability).

8   Employees must be permitted to take *unpaid* sick leave if they are working for a business with 50 or more employees or a public agency. The absence of paid sick leave in many businesses led undiagnosed sick workers to continue working if their business was open during the COVID-19 pandemic.

References

American Association of University Professors (2017) 'Trends in the Academic Labor Force, 1975–2015', https://www.aaup.org/sites/default/files/Academic_Labor_Force_Trends_1975-2015.pdf

Appel, S. and Zabin, C. (2019) 'Truck Driver Misclassification: Climate, Labor, and Environmental Justice Impacts', August, Center for Labor Research and Education, University of California, Berkeley, http://laborcenter.berkeley.edu/truck-driver-misclassification/

Bureau of Labor Statistics (2018) Contingent and Alternative Employment Arrangements Summary, 7 June, https://www.bls.gov/news.release/conemp.nr0.htm

Carr, F. (2015) 'Destandardization: Qualitative and Quantitative', in Edgell, S., Gottfried, H. and Granter, E. (eds) *The SAGE Handbook of the Sociology of Work and Employment*, London: Sage, pp 385–405.

Chambel, M.J. and Castanheira, F. (2006) 'Different temporary work status, different behaviors in organization', *Journal of Business and Psychology*, 20(3): 351–367.

Club Industry (2017) 'Gold's Gym Trainers in Los Angeles Vote Down Union', 28 April, https://www.clubindustry.com/news/gold-s-gym-trainers-los-angeles-vote-down-union

Covert, B. (2015) 'Why Your Beauty Salon Likely Doesn't Have Any Employees, *ThinkProgress*, 3 June, https://archive.thinkprogress.org/why-your-beauty-salon-likely-doesnt-have-any-employees-dcb01d801bc4/

Davis-Blake, A. and Uzzi, B. (1993) 'Determinants of employment externalization: A study of temporary workers and independent contractors', *Administrative Science Quarterly*, 38(2): 195–223.

De Cuyper, N., De Jong, J., De Witte, H., Isaksson, K., Rigotti, T. and Schalk, R. (2008) 'Literature review of theory and research on the psychological impact of temporary employment: Towards a conceptual model', *International Journal of Management Reviews*, 10(1): 25–51.

Dubal, V.B. (2017) 'Wage slave or entrepreneur? Contesting the dualism of legal worker identities', 105 *California Law Review*, 101: 65–124.

Esbenshade, J., Shifrin, E. and Rider, K. (2019) 'Leveraging liminality: How San Diego taxi drivers used their precarious status to win reform', *Labor History*, 60(2): 79–95.

Eurofound (2017) *Fraudulent Contracting of Work: Bogus Self-employment (Czech Republic, Spain and UK)*, Dublin: Eurofound.

Foxhire team (2016) 'What's the difference between a contractor and a temp?' available at https://www.foxhire.com/blog/what-s-the-difference-between-a-contractor-and-a-temp/

Galais, N., and Moser, K. (2009) 'Organizational commitment and the well-being of temporary agency workers: A longitudinal study, *Human Relations*, 62(4): 589–620.

George, E. and Chattopadhyay, P. (2005) 'One foot in each camp: The dual identification of contract workers', *Administrative Science Quarterly*, 50(1): 68–99.

Internal Revenue Service (2019) 'Minimum value and affordability', available at https://www.irs.gov/affordable-care-act/employers/minimum-value-and-affordability

International Labour Organization (2018) *Women and Men in the Informal Economy: A Statistical Picture (3rd edition)*, Geneva: International Labour Office.

Kalleberg, A.L. (2000) 'Nonstandard employment relations: part-time, temporary and contract work', *Annual Review of Sociology*, 26: 341–365.

Kunda, G., Barley, S.R. and Evans, J. (2002) 'Why do contractors contract? The experience of highly skilled technical professionals in a contingent labor market', *Industrial and Labor Relations Review*, 55(2): 234–261.

Lane, C.M. (2011) *A Company of One: Insecurity, Independence, and the New World of White-Collar Unemployment*, Ithaca, NY: Cornell University Press.

Leberstein, S. and Ruckelshaus, C. (2016) 'Independent Contractor vs. Employee: Why Independent Contractor Misclassification Matters and What We Can Do to Stop It, National Employment Law Project Policy Brief', May, https://s27147.pcdn.co/wp-content/uploads/Policy-Brief-Independent-Contractor-vs-Employee.pdf

Monteith, W. and Giesbert, L. (2017) ' "When the stomach is full we look for respect": Perceptions of "good work" in the urban informal sectors of three developing countries', *Work, Employment and Society*, 31(5): 816–833.

MortgageOrb Contributors (2006) 'Loan Officer Compensation Rules Pose Difficulties', available at https://mortgageorb.com/loan-officer-compensation-rules-pose-difficulties

MOW International Research Team (1987) *The Meaning of Working*, London: Academic Press.

Muehlebach, A. and Shoshan, N. (2012) 'Post-Fordist affect: Introduction', *Anthropological Quarterly*, 85(2): 317–343.

National Conference of State Legislatures (2020) 'Employee Misclassification', available at https://www.ncsl.org/research/labor-and-employment/employee-misclassification-resources.aspx

Sennett, R. (1998) *The Corrosion of Character*, New York, NY: W.W. Norton & Company.

Smith, V. (1998) 'The fractured world of the temporary worker: Power, participation, and fragmentation in the contemporary workplace', *Social Problems*, 45(4): 411–430.

UpCounsel (2020) 'Internal Contractor: Everything You Need to Know', available at https://www.upcounsel.com/internal-contractor

US Dept. of Labor (n.d.) Vacation leave. https://www.dol.gov/general/topic/workhours/vacation_leave

Weeks, K. (2011) *The Problem with Work: Feminism, Marxism, Antiwork Politics, and Postwork Imaginaries*, Durham, NC: Duke University Press.

Weil, D. (2014) *The Fissured Workplace: Why Work Became So Bad for So Many and What Can Be Done to Improve It*, Cambridge, MA: Harvard University Press.

Weil, D. (2019) Why the Fissured Workplace Is Bigger Than the Contingent Worker Survey Suggests, *The American Prospect*, 14 May, https://prospect.org/economy/future-real-jobs-prospect-roundtable/

World Economic Forum (2018) *The Future of Jobs Report 2018*, Cologne/Geneva: World Economic Forum.

PART II

Resignations

4

Wilful Resignations: Women, Labour and Life in Urban India

Asiya Islam

When I first met Chandni[1] in December 2016, she had just left her job working behind the till at a cafe in South Delhi. Although she was initially excited about this work, she told me her enthusiasm had been dampened by the manager's condescending attitude towards her and other workers. Within just a few weeks of joining the cafe, Chandni resigned when the manager refused to grant her time off to celebrate her anniversary with her boyfriend. Her friend, Prachi, who worked at the same cafe was supportive of Chandni's decision; she said, "We're not the kind of people who would back down because we only ask for what we should get, what we know is right. *How can you expect a person to work for seven days?*"[2] In the few months after her impulsive resignation, Chandni only managed to find brief periods of ad hoc work for a car company, which involved calling customers to invite them to promotional events. Eventually, one of Chandni's contacts invited her to paid participation in market research groups. Chandni agreed, hoping that this would eventually lead to full-time employment as a recruiter in the marketing company. But when this did not materialize, Chandni decided to quit in order to focus on her studies instead. At the time, Chandni was pursuing an undergraduate degree through distance learning and was keen to pass her exams. While studying at home and occasionally attending weekly classes on the university campus, Chandni was also responsible for managing the household after her mother temporarily moved away to work as a live-in nanny. When I visited Delhi in July 2018, six months later,

Chandni had finished her undergraduate degree and was employed in a data entry job in an office.

Drawing on nine months of ethnographic fieldwork, this chapter examines the lives of young lower middle class[3] women as they wilfully moved in and out of employment in the new economy[4] of urban India. As Chandni's account demonstrates, young women were inclined to short-term employment across a range of new economy jobs in cafes, call centres, shopping malls and offices, rather than to careers in specialized fields. In other words, while they were entering employment in the new economy, their participation was often not sustained. This movement might suggest easy availability of employment but this was not the case, with women often struggling for months to secure their next job. I became curious about these young women's wilfulness in quitting paid work given that their incomes, although not entirely indispensable, were significant for their low-income families. I use the term 'wilfulness' to indicate the voluntary, even assertive, nature of these young women's resignations. The most common reasons for quitting work included not being allowed time off, being disrespected or sexually harassed by managers or colleagues, and disliking the work environment. Importantly, during their periods of unemployment, young women were compelled to increase their participation in housework, primarily cleaning and cooking. When possible, they also enrolled in short-term training courses at skill centres in their neighbourhoods to keep themselves occupied, to further develop their employability and enhance their chances of realizing the next job opportunity.

There is an emerging ethnographic literature on young men's under- and unemployment in contexts of neoliberal precarization (Mains, 2007; Jeffrey, 2010; Di Nunzio, 2019). However, women's exit from employment remains relatively unexamined, to the detriment of our understanding of gendered experiences of precarity and work. This lacuna is exacerbated by a general and overly simplistic understanding that women leave work because of their commitment to homes and families, thus subsuming women's unemployment into domesticity. While I do not dispute the pressures that women may navigate between 'home' and 'work', the experiences of the young women in this chapter show that these are neither discrete nor linear categories. Indeed, their experiences make visible the constant back-and-forth to sustain livelihoods through multiple strategies at various sites, including but not limited to home and workplaces. What can these young women's wilful resignations from formal wage employment then offer us in terms of understanding work? In this chapter, I deploy young women's resignations as moments that reveal the intersecting power structures, particularly of gender and class, within which women navigate their subjectivities vis-à-vis work. These acts provide important insights into young women's emerging understandings of, and ways of relating to, work, highlighting gendered and classed experiences of emerging forms and processes of work.

In the following section, I provide an introduction to the 'new economy' in urban India and discuss the issue of unexpected 'de-feminization' of labour in recent years. I then outline methodological concerns around studying women and work and methodological strategies I deployed for my study on young women's experiences of the new economy. Following this, I focus on women's negotiations of 'respectability' in the workplace and the compulsion to domesticity at home. Through their narratives, I demonstrate that young women invest in multiple life strategies simultaneously to secure their futures amidst precarity of life and labour.

Precarity and de-feminization in the new economy of urban India

The changing nature of work in post-liberalization India has been the subject of considerable academic debate (Gooptu, 2009; Chakrabarti, 2016; Nayyar, 2017). In the 25 years following economic restructuring, the service sector has become the largest contributor to the country's GDP, outperforming agriculture and manufacturing.[5] The service sector boom – owed in large measure to the growth of information technology and dependent services – has been credited with the emergence of a 'New Middle Class' in India. This New Middle Class is qualitatively 'new' in its emergent social, economic and cultural practices – particularly in its rejection of state-led development in favour of market-driven growth (Fernandes, 2006; Lukose, 2009). Closely related to new class formations are changing ideals of gender relations – as capital for the bourgeoning economy, young women are central to the image of India as a modern nation (Oza, 2006; Dhawan, 2010; Lau, 2010). However, many scholars identify a gap between the discursive constructions and material realities of post-liberalization India. The majority of the so-called New Middle Class struggle in the precarious economy with low pay and no job security while only the securely middle and upper class are able to access high-level, high-pay jobs in the new economy (Fernandes, 2000; Ganguly-Scrase and Scrase, 2009). Further, contrary to expectations, the boom in services has not resulted in increased rates of labour force participation among women. Indeed, researchers have been preoccupied with the low and declining participation of women in the workforce, currently at only 15.9 per cent in urban areas (Periodic Labour Force Survey (PLFS) Annual Report, 2019). Some scholars have suggested that there is a U-shaped relationship between female labour force participation rate and household income in India, that is, women withdraw from the labour market as the household income increases, eventually returning at the high end of household income (Mammen and Paxson, 2000; Bhalla and Kaur, 2011; Das et al, 2015). However, evidence for this hypothesis is inconclusive (Mazumdar and Neetha, 2011; Abraham, 2013). Further, it is interesting to note that in urban areas, the highest rates of unemployment are found among women educated above secondary level (19.8 per cent as compared to 9.2 per cent for men educated to the same level (PLFS Annual Report, 2019)).

I suggest that analysis of the low and declining female labour force participation rate – largely reliant on survey data from the National Sample Survey (NSS) – suffers from three main shortcomings. One, while survey data is useful in providing headline statistics, they do not convey the complexities of availability and quality of employment opportunities in economically diverse settings of Indian cities (Sudarshan and Bhattacharya, 2008). Two, they do not offer an insight into women's own decision making about participation in employment. And finally, survey classifications do not capture the non-linearity of women's participation in work. The NSS records the following categories of employment: regular or waged, casual, and self-employment. While the young women centred in this chapter would fall into the category of 'regular or waged' work when employed, their movement from one activity to another, between paid work and domestic work, as well as often juggling multiple forms of 'work', belies that classification, blurring the boundaries between regular/irregular work.

Scully (2016, 298) paints a similar picture in his research on precarity in South Africa:

> ... precarious workers have complex economic lives, relying on a combination of diverse income sources, including, but not limited to, their own wage in order to gain a livelihood. The primary site through which incomes are combined and livelihoods are produced is the precarious workers' households. As a result, these workers' material interests are centred on their household livelihood strategies rather than their workplaces.

This recognition of the aggregation of 'diverse income sources' as an approach to mitigating precarity finds resonance in feminist scholarship, which argues that women have always had a precarious relation to waged labour (Precarias a la deriva, 2004; Federici, 2006; Betti, 2016). To nuance the picture, women have always been engaged in multiple forms of labour for the maintenance of households. In young women's strategies for securing livelihoods, it is, therefore, not so much a *shift* to the site of the household (as Scully, 2016 suggests) but instead the further diversification of labour through participation in education, skills training, and employment compelled by the new economy. In particular, women's precarity emerges in relation to 'flexible job market and less flexible societal structures affecting their lives, such as heterosexual marriage, maternity, care-work ...' (Fantone, 2007, 8). Rather than implying the simple absorption of women into domesticity, these very conditions inform women's decisions about employment in intersecting and overlapping ways. The multi-sited labour of the young women in this chapter then points towards the need to develop a language and understanding of work that accounts for its ordinary everyday experiences. Only by considering wage employment as *one among many* strategies of navigating the complex web of labour and life conditions are we able to generate a more comprehensive and sophisticated understanding of women's impulsive and assertive decisions to leave employment.

Researching women and work in New Delhi, India

Contrary to much of the existing research on women in India's 'New Middle Class', this chapter focuses on the category of *lower middle class women*. Building on research that highlights the precarity of employment in the new economy and the lack of stability and security it affords its workers (Gooptu, 2013; Maiti, 2013; Rogan et al, 2018), it is important to study the experiences of those who are not comfortably middle class. In aspiring to the opportunities promised by the new economy, notably new consumer choices and access to higher education (Osella and Osella, 1999; Jeffrey, 2010; Dickey, 2012), the 'work' practices of the lower middle classes offer relatively underexplored insights into the changing dynamics of class and gender. Among the lower middle classes, attempting to distance themselves from livelihoods of necessity, women's employment may be particularly contested. In contrast to Papanek's historical observation that 'men in many societies boast that "my wife doesn't have to work" when they want to demonstrate middle-class status' (Papanek, 1979, 779), in contemporary India, 'the public visibility of women and their relative freedom to pursue careers' is emerging as a marker of *middle-classness* (Ganguly-Scrase, 2003, 554). That this is a transition is evident in contestations over the subject of the 'working woman', particularly lower middle class women neophyte workers in the service economy. For example, Patel (2010, 4) points out through her study of women call centre workers that 'As global customer service workers, women must now traverse the nightscape' and, therefore, negotiate judgement, disdain and violence as women 'out of place'. Similarly, among workers in a small-town BPO (Business Process Outsourcing) centre near Bangalore, India, Vijaykumar (2013, 778) finds that young women feel the need to distance themselves from both 'old-fashioned housewives and promiscuous urban call center girls'. These negotiations reveal how such emerging work in the service economy simultaneously promises professional respectability while threatening the community respectability of lower middle class women. Interrogating the situated nature of women's engagement in various forms of work, my research framework prioritized fine-grained insights built through long-term ethnographic research with young lower middle class women in South Delhi.

I started by adopting the classic approach of ethnographies of work by embedding myself in particular workplaces (Smith, 2001; Brannan et al, 2007; Platt et al, 2013). I established access to a cafe in South Delhi, *Cuppa n Cake*, an Indian cafe chain. With its air-conditioned interiors, serving coffee and cakes, the cafe chain is representative of a distinctly modern, urban and global India. By frequenting the cafe, I became a familiar face to Prachi and Sheela, who worked the day shifts there, arriving at 8 am and leaving after 6 pm. Chandni, whom I introduced at the start of the chapter, had also worked at the same cafe, but left shortly before I became a customer there. I told Prachi and Sheela that I was a researcher and hoped that the cafe could be the primary site for my ethnography of work. However, a few weeks later, Prachi too quit the cafe over an argument with the manager. Prachi's decision to leave her cafe job was in part informed by the understanding that this work was only temporary and could be potentially substituted by another equally paid job; she explained, "Right now, we are not working to build *careers*, we are working because we need to."

Arendt (1998) identifies 'labour' and 'work' as distinct categories on the simple basis that most European languages contain different terms for these seemingly similar activities. Through their historical and contemporary usage, and reliance on a Marxist understanding, Arendt (1998, 7) proposes that labour is natural, while work is artifice; 'The human condition of labour is life itself'. Labour is then a broader conceptualization, akin to this volume's proposed concept of 'ordinary work'. In Hindi too, there are various terms in circulation, for example, Parry (2013) describes how workers in a public sector Indian steel plant differentiated between *naukri* as secure employment and *kam* as insecure wage labour, resulting in social distinctions between the two groups. The participants in this research used the English words 'jobs' to refer to short-term work, 'career' to refer to long-term professional engagement that yields higher material rewards, and 'labour-type' work to refer to manual work, such as the kind of cleaning work that some of their parents did, but which they firmly rejected as not commensurate with their education level. In referring to their employment as 'jobs' rather than 'careers', young women participated in waged employment not as a discrete form of labour but as one of many labours to build and secure their lives, including skills training, education, housework, maintenance of respectability and so on.

Upon learning that young women participated in formal employment on a short-term and intermittent basis, it became apparent that I needed to extend my research into women's lives beyond their workplaces. I hired one of my early contacts, Pooja, as a research assistant. She proved to be instrumental in enabling me to shift the focus *from work to working lives* by introducing me to her friends and others in their residential neighbourhoods – Dakshinpuri and Khanpur. The move from workplaces to neighbourhoods (Scully, 2016; Sen and Sengupta, 2016) was central to gaining a comprehensive understanding of decision making about employment within the structures of their lives. Dakshinpuri and Khanpur are adjacent low-income neighbourhoods in South Delhi, inhabited by a Hindu majority population, ranging from middle to low castes and comprising the lower middle classes. A *basti* or slum in the area called JJ Camp is home to a working class population. The narrow roads of Dakshinpuri and Khanpur are lined by three-storey houses, which are split into either privately owned or rented one-bedroom flats on each floor. Through snowballing, I came to know a group of young women in these neighbourhoods, all of whom were either employed or had been employed in the last six months in new service economy work.

These young women, aged 19–23 years old, were unmarried and living with their families, usually composed of parents and siblings, and sometimes paternal grandparents. They had grown up in Delhi and identified themselves as urban women in contrast to those from their parents' villages in the states of Uttar Pradesh, Uttarakhand, Bihar and Rajasthan. They were either pursuing or had completed undergraduate degrees through distance learning from Delhi University although they regularly missed the weekly on-campus classes due to work and exhaustion. Nevertheless, acquiring an undergraduate degree was significant for them, particularly because this exceeded their parents' educational opportunities. These women's qualifications are in consonance with the narrowing gender gap across all levels of education in India. While in 1990–91, 46 girls per 100 boys were in higher education, in 2015, this increased to 85 girls per 100 boys (Education Statistics at a Glance, 2016). On the basis of these newly acquired qualifications and skills, young women distanced themselves from their mothers' occupations as housewives and domestic workers. The rhetorical question I frequently heard was "Why would we do that [become domestic workers or housewives] when we're educated?!" Further, these young women also enrolled in other vocational skills courses, such as spoken English, basic computers and retail management, which have become integral requirements for entry into the new economy (Nambiar, 2013). The young women worked in a range of workplaces – cafes, shopping malls, call centres and offices of varying sizes, and carried out a variety of roles including retail, data entry and telecommunications work. Their incomes were between Rs.8,000 and Rs.12,000 per month (GBP 80–120), which was close to the minimum wage for semi-skilled workers in New Delhi (Rs.10,764 or GBP 110).

After shifting the focus away from workplaces, I hung out with respondents in their spare time, in malls, markets and parks. I also visited the homes and workplaces of young women when I was invited and had informal conversations with some respondents' families, workplace managers and skills training providers. In the second phase, I carried out in-depth semi-structured interviews with 18 women, including the group of women I had been hanging out with. I met most women more than once; in cases where only one meeting was possible, I continued conversations about their work and families through WhatsApp messages. In conducting this fieldwork, I relied on my 'insider' position as a young Indian woman with native fluency in Hindi. Our class difference, however, was obvious and acknowledged on both sides; indeed it provided fertile material for our discussions on class identifications. Deploying me as a reference point in our conversations, many respondents pointed out that I was 'high class' (based on my clothes, manner of speaking, and especially my residence in the UK) while they were just about 'middle class'. Although only one respondent specifically used the term 'lower middle class', most of them were tentative in their claims to middle-classness. The analysis that I present in the following sections is steered by young women's narratives, informed by the understanding that they are the experts on their own lives (Sosulski et al, 2010). I use these narratives to establish micro–macro links between women's working lives and wider socio-economic change in urban India.

Resignations and respectability

On one of the days I spent in *Cuppa n Cake*, where Sheela and Prachi were then employed, I witnessed an area managers' meeting. Dressed in shirts and black trousers, a group of men pulled tables and chairs together to sit in a boardroom format. The cafe workers – with titles like 'brew master' and 'housekeeper' – were behind the counter dressed in t-shirts and trousers. The gender differentials in the cafe were stark: all the area managers around the table were men, whereas two out of three workers behind the counter were women. I made the observation to Sheela; she smiled, shrugged and responded; "That's how it is." Sheela told me that she had heard about one woman who had been promoted to the position of an area manager for *Cuppa n Cake* but that otherwise, it was known that despite the large number of women employed as 'team members' in these cafes, it was mostly only men who made it to managerial positions.

Sheela was one of the few respondents who worked for an extended period in one job, around 18 months. During this time Sheela was promoted just once. While her title changed from 'team member' to 'brew master' (or 'TM to BM' in the cafe lingo), the promotion was not accompanied by a significant pay rise. In addition, she was once awarded 'Employee of the Month' for which she took home a coffee hamper. Sheela took pride in her work and all that it allowed her to do; she enjoyed learning how to do coffee art, her income paid in part for her younger siblings' education, and she showed me the smartphone that she bought after saving small amounts of her salary each month. In that, Sheela was representative of other respondents, who asserted their professional respectability through these new economy 'jobs'. However, the deliberate strategy of professionalizing these jobs through titles such as brew master, executive assistant, sales executive and so on was mismatched with long hours, low pay and low value characterizing this work. Despite being contracted to work five days a week they were often expected to work six or seven days a week for which they did not receive additional payment. Overtime work was seen as an obligation and while the employees complained about it to each other and to me, they did not raise this with the managers.

Young women were conscious of their lower status in the workplace in relation to their overwhelmingly male managers. While workplace hierarchies are very much the norm, for these young women, these hierarchies were felt as 'injuries' given their vulnerable position as 'working women' from lower middle class families. Despite their own sense of the changing role of paid work in their lives – that they asserted through their *choice* to be in employment – they were conscious that managers may see them as women who had been sent to work by their families out of necessity. Prachi quit her cafe job within a few months after feeling disrespected by managers and colleagues and expanded on these gendered and classed expectations: "They say girls who are 'good', work silently ... I'm not like this. I do what I think is right. I don't want to do the kind of work where I feel insulted, where I work hard and still can be told whatever ..."

Instances in which women felt insulted were varied and included sexual harassment, even though it was not necessarily named as such. Prior to working at *Cuppa n Cake* Prachi had a job in a boutique, but had to quit this work after a fellow male employee had started 'liking' her, and persistently contacted her outside work hours. With no worthwhile recourse to report his behaviour, she felt that the situation would escalate if she continued working at the shop. She had not considered reporting his behaviour to either her manager or her parents. She thought that the manager may put the blame on her and that her parents might tell her to stop working altogether. Such situations were exacerbated where the managers themselves sexually harassed the employees. Chandni told me that she had left a previous job in a call centre on account of low wages and the manager's misbehaviour. When I asked whether she had thought about complaining, Chandni responded, "No, he was the *boss* of the *office*. He tried to be *extra friendly* with me once, so I said to him, *sir*, you know you're like my father ... He didn't touch me but he tried to be *over friendly* ... I didn't say much, but I said this much."

Given these workplace hierarchies along lines of gender and class, young women did not have an avenue to resist or complain about their managers. Crying therefore became a form of veiled protest. Women reported shutting themselves in the toilet and crying after being unfairly told off or insulted in front of colleagues and customers. Prachi told me she cried in the cafe toilet when Sheela told her what other colleagues had been saying about her behind her back. Chandni had also emerged with 'red puffy eyes' from the toilet after the manager refused her time off. While crying may seem like a fairly innocuous reaction to unfair and even hostile conditions of work, young women were aware that this response could make their managers conscious of their behaviour without explicitly challenging them and workplace hierarchies. For these young women, crying was therefore an acceptable way to express their unhappiness about being treated disrespectfully while remaining within class and gender norms.[6] Lacking avenues for protest, such as unions, strikes and workplace disciplinary procedures, women sought to gain control in the workplace by prudently signalling that they were unhappy, rather than overtly challenging patterns of discrimination.

The need to signal discontent in order to be heard also underpinned women's wilful decisions to resign from their posts when they felt they had reached a breaking point. The young women I got to know rarely resigned 'formally', that is, by tendering a resignation letter and working their notice period. Instead, following an unpleasant incident at work that undermined their respect, young women chose not to show up to work the next day, and thereby terminated their contracts spontaneously. In retrospective discussions, such incidents were identified as breaking points and referred to in the context of longer-term conditions of workplace inequality. For example, Sheela quit the cafe after 18 months of employment over an argument with a new member of staff. This member of staff, Sheela told me, came from a 'good family', that is, from a well-off family. This, Sheela thought, gave her the impudence to behave badly. Partly because of her bad behaviour and partly because the manager did not defend Sheela, she impulsively decided to quit work. When she did not show up at work the next day, the manager called and requested her to come back. When she did not acquiesce to his request, she got a call from a head office representative who offered to transfer her to another cafe nearby to resolve the conflict with her colleague, and consequently her manager. She accepted the offer, working at the nearby cafe for a brief period, before she eventually quit in order to return to studies.

Other women had also engaged in similar negotiations following their resignations from work, which enabled them to gain an upper hand over their managers, even if only briefly. Although the young women were not indispensable, managers did seem to be affected by their exit from work. This may be due to the costs of training new staff but it might also be the case that a consistently high turnover of staff would have reflected badly on the managers' performance. When women quit impetuously, managers attempted to pacify them, although these efforts did not entail offers of higher pay. Therefore, through their resignations, women did not seek to negotiate material gains. Rather, their wilfulness in leaving work helped them to assert to their managers that, contrary to their manager's assumptions, they did not *need* this job. Through their resignations, young women attempted to re-establish the respectability which they perceived was continually undermined in low-end service work.

Strategies for sustaining lives

While Sheela was still working at *Cuppa n Cake*, she told me that she had decided to seek employment after Class XII, her last year of high school, to enable her younger siblings to continue their studies. Her father was a carpenter by trade but had not had any work for the last two to three years. Her mother had previously been a housewife but since her father's loss of income, she had started working as a domestic worker in multiple households, earning around Rs.5,000 (GBP 50) per month. Sheela had not given up on higher education as she believed that gaining an undergraduate degree would help her to secure other, perhaps better, jobs in the future. She was uncertain about her English language skills and therefore nervous about enrolling for a degree taught and examined in English. When I suggested that she could do it in Hindi, Sheela replied:

> 'No, but I also don't like Hindi. And here all my work is in *English*. I don't know *English perfectly*. So I'll have to continue. This year, there was this situation, so I couldn't do it. *Mummy* had to go to the village and we had to send money to her, so I thought I'll start next year.'

Aiming to improve her English skills, and therefore her employability, Sheela enrolled for an undergraduate degree through distance learning after leaving work from *Cuppa n Cake*. She contextualized her decision by telling me that her younger sister had managed to find employment in an office and could substitute her income for the family, at least for a few months. This arrangement, whereby another family member could compensate for the loss of income, was crucial to young women's impulsive resignations. Through an aggregation of incomes at the site of the family, young women were able to repudiate employment when they reached a breaking point. This familial interdependence is apparent in the considerations that Sheela engaged with in making decisions about employment; the promise of a better life through education, the need for money for everyday maintenance of the household, and the imperative to oblige extended families in villages. Interestingly, young women seemed to make these employment decisions in conjunction with their mothers and sisters, the female members of their households.

Sheela relied on her younger sister's ability to find employment while Chandni, whom I mentioned earlier in the chapter, was able to focus on her studies when her mother took up employment as a live-in nanny. Similarly, Prachi was able to study because her elder sister had started working early. After she quit her job from *Cuppa n Cake*, Prachi's family was worried about paying back instalments on the loan they had taken out for house repairs. Although Prachi struggled to find a suitable replacement job, her younger sister did manage to secure employment as a sales assistant in a groceries store in the mall to support the family income.

These female networks within families did not, however, facilitate straightforward or discrete exchanges of labour. Instead, such exchange was possible – often at a moment's notice – because the women were *simultaneously* involved in multiple activities to sustain their present and future lives. These multiple activities included various kinds of work in which women were compelled to participate in order to comply with gender norms and social obligations. While employed, both Sheela and Chandni had managed to mostly (but not completely) avoid housework responsibilities. However, once they quit, they were expected to pick up the housework that their mothers were responsible for. Further, these young women were aware that once married, the responsibility for housework would be inevitable. At times, these conflicting obligations, combined with the inability to get time off from work, pushed women out of employment, even if only intermittently. Some respondents referred to 'personal problems' in explaining their exit from previous jobs. These commonly included attending weddings, preparations for upcoming festivals, and family visits to the village. Such distinctly gendered activities broadly fall within the category of what Papanek (1979) calls 'status production work' or work done by women to maintain the status of families, beyond the everyday work of cooking, cleaning and caring. Papanek suggests that for families seeking social mobility, these activities may assume even greater importance, requiring women's compulsory participation. The routine of employment in services, characterized by long work hours, weekend work and lack of benefits such as sick pay and annual leave, does not accommodate such activities. Unable to get time off from work and compelled to participate in such activities, women would, therefore, temporarily withdraw from employment. Their exit from employment, while seemingly dramatic in its impulsiveness, needs to be placed and understood within the web of the many labours women engage in to sustain lives. They seek employment asserting their subjectivities as educated, urban professional women. But the low-end service employment that they access offers limited security of life. It is, therefore, interchangeable with other gendered labours of life making, including domestic, care and status-production work. In other words, for young women, 'Waged work and reproductive labour come together as possible strategies for enabling life', demonstrating that 'in fact it is waged work that serves reproductive labour and reproductive labour that is the over-arching mode of all economic activity' (Bhattacharyya, 2018, 52).

Conclusions

The experiences of Sheela, Prachi and Chandni demonstrate the participation of young Indian women in a broad range of 'work' beyond paid employment, including further study and skills training for employability, unpaid housework and family obligations to maintain status. Although many of these activities did not generate a direct income, they were seen as instrumental for the future. The multiplication of livelihood strategies has been described as a more general phenomenon among young people navigating precarious socio-economic conditions (Scully, 2016; Ferguson and Li, 2018), and yet the compulsion to provide reproductive labour falls disproportionately on women, which needs to be better contextualized in order to develop a comprehensive and gendered understanding of how precarious lives are sustained. Sheela, Prachi, Chandni and other respondents repeatedly emphasized that they did not want to become 'housewives' (Islam, 2020). In other words, they did not leave employment because of 'attachment' to, or preference for, reproductive labour, as has been historically argued for women (Sen, 1999; Betti, 2016). Rather, this discussion shows how women's changing role in the market in conjunction with an almost unchanging role in the family informed how they related to, and made decisions about, work.

The decisions of young women to quit wage employment were informed by a precarious web constituted by conditions of work, family compulsions and the need to secure respectability. Their attempts to establish a temporal routine and a regular income to sustain their present and future lives through employment rubbed up against the precarious realities of India's new economy – low pay, long hours, insecure contracts – exacerbated by a lack of progression, gendered hierarchies and the need to retain 'respect' as lower middle class women at work. These conditions, in combination with rigid expectations to conform to gender norms, generated precarity not only of labour, but also of life (Nielsen and Waldrop, 2014; Millar, 2017). I therefore argue that women's exit from employment cannot be isolated from the plurality of their labour, which extends beyond workplaces.

From the vantage point of gender, this research generates several insights into the broader formulation of 'ordinary work', as proposed by this volume. While young women engaged with emerging and contested subjectivities as they entered employment in the new economy, they were conscious of structural constraints of class and gender that limit their progression in workplaces, and subsequently, in life. It is therefore not surprising that they rejected such employment themselves, initially by distinguishing these 'jobs' from 'careers' and eventually by resigning. However, the picture is complicated by the non-linearity of women's employment and unemployment. By treating employment and unemployment as discrete categories, a sophisticated understanding of how people live ordinary lives becomes elusive. These young women's narratives show that they made decisions about employment on a continuum along with a number of life-sustaining and future-promising activities, including non-income-generating activities. While young people in general may invest in education to secure opportunities, women are also compelled to reproduce gender norms by participating in unpaid housework and status-production work. These young women's lives thus contribute to a conceptualization of *ordinary work as livelihood strategies that are both facilitated and constrained by socio-economic conditions.*

This wider conceptualization of ordinary work challenges the focus on paid employment in the scholarship on precarity (see Kalleberg, 2009; Standing, 2011). Assessing the conditions of employment in general limits our understanding of the interconnections between labour and life, which is detrimental to policy formulations for tackling underemployment and unemployment. This is reflected in the proliferating but incomplete and largely ineffective discussion on the declining rate of female labour force participation in India. In discussions on unemployment, the wide use of the category 'NEETs' or young people 'Not in Education, Employment, or Training' tends to neglect the value of non-income-generating reproductive labour that contributes to sustaining lives amidst precarious conditions. Accounting for non-income-generating reproductive labour as part of 'ordinary work' would facilitate the development of long-term and sustainable policy measures aimed at augmenting people's capacities rather than merely increasing rates of employment.

Acknowledgements

I am grateful to the Gates Cambridge Trust and the Department of Sociology, University of Cambridge for providing funding that enabled this research. I am indebted to Ms Pooja Pacherwal, my research assistant, who greatly enriched my fieldwork.

Notes

[1] All names of individuals and workplaces have been changed to preserve anonymity.

[2] The conversations and interviews were conducted primarily in Hindi, with participants occasionally using English words, phrases and sentences. These have been italicised in the quoted text.

[3] Deploying the category 'lower middle class' does not suggest that it is a unified category in an abstract sense or even in India. To the contrary, there can be wide variations between income, consumption and life-styles of those in the liminal margin between the poor and the securely middle class, which is demonstrated by research on lower middle classes in different regions of India by various scholars (see, for example, Ganguly-Scrase, 2003; Jeffrey, 2010; Dickey, 2016).

[4] Although the 'new economy' is an imprecise term, it is useful to capture professions in the services sector that have emerged in India in the last three decades. At a low level, these include a wide range of work – retail, telecommunications, data entry – across various workspaces, such as shopping malls, cafes, call centres, and offices (examples of types of offices that the respondents for this research were employed in include offices for a tourism company, a tele services provider, a car company, customer services for a manufacturing company, and so on).

[5] According to the Economic Survey 2017–18 (Ministry of Finance, 2018) the services sector accounts for 72.5 per cent of the Gross Value Added (GVA) to the Indian economy.

[6] In her study of neophyte factory women in Malaysia, Ong (2010, 165) notes the phenomenon of women workers' emotional outbursts: 'a female office worker noted that when foremen scolded the operators, the latter were not allowed to respond but had to be "very polite" … Crying sometimes seemed the only way to seek relief from being reprimanded and to obtain pardon' (also see, Ngai, 2005, 165–188).

References

Abraham, V. (2013) 'Missing labour or consistent "de-feminisation"?', *Economic & Political Weekly*, (31): 99–108.

Arendt, H. (1998) *The Human Condition* (2nd edn), Chicago: University of Chicago Press.

Betti, E. (2016) 'Gender and precarious labor in a historical perspective: Italian women and precarious work between Fordism and post-Fordism', *International Labor and Working-Class History*, 89: 64–83.

Bhalla, S. and Kaur, R. (2011) *Labour force participation of women in India: some facts, some queries*, LSE Asia Research Centre Working Papers. London: London School of Economics.

Bhattacharyya, G. (2018) *Rethinking Racial Capitalism: Questions of Reproduction and Survival*, Cultural Studies and Marxism, London: Rowman & Littlefield.

Brannan, M, Pearson, G. and Worthington, F. (2007) 'Ethnographies of work and the work of ethnography', *Ethnography*, 8(4): 395–402.

Chakrabarti, A. (2016) 'Indian economy in transition', *Economic & Political Weekly*, 51(29): 61–67.

Das S., Jain-Chandra, S., Kochhar, K. et al (2015) 'Women Workers in India: Why So Few Among So Many?' *IMF working Paper* WP/15/55.

Dhawan, N.B. (2010) 'The married "new Indian woman": Hegemonic aspirations in new middle-class politics?' *South African Review of Sociology*, 41(3): 45–60.

Di Nunzio, M. (2019) *The Act of Living: Street Life, Marginality, and Development in Urban Ethiopia*, Ithaca, NY: Cornell University Press.

Dickey, S. (2012) 'The pleasures and anxieties of being in the middle: Emerging middle-class identities in urban South India', *Modern Asian Studies*, 46(03): 559–599.

Dickey, S. (2016) *Living Class in Urban India*, New Brunswick, NJ: Rutgers University Press.

Economic Survey 2017–18 (2018) Delhi: Ministry of Finance, Government of India.

Education Statistics at a Glance (2016) Ministry of Human Resource Development, Department of School and Education, Government of India.

Fantone, L. (2007) 'Precarious changes: Gender and generational politics in contemporary Italy', *Feminist Review*, 87(1): 5–20.

Federici, S. (2006) *Precarious Labor: A Feminist Viewpoint*, Lecture, available at https://inthemiddleofthewhirlwind.wordpress.com/precarious-labor-a-feminist-viewpoint/

Ferguson, J. and Li, T.M. (2018) 'Beyond the "proper job:" Political-economic analysis after the century of labouring man', Working Paper 51. PLAAS, UWC: Cape Town.

Fernandes, L. (2000) 'Restructuring the new middle class in liberalizing India', *Comparative Studies of South Asia, Africa and the Middle East*, 20(1–2): 88–112.

Fernandes, L. (2006) *India's New Middle Class: Democratic Politics in an Era of Economic Reform*, Minneapolis, MN and London: University of Minnesota Press.

Ganguly-Scrase, R. (2003) 'Paradoxes of globalization, liberalization, and gender equality: The worldviews of the lower middle class in West Bengal, India', *Gender & Society*, 17(4): 544–566.

Ganguly-Scrase, R. and Scrase, T.J. (2009) *Globalisation and the Middle Classes in India: The Social and Cultural Impact of Neoliberal Reforms*, Oxford: Routledge.

Gooptu, N. (2009) 'Neoliberal subjectivity, enterprise culture and new workplaces: Organized retail and shopping malls in India', *Economic & Political Weekly*, 44(22): 45–54.

Gooptu, N. (2013) 'Servile sentinels of the city: Private security guards, organized informality, and labour in interactive services in globalized India', *International Review of Social History*, 58(1): 9–38.

Islam, A. (2020) '"It gets really boring if you stay at home": Women, work and temporalities in urban India', *Sociology*, 54(5): 867–882.

Jeffrey, C. (2010) *Timepass: Youth, Class, and the Politics of Waiting in India*, Stanford, CA: Stanford University Press.

Kalleberg, A.L. (2009) 'Precarious work, insecure workers: Employment relations in transition', *American Sociological Review*, 74(1): 1–22.

Lau, L. (2010) 'Literary representations of the "new Indian woman": The single, working, urban, middle class Indian woman seeking personal autonomy', *Journal of South Asian Development*, 5(2): 271–292.

Lukose, R. (2009) *Liberalization's Children: Gender, Youth, and Consumer Citizenship in Globalizing India*, Durham, NC: Duke University Press.

Mains, D. (2007) 'Neoliberal times: Progress, boredom, and shame among young men in urban Ethiopia', *American Ethnologist*, 34(4): 659–673.

Maiti, D. (2013) 'Precarious work in India: Trends and emerging issues', *American Behavioral Scientist*, 57(4): 507–530.

Mammen, K. and Paxson, C. (2000) 'Women's work and economic development', *The Journal of Economic Perspectives*, 14(4): 141–164.

Mazumdar, I. and Neetha, N. (2011) 'Gender dimensions: Employment trends in India, 1993–94 to 2009–10', *Economic & Political Weekly*, 46(43): 118–126.

Millar, K.M. (2017) 'Toward a critical politics of precarity', *Sociology Compass*, 11(6): 1–11.

Nambiar, D. (2013) 'Creating enterprising subjects through skill development: The network state, network enterprises, and youth aspirations in India', in Gooptu, N. (ed) *Enterprise Culture in Neoliberal India: Studies in Youth, Class, Work and Media*, Oxford: Routledge, pp 57–72.

Nayyar, D. (2017) 'Economic liberalisation in India: Then and now', *Economic & Political Weekly*, 52(2): 41–48.

Ngai, P. (2005) *Made in China: Women Factory Workers in a Global Workplace*, Durham, NC and London: Duke University Press.

Nielsen, K.B. and Waldrop, A. (eds) (2014) *Women, Gender and Everyday Social Transformation in India*, London and New York, NY: Anthem Press.

Ong, A. (2010) *Spirits of Resistance and Capitalist Discipline* (2nd edn), Albany, NY: SUNY.

Osella, F. and Osella, C. (1999) 'From transience to immanence: Consumption, life-cycle and social mobility in Kerala, South India', *Modern Asian Studies*, 33(4): 989–1020.

Oza, R. (2006) 'The new liberal Indian woman and globalization', in *The Making of Neoliberal India: Nationalism, Gender, and the Paradoxes of Globalization,* New York, NY: Routledge, 21–44.

Papanek, H. (1979) 'Family status production: The "work" and "non-work" of women', *Signs: Journal of Women in Culture and Society*, 4(4): 775–781.

Parry, J. (2013) 'Company and contract labour in a central Indian steel plant', *Economy and Society*, 42(3): 348–374.

Patel, R. (2010) *Working the Night Shift: Women in India's Call Center Industry*, Stanford, CA: Stanford University Press.

Periodic Labour Force Survey (PLFS) Annual Report (2019) May. Ministry of Statistics and Programme Implementation, Government of India.

Platt, J., Crothers, C. and Horgan, M. (2013) 'Producing ethnographies: Workplace ethnographies in history', *Journal of the History of the Behavioral Sciences*, 49(1): 45–62.

Precarias a la deriva (2004) 'Adrift through the circuits of feminized precarious work', *Feminist Review*, 77: 157–161.

Rogan, M., Rover, S., Chen, M.A. and Carre, F. (2018) 'Informal employment in the global South: Globalisation, product relations and "precarity"', in Kalleberg, A.L. and Vallas, S. (eds) *Precarious Work* (Vol 31), Bingley: Emerald Publishing Limited, pp 307–334.

Scully, B. (2016) 'From the shop floor to the kitchen table: the shifting centre of precarious workers' politics in South Africa', *Review of African Political Economy*, 43(148): 295–311.

Sen, S. (1999) *Women and Labour in Late Colonial India: The Bengal Jute Industry*, Cambridge: Cambridge University Press.

Sen, S. and Sengupta, N. (2016) *Domestic Days: Women, Work, and Politics in Contemporary Kolkata*, New Delhi: Oxford University Press.

Smith, V. (2001) 'Ethnographies of work and the work of ethnographers', in Atkinson, P., Coffey, A., Delamont, S., Lofland, J. and Lofland, L. (eds) *Handbook of Ethnography*, London: SAGE Publications Ltd, pp 220–233.

Sosulski, M.R., Buchanan, N.T. and Donnell, C.M. (2010) 'Life history and narrative analysis: Feminist methodologies contextualizing black women's experiences with severe mental illness', *Journal of Sociology & Social Welfare*, XXXVII(3): 29–57.

Standing, G. (2011) *The Precariat: The New Dangerous Class*, London: Bloomsbury.

Sudarshan, R.M. and Bhattacharya, S. (2008) *Through the Magnifying Glass: Women's Work and Labour Force Participation in Urban Delhi*, ILO Asia-Pacific working paper series. New Delhi: International Labour Organization, Subregional Office for South Asia.

Vijayakumar, G. (2013) 'I'll Be Like Water', *Gender & Society*, 27(6): 777–798.

5

"Be Your Own Boss": Entrepreneurial Dreams on the Urban Margins of South Africa

Hannah J. Dawson

South Africa has one of the highest youth unemployment rates in the world. With two thirds of young people excluded from employment, turning jobless youth into self-made entrepreneurs has become the mantra of the state, NGOs and the Church. In June 2015, at a government-funded 'career exhibition' targeting unemployed youth in Zandspruit informal settlement in Johannesburg, the leader of a youth-run NGO told the young people gathered not to wait for jobs but to start their own businesses. "Your future is in your hands, not government's hands," Sibongile shouted, valorizing individual entrepreneurship as the solution to the crisis of youth unemployment.

During my time in Zandspruit, I found that many young people promoted the idea and aspiration of starting their own business. One young man by the name of Itumeleng wrote a self-help book called *Be the Boss of your Future*. In the introduction he writes: 'A bit of shocking South African statistics. Only one out of every nine matriculants (14%) will get formal, salaried jobs. Only 9% will undergo tertiary education. As many as 80% will remain officially unemployed. To survive in such a harsh environment you need to start your own business' (Dithupe, 2016, 32). Echoing the entrepreneurial messages from the state, Itumeleng presents self-employment as the solution to unemployment but also as a way to obtain economic independence and social mobility. The framing of entrepreneurship in the 'township economy' (or informal entrepreneurship) as a route to improved life chances rather than a 'coping strategy' (Rakodi, 1995) reflects important shifts in the ways in which researchers and policy makers conceptualize the informal economy. At the time of the career exhibition in Zandspruit, there was much talk about the Gauteng provincial government's Township Economy Revitalisation Strategy, which frames the 'township economy' as a generator of jobs, entrepreneurship and economic inclusion, rather than poverty and marginalization. This shift reflects the emergence of a new development paradigm that views the informal economy through the neoliberal lens of entrepreneurship and job creation (Roy, 2010; Dolan and Rajak, 2016; 2018).

Drawing on ethnographic fieldwork in Zandspruit, this chapter examines the question of why young un- and underemployed young men in the South African informal economy express a preference for self-employment. By documenting the work histories of two informal entrepreneurs – Hloni, who makes a living as a mechanic, and Thatho, whose livelihood comes from wiring illegal electricity connections – I examine the appeal of the 'be your own boss' discourse and the factors that lead young people to embrace informal entrepreneurship. In so doing, I highlight the social, relational and reciprocal dimensions of self-employment as experienced by young men in South Africa that are often missing in the literature on entrepreneurship with its focus on individual agency and self-reliance. Drawing parallels with Kathleen Millar's work in Brazil (2014) and Tatiana Thieme's work in Nairobi (2013; 2018), I consider how self-employment blurs the boundaries between 'work' and 'non-work' and thus enables young men to weave together diverse forms of working and socializing. I argue that while young men's preference for self-employment encompasses the neoliberal or individualistic ideal of getting ahead, it must also be read as an expression of discontent with a racially segmented economy that incorporates young Black men on degrading terms that make it very difficult to combine having a job with having a decent life. I argue that low-end wage work disrupts the rhythms of life in Zandspruit, where having time to build, maintain and extend profoundly local relations is essential to achieving socio-economic prosperity.

Entrepreneurism in the 'informal economy': from condemnation to celebration?

Entrepreneurship in the informal economy has acquired increasing prominence in South Africa's public and policy debates in the last decade. It was not always like this. For much of the twentieth century, self-employment in the informal economy was strongly discouraged (even outlawed for certain trades) by apartheid legislation. A range of influx laws sought to force specifically Black South Africans into wage labour and, often ineffectively, restrict urban residence to those with state-recognized employment. These laws were frequently tied to a concern with 'idleness', especially among unemployed township youth, which underpinned the criminalization of informal entrepreneurship. In 1962 the government's Botha commission characterized those who refused to do arduous manual labour and instead made money informally through notions of crime, idleness and parasitism (Seekings and Nattrass, 2005, 170). This concern with 'idle youth' and 'informal' money-making activities that fell outside the regulation of the state was not unique to apartheid South Africa. As Dolan and Gordon (2019, 304) note, 'the presumed "idleness" of Africans was the subject of searing colonial commentaries that cast informal livelihoods as a threat to economic development and moral rectitude'.

The portrayal of informal entrepreneurship as criminal, deviant and unproductive reflects a long-standing association between development and the universalization of waged or salaried work (Li, 2010; 2017). On this reading, the informal sector was viewed as a temporary holding space on a teleological transition that would result in the gradual disappearance of the 'backward' or 'traditional' informal sector as the economy was transformed by 'modern' and 'productive' capitalist modes of production. The expansion of capitalist wage labour was thus central to mainstream visions of social order and development (Barchiesi, 2011; Weeks, 2011). As Franco Barchiesi points out, wage labour has long been viewed as an 'image of social discipline' and a technique of governance to regulate 'uncivilised' and 'unruly' African populations, with a particular emphasis on youth (Barchiesi, 2012, 243). Despite a growing critique of the idea of wage labour as the 'presumed norm or telos of "development"' (Ferguson and Li, 2018, 1), the dualist logics of these earlier debates continue to linger in South Africa's policy discourses.

The term 'informal sector' was first introduced by Keith Hart's (1973) seminal work in Accra, Ghana that made the case for studying the varied economic activities of the urban poor. Hart used the term to draw attention to a vast array of money-making activities that fell outside the regulation of the state and, importantly, did not feature in government statistics. However, the term was often used by governments and researchers in ways that problematically conflated formal employment with prosperity, and informal entrepreneurship with precariousness and abjection. For example, the 'two economies' thesis promulgated by former South African President Thabo Mbeki in the early 2000s portrayed the poor as trapped in a 'second economy' structurally disconnected from the 'first' or mainstream economy (du Toit and Neves, 2007). According to the presidential letter of 2003, poverty was understood as a function of exclusion from formal systems of production, and thus poverty alleviation could only occur when those in the 'second economy' are incorporated into the modern economy via wage labour.

In more recent years, the phenomenon of 'jobless growth' and unemployment (Hull and James, 2012) has prompted the South African government to reassess its position on the informal economy and value its role in creating work and sustaining livelihoods. The current National Development Plan (NDP), for example, projects the informal economy will generate almost 2 million jobs by 2020. The NDP does not, however, offer any specific plans or proposals to support this expansion (Fourie, 2018). The Gauteng provincial government is at the forefront of a reconceptualization of the informal economy. The Township Economy Revitalisation Strategy seeks to 'revitalise township economies' in the hope of turning the unemployed into entrepreneurs. The strategy uses the term 'township economy' to draw attention to the role of enterprises based in townships and informal settlements such as Zandspruit – spaces that are characterized by high levels of poverty, unemployment and marginalization from centres of economic activity – in helping to create an 'inclusive, labour-absorbing and growing economy'. It thus reflects the rise of a neoliberal development paradigm – promulgated by the World Bank – that has reinterpreted the informal economy as a space in which the jobless are transformed into self-made entrepreneurs (Maloney, 2004; Dolan and Rajak, 2018). Critically, this revalorization of the informal economy is occurring at a time when unemployment rates are at an all-time high, and growing numbers of people – especially young people – enter a labour market with little, if any, prospect of acquiring formal sector jobs.

At the time of my fieldwork in Zandspruit in 2015, there was much talk about the Township Economy Revitalisation Strategy and its commitment to supporting young, Black township entrepreneurs (Govender, 2017). Sibongile, who addressed young people at the government-funded 'career exhibition', was well versed in this initiative and lauded the government's attempts to direct public sector procurement spending to local township businesses. One such initiative, the *Jozi@Work* scheme, awarded 'work packages' to local cooperatives and businesses in the community for various local government functions, including waste removal and garden maintenance. Sibongile saw the programme as offering youth opportunities to, as he put it, "meet the government half way" instead of "waiting for the government to give us jobs." He saw himself as leading the way, having already registered a cooperative and construction business himself. Sibongile estimated he could profit from these smaller work packages, while also eying larger government contracts related to much-promised (yet elusive) infrastructural and housing developments. However, others in Zandspruit were more sceptical and saw the programme as benefiting those who already had government 'connections' rather than new entrants to the economy. One young man I got to know insisted that the project was effectively a way to cut costs by outsourcing various local government functions to community co-ops to avoid the cost of hiring workers directly.

The township strategy is focused on producing successful Black entrepreneurs who graduate from 'necessity' enterprises in the informal economy to 'opportunity' enterprises in the formal economy. However, this opportunity–necessity dichotomy – well established in the literature on entrepreneurship – does not provide us with the conceptual tools to understand why young people might choose to voluntarily exit the formal economy and take up self-employment in the informal economy (Langevang et al, 2012). Doing so requires a different approach that enables us to reconnect the dots between work and life through a broader framework of 'life-work' (Thieme, 2018) or 'forms of living' (Millar, 2018) in order to advance policy and academic debate on entrepreneurship.

In the section that follows, I examine the various factors that attract young people to informal self-employment, challenging the World Bank's individualistic and self-enterprising understanding of entrepreneurship. By tracing the work histories of Hloni and Thatho, two young men who live and work in Zandspruit informal settlement, I pay particular attention to the importance of sociality and redistribution in young men's preference for informal entrepreneurship over precarious and degrading forms of wage employment. This chapter reveals how waged work disrupts the rhythms of socio-economic life in Zandspruit, where having time "to communicate with people" and maintain social relations is critical to operating in the informal economy. In other words, the aspiration and preference of many youth to 'be your own boss' is attractive insofar as it provides young people with the autonomy and flexibility to invest in valued relationships.

Life and labour in Zandspruit

This chapter is based on 12 months of ethnographic research with unemployed and marginally employed young men in Zandspruit informal settlement on the outskirts of Johannesburg's northern suburbs. Zandspruit began as a small squatting community on private agricultural land in 1994 and grew exponentially over the following decade as people flocked to Johannesburg in pursuit of employment and better lives. Only 25 per cent of Zandspruit's residents were born there: over half migrated from South Africa's other eight provinces, and 19 per cent are immigrants from other African countries (StatsSA, 2011). The settlement now has over 30,000 residents who are almost entirely Black African and predominantly young (55 per cent of residents are aged between 15 and 34).

Zandspruit is closely located to shopping malls, office parks and industrial areas; areas that generate formal employment opportunities – however precarious – for people in the community. The 2011 census data revealed that 45 per cent of Zandspruit's residents were engaged in some form of economic activity – a figure that was 4 per cent higher than other informal settlements in Gauteng province and notably higher than South Africa as a whole. While South Africa's employment data is more reliable than that of many other African countries, it should be used with caution. This data suggests that of the economically active in Zandspruit, 62 per cent work in the formal economy, 13 per cent in the informal economy, and 21 per cent in private households (generally as informal domestic workers and home-based workers) (StatsSA, 2011). However, such statistics produce a very stratified picture of the economy, which is unhelpful for two reasons. First, they conceal the connections between the formal and informal economies. Second, they reduce people's economic lives to the dualist categories of active/inactive, waged/unwaged, and formal/informal.

In reality, the majority of people in Zandspruit combine formal wage labour with informal wage labour and self-employment, while also leveraging distributional claims on others both inside and outside of their households. Many of the young men I got to know in Zandspruit were technically unemployed but got by through a diverse range of income-generating activities, many of which blurred the lines between formal and informal, legal and illegal, and were left out of official statistics. The fact that many people straddled and combined different modes of work underlines the importance of viewing Zandspruit as part of what James Ferguson has termed a 'system of distributed livelihoods' (2015, 94) in which the formal and informal economies are viewed as part of a 'differentiated whole' (du Toit and Neves, 2007; Callebert, 2014).

To understand young people's preference for informal self-employment, it was important to grasp the full range of economic options available to them and the factors that shaped their decisions. To attain this bigger picture, I spent the first two months of my fieldwork in 2015 conducting a survey with 100 young people and a mapping exercise of the local economy including semi-structured interviews with 40 local enterprise owners. This was followed by sustained participation in the everyday life worlds of young people, along with life and work history interviews with 37 youth, each of whom I interviewed between two and four times. In this chapter I draw heavily upon informal conversations and in-depth interviews with two of my interlocutors – Hloni (age 34) and Thatho (age 21) – who were both long-standing residents of Zandspruit. Hloni and Thatho both lacked post-secondary qualifications, had worked intermittently in the formal economy and, at the time of my research, had purposely left formal wage employment in favour of self-employment in the informal economy. I focus on them because their economic choices typify the growing trend of young people (especially men) rejecting jobs at the bottom end of the formal labour market in favour of pursuing alternative livelihoods in the informal economy (Mains, 2012; Dawson, 2019; Zizzamia, 2020).

Hloni: the fixer

I first met Hloni in 2011. His tall, slim frame was bent over the engine of a maroon *bakkie* (pick-up-truck) parked outside his yard. I later learned that if a car was outside with the bonnet up, he had work to do and liked to be left alone. However, on the days when he had no cars to fix, Hloni spent most of his time watching old action films inside his shack. I spent many afternoons with Hloni and his friends socializing, drinking and passing what often felt like an abundance of time. He grew up in a rural part of Limpopo province but moved to Zandspruit (where his mother lived) in 2005 at the age of 19. His mother worked as a domestic worker for a White family in a nearby suburb for most of her life and was part of the first group of people to start living in the area. She bought a stand in Transit Camp (the oldest section of the settlement) in the late 1990s – the stand where Hloni now lives with his older sister and her two children. The yard has four shacks: one for his sister, one for him and two they rent out as a source of income.

Prior to 2010, Hloni had worked first as a panel beater and then a mechanic for an auto-repair garage in a nearby industrial area where he earned around R6,000 ($380) a month for working six days a week. This would have been considered a relatively good wage at the time, especially when compared to the average earnings of formally employed people in Zandspruit. However, two years into his job at the auto-garage, Hloni started his own informal mechanic business to supplement his wages. He began fixing the cars of friends and neighbours but soon developed a wider network of customers and patrons. A year later, in late 2010, he quit his waged job and started working as a mechanic from his yard full time. Hloni did not start his informal enterprise as a result of economic necessity, but rather to enable him to escape a job where he felt, in his words, "ripped off". When I probed his decision to walk away from a relatively stable job and start his own business, he voiced his frustration with the inequalities of employment in the post-apartheid workplace: "To work for someone else is going to be difficult. Today you say two or three cars, maybe I do R100, 000 for those three cars but you give me R6,000 a month. It's not what I want. You make someone else rich. How do I get profit?" Hloni described how he would fix three or four cars a week – generating the business R100,000 ($6,400) or more – but never pocketed more than his salary of R6,000 ($380). "How do I profit?" he asked rhetorically, expressing a widely held frustration with formal waged employment that is seen to generate surplus value for the boss at the expense of the worker. This sense of being perpetually cheated and unable to move up the ranks or accumulate more of the value he was generating ultimately led to Hloni quitting his job.

Hloni has worked for himself since 2010. During my fieldwork, I was often puzzled as to how Hloni made enough money to survive. He worked intermittently and often in short bursts, when he had a car to fix or clients with money to pay him. He was busiest in the first two weeks of the month – after payday. Towards the end of the month, when business was quiet, he spent a great deal more time at home alone or with his friends. Some of his customers would leave their cars outside his house for a day and collect them as soon as the problem was fixed. Others would park their cars outside his yard for weeks and sometimes months at a time. This was more common when the problem was more complicated or costly, or when a customer could only afford to pay for part of the repair. Hloni's experience of self-employment thus enabled him to mould his work around his life in ways that were not possible in his previous job, subverting the spatial and temporal boundaries of waged employment. Furthermore, his entrepreneurial activities were more socially 'thick' than his waged job insofar as these involved the negotiation of a range of different relationships and exchanges (Ferguson, 2015). Hloni rarely got paid in one payment for work completed. Instead, his money came in dribs and drabs due to the multi-staged nature of the repairs and the precarious financial situation of many of his clients. Consequently, he became more selective about whose cars he fixed, having learned of the dangers of working in return for unfulfilled 'favours'.

Given the precariousness of his livelihood, it took me time to realize that what he valued most about working for himself was not the money (even though he claimed to make more working for himself than the R6,000 ($380) he earned working for someone else). It was rather his sense of autonomy and control over his time. He emphasized that more than anything, the advantage of working for himself was being able to work without a boss telling him "when I can or cannot take a coffee break". Moreover, unlike in his former job, Hloni found business when he wanted or needed it, and felt that the money he made was a fair reflection of the effort he invested. While self-employment did not provide an escape from precariousness and insecurity, it did offer him what formal employment could not: a self-directed capacity to earn money and greater control over his time. Hloni's story allows us to see that the widely held desire to be one's own boss is not only a reaction to the intolerability of exploitative and degrading work (Bourgois, 2003), but also an expression of entrepreneurial agency and the desire to fashion a life for oneself on one's own terms.

Thatho: the 'connector'

I first met Thatho on the top street in Transit Camp, where he grew up. He stood out with his red suede Carvela shoes (a high-end designer brand) that are associated with the youth sub-culture I'khothane.[1] I was introduced to Thatho through a mutual friend who knew I wanted to talk to someone who made a living as a 'connector' in the informal electricity market. He is short and wiry with a diamond stud in his left ear, and two gold-capped front teeth – a fashion trend resurrected in recent years by the hip hop industry. Thatho's mother, who works at a nearby crèche, was also one of the original settlers in Zandspruit in the mid-1990s. In 2015, at the age of 21, Thatho lived in a backyard shack in his mother's yard. This provided him with a measure of independence and a significant saving on rental costs: something many newer residents did not have.

Thatho became involved in fixing illegal connections in his second year of high school. At first, he concentrated on the less dangerous work of repairing people's wires inside their shacks. Over time he learned how to tap electricity from the neighbouring plots and municipal poles and connect new shacks to the grid: a dangerous and sometimes deathly task. In Thatho's last few years of high school, he charged a one-off fee of R150 ($9) to connect each new shack. The money he earned was small and intermittent but enough to go out, drink and keep up with the latest fashion trends, which was more than what his teenage friends had. But it was not enough to support his mother and siblings and fulfil the role of provider – a role closely linked to ideas of masculinity and social membership in the region (Hunter, 2010; Ferguson, 2015).

Thatho finished high school in December 2013 and had no aspirations to further his education. However, in 2014 he agreed at his mother's urging to attend a job readiness programme run by a local NGO. Job readiness training programmes have proliferated in recent years, often run by local NGOs and churches. These programmes focus on teaching youth the kinds of skills and decorum required by service sector jobs and matching their top students with employers searching for 'reliable' employees – a category that can be traced back to colonial ideas of the disciplined waged subject (Barchiesi, 2011). A few weeks after the training, an old friend found Thatho a job selling sports equipment at a nearby shopping centre. He took it grudgingly. It required him to work long hours including weekends (a prerequisite in retail) and paid him "peanuts". When I asked him about the job, he told me that he hated being bossed around and made to feel "useless":

> 'That guy [boss] is yelling at me for five days. On the sixth day I realized no it's too much. I can't do this. I'm trying my best. I'm sweating and still this guy [boss] can't see what I'm doing. No, if you can't see what I'm doing and you saying I'm useless. I'm just adding a number in the company. It's better if I left the company cause it's painful when you work hard and someone says you not doing anything.'

After six months Thatho quit and "sat at home" for a prolonged period. His short stint in the job confirmed his suspicion that formal wage work not only failed to provide a decent and dependable livelihood, but also involved being subjected to bosses who saw it as their job to discipline and demean their employees. Other residents in Zandspruit pointed to the racialized nature of employer–employee relations in

South Africa's low-end wage economy, concluding that White bosses "use Black people to make them rich without caring about their well-being" and that "they want to keep Blacks at the bottom of the ladder and Whites at the top." Within this context, it is not surprising that entrepreneurial narratives that link self-employment with Black ownership and independence draw wide appeal.

Thatho's experience in the retail job was instrumental in his decision to turn his back on low-end jobs in South Africa's formal economy and instead focus on establishing a livelihood as a 'connector' in the informal electricity market. In the months that followed, Thatho and his friend Sandile, who had also been connecting electricity since he was a teenager, decided to work together and, in Thatho's words, "make a living out of this". He explained, "The other thing that made me leave [the job] is that when I look at the salary and the *izinyoka* [illegal connections] money. In the *izinyoka* I get triple the Sportsman's warehouse money so it's not worth it." Like Hloni then, Thatho sought out more profitable opportunities in the informal economy. He transformed his business from simply connecting shacks to the grid for a small one-off fee to providing a subscription service to customers who pay a monthly fee:

> 'It changed I think around when I was doing matric. Before we used to connect electricity and someone [would] pay us R150 as a joining fee and then use electricity for free. And then when the wires are burnt we [would] go and collect R20 from each house to buy new wires and then connect. That was the case until we realized that we could make a living out of this. [Then] people started paying a monthly premium of R100. It started at R100 and then we increased our price to R150. Our joining fee is R200 and then every month R150 because there are people who we connect electricity for who live a little bit far so we have to buy a lot of wire to get electricity that side.'

One of the things that struck me most in my conversations with Thatho was his use of the global language of entrepreneurship. On more than one occasion he referred to Sandile and himself as 'entrepreneurs' and 'business partners'. Furthermore, he referred to the households whose electricity wires he repairs and maintains as 'customers', who pay 'joining fees' and 'monthly premiums'. It took me some time to understand the significance of Thatho's use of commercial language. The language of entrepreneurship enabled him to cultivate an image of himself as an enterprising individual in pursuit of opportunities rather than a social bandit engaged in illegal activity, generating a sense of self-worth and respectability. As Tatiana Thieme writes of the hustle economy, Thatho's testimony 'combined the urgency of everyday economic survival with aspirational urban identities' – such as that of the successful entrepreneur – in order to make the everyday struggle 'meaningful and culturally significant' (2018, 541). Low-end wage employment was seen to provide no such opportunities.

The commodification of the electricity network 'from below' should be understood in relation to the massive expansion of the illegal electricity market after 2010, largely the result of the government's failure to bring formal electricity to the area. Today, illegal connections criss-cross the entire settlement, with at least 60 per cent of households illegally connected. Informal electricity wires are maintained and controlled according to street- and neighbourhood-level youth groups that are reminiscent of the territory-based youth street gangs in Soweto in the 1970s (Glaser, 2000). In the area where Thatho and Sandile operate, for example, there are seven groupings of young men who control the network that diverts power from the transformer on Marina Drive next to a shopping centre. The social and economic organization of the informal electricity network also resembles the garbage collection groups in Nairobi's slums, which territorially mark different sub-neighbourhoods in 'gang-like formations' (Thieme, 2018, 11).

Residents have mixed views about the informal electricity market and the role played by 'connectors' such as Thatho. Most of the residents I spoke with recognized that the connectors provide power at significant risk to their own lives, while also complaining about the significant fees they charge, the anticipation of blackouts and breakdowns, and the abuse they receive should they not pay. Some residents chastized local connectors for further impeding the government's plans to incorporate the area into the formal electricity grid. Others actively opposed illegal connections because of the association of 'connectors' with corruption and theft. The illegal electricity network is often referred to as *izinyoka* (isiXhosa/isiZulu for 'snake'). Following a series of adverts run by the electricity supplier Eskom in the early 2000s, 'connectors' were labelled *izinyoka* in an attempt to brand them as criminals.

Thatho did not see his work as criminal, but rather as a form of social entrepreneurship that allowed him to profit while at the same time "helping" the community. He often emphasized the benefits his work brings to the community: improved safety, a reduction in shack fires, and cost savings if compared to the cost of prepaid electricity should the government deliver on its promise to electrify the settlement. I asked

Thatho if he has any difficulty getting residents to pay. To my surprise, he told me 95 per cent of residents pay him on time, with only 5 per cent "causing trouble". It was unclear how successful Thatho was at collecting fees from this group or how exactly he went about this. What was clear is that Thatho's ability to profit from wiring illegal connections was intimately tied to his ability to discern, and negotiate, multiple modes of local authority including gangs and street patrollers that have a long history of subverting the state, laws and the police in Johannesburg, often via violence or the threat of violence. Within this context, Thatho deploys entrepreneurial discourses to bring a degree of respectability to his work as a 'connector' and to legitimate his interactions with residents who often have little choice but to pay the monthly premiums.

In early 2016, Thatho and Sandile had 90 customers in the sub-section of Zanspruit they control. While this is only a small fraction of the overall market, they were each making around R9,000 ($580) per month: roughly three times what Thatho made in retail working six days a week. Yet unlike Hloni, who had come to appreciate his life as an informal mechanic in Zandspruit, Thatho did not see a long-term future for himself as a 'connector'. He dreamed of leaving Zandspruit and living a life in the more affluent suburbs that surround him but understood that for as long as he worked as a 'connector' he was unlikely to leave.

Time, obligation and flexible reciprocity

Self-employment in the informal economy offered young men in Johannesburg something that precarious waged employment cannot: a self-directed capacity to generate money while retaining control over their time. For Hloni and Thatho, a large part of the appeal of working for themselves lay in the ability to adjust their work schedules in ways that allowed them to invest in valued relationships – something that the rigidity of low-end wage employment denied them. Both of their previous jobs required them to leave the settlement early in the morning and come back after dark, thus leaving them with little time to pursue alternative socio-economic activities or spend time with friends and family.

Self-employment in the informal economy enabled Hloni and Thatho to blur the spatial and temporal distinctions between work and non-work. Hloni's intermittent work schedule allowed him to spend a great deal more of his time watching films and socializing with friends and occasional customers. Meanwhile, Thatho was able to spend the bulk of his time hanging out with a group of young men who provided a degree of protection for his business. Street corners in Zandspruit provide a space for groups of young men to gather to pass time, drink, listen to popular music, gamble and strategize ways to make money. Corners thus provide young men like Thatho with sustained forms of sociality, or what Masquelier (2013) describes as 'surrogate kin'. Similarly, the men who gathered around Hloni's shack to watch films and engage in lively debates about frustrations, politics and dreams also engaged in various forms of mutual sharing. Buying and sharing alcohol provided an important way for men to cement friendships but also practise reciprocity, much like the young men Daniel Mains (2013) describes in Jimma, Ethiopia. These networks of support equipped young men with an informal kind of "insurance" against social isolation and impoverishment, as one of my interlocutors put it, as well as networks that provide alternative opportunities for pocketing cash.

We cannot fully understand the time that Hloni and Thatho spent in the yard and on the street corner as dead time or 'leisure time' – concepts derived from the separation of work and life associated with wage employment. Instead, they understood this time to be fundamental to building and maintaining a wide array of relationships, diversifying income streams and mitigating risk. For example, Thatho's work as a 'connector' required him to continuously maintain relations with local power brokers, street committees, gangs and connectors, as well as residents and police. The maintenance of these relationships required considerable time and effort, as well as the type of tacit knowledge that is acquired from being embedded in such relationships – and the ability to respond to spur-of-the-moment opportunities and threats – over an extended period of time.

In December 2015, Thatho returned briefly to a job at the sports shop in order to make extra money. It was a six-week post over the busy Christmas period. He quit three weeks into the contract, or, more accurately, he simply did not turn up for work. The reasons he provided were similar to before: he hated the long hours and being bossed around. When pushed, he explained that working six days a week morning till night left him with little time to "communicate with people" and thus maintain key relationships for his business as a connector. For example, in March 2016, Eskom, the South African electricity public utility, in conjunction with the South African police, destroyed some of the informal electricity infrastructure that Thatho had constructed. This was part of a government clamp-down on electricity theft. Thatho and other connectors were notified immediately and began repairing the network within minutes of the police leaving. Had Thatho not been there to repair the infrastructure and defend his sub-section of the network at this key juncture he would have risked losing his livelihood. The importance of shrewd improvisation and an ability to seize the moment is also reflected in the work of Marco Di Nunzio (2012) in Ethiopia, Jeremy Jones (2010) in Zimbabwe, and Tatiana Thieme (2018) in Kenya, where hustling for a living often depends on being 'in the right place at the right time' (Jones, 2010, 292). However, as Thatho's case shows, such acts of movement and improvization are often incompatible with the rigid spatial and temporal regimes imposed by low-end wage employment.

In a sense, being in full-time wage work came with the risk of forsaking, or being cut off from, a complex range of relationships that underpin livelihoods in the 'hustle economy' (Thieme, 2018). This was not only the case for those who operate in the informal economy, but also for persons who sought out relations of patronage with the state or NGO actors. For example, Sibongile, who ran the local NGO mentioned earlier, decided to quit his call centre job to provide himself with sufficient time to work in the community to build a constituency before standing in the local elections. I was struck by the extraordinary amount of time and energy he spent tending to relationships and investing in the NGO and other institutions. Had he kept his waged job, he would not have had the time or flexibility required to attend meetings, events and briefings, many of which occurred during the week.

Kathleen Millar (2014; 2018) emphasizes the relative flexibility and autonomy provided by wageless work in her research with *catadores* (waste pickers) in Rio de Janeiro, Brazil. She argues that the *catadores'* ability to come and go from the dump and adjust the intensity and frequency of their work makes it difficult for them to return to the structure and rigidity of the wage economy. Millar develops the concept of 'relational autonomy' to draw attention to the ways in which working on the dump involves an adjustment to a different 'temporality of work'. As in Zandspruit, informal work provided the *catadores* with greater control over their time to maintain relationships, fulfil social obligations and build life projects in a context of pervasive insecurity.

However, there is an important difference between Thatho and Hloni and the *catadores* Millar describes in Rio de Janeiro. The *catadores* are primarily women who desire the autonomy to combine work with taking care of children, running a home, fulfilling social obligations and managing a multitude of 'everyday emergencies'. In contrast, young men such as Thatho and Hloni are largely absolved of such domestic responsibilities. While young men might still depend on their mothers, girlfriends and sisters for assistance with cooking and cleaning, they often live alone and have few dependants of their own. Their social networks were predominantly comprised of men who were able to provide connection and assistance premised on an understanding of flexible reciprocity whereby those who have temporary access to resources are expected to help out those who do not (Mains, 2013; Dawson, 2014).

Informal work also enabled young men to escape some of the obligations associated with wage employment. For example, when I asked Thatho how much he gave to his mother, siblings and girlfriend, he responded, "It's up to me, but if you have a job there is more responsibilities. They will say 'Ah, he is working he must do this and this and this ....'"

Mandla, another of my interlocutors, put it like this: "Having a job, especially for men, carries a big weight, a big burden ... but when you're hustling there is no fixed time [when people know] I have X amount of money in my bank account." "But," he continued, "if you have a job, even the extended family, they will know that at the end of the month Mandla is going to get paid. ... But when you're hustling there isn't really a plan to say 'Hey, listen – we know you've got money'." Seen this way, the temporal stability of the wage was often seen as a burden rather than an advantage for the young men I spent time with. At the same time, the erratic and unpredictable nature of informal earnings allowed them to hold on to more of their limited resources and, in some cases, have more say over what they did with their money.

Thus, part of the appeal of being one's own boss relates to the possibility it provides to evade the burden of social obligations to siblings, parents, girlfriends and children. While the wage has often been conceptualized as a mode of government surveillance (Mbembe, 2001; Barchiesi, 2011), it has rarely been thought of as a form of social surveillance; as something that renders young men accountable to their families. Self-employment thus made it easier for young men to defer or escape the social demands associated with the wage while providing them with valued forms of male sociality and mutual dependence. Men's longing for flexibility and autonomy also animated their preference for forms of self-employment. The sense of agency and control acquired though informal livelihoods stems from an ability to escape the rigid separation of 'work' and 'home' that is forged through formal waged employment. Both Thatho and Hloni worked sporadically and spent a great deal of time combining social and economic activities in ways that were not possible in their formal jobs. Such flexibility provided them with greater autonomy over their day-to-day lives and obligations. Furthermore, the ambiguity of this work enabled them to narrate it in ways that rendered the everyday struggle 'meaningful and culturally significant' (Thieme, 2018, 541) through appeals to 'be[ing] your own boss'.

'Be your own boss': on the appeal of wageless life

Unlike Keith Hart's (1973) descriptions of the large swaths of the urban population in Accra in the 1970s, Hloni and Thatho both had access to wage labour. Indeed, their experiences of degrading and exploitative low-end jobs are critical to understanding their turn to self-employment in the informal economy. These experiences put an end to the idea that wage employment offers an escape from poverty and a pathway to social mobility through integration into the 'modern' economy. In fact, like many of the young people I got to know, Hloni and Thatho understood employment at the bottom end of the formal labour market as a mechanism of subordination and exclusion rather than mobility and development – an understanding reinforced by the rise in casualized and flexible work arrangements in Zandspruit (Kenny and Webster, 1998; Paola and Pons-Vignon, 2013) and a reality of pervasive insecurity and exploitation. Within this context, most young people's experiences of wage employment were limited to short-term contract work in fast food restaurants, as private security guards, cleaners, retail workers and call centre agents. Many were contracted through labour brokers that typically offer little or no job security or benefits (Patel et al, 2016; Dawson, 2019; Zizzamia, 2020) and it was unusual to stay in a job for longer than a year. In most instances, this was because of the short-term nature of the contract. Yet, in a surprising number of instances this was due to youth voluntarily quitting jobs. The most common reasons for quitting included the following: pay that is too little to cover basic expenses; negative experiences in the workplace including racial abuse and exploitation; and limited prospects for meaningful social mobility (Dawson, 2019; Zizzamia, 2020).

While many young people in Zandspruit may sympathize with Hloni and Thatho's experiences, few have an alternative source of income that would allow them to consider quitting. Thatho and Hloni's ability to walk away from their jobs was thus contingent on their relative privilege, in terms of having rent-free accommodation, few dependants and the connections required to cultivate alternative sources of income. Their decision to leave waged work in favour of informal livelihoods was motivated by the importance of social relationships and redistribution, on the one hand, and a desire for greater autonomy and social advancement, on the other. Their pursuit of informal self-employment therefore reveals how informal livelihoods are not necessarily a 'last resort' or a substitute for a 'proper job' (Millar, 2014, 33) but might, in some instances, be preferable to waged employment in the formal economy. However, in contrast to the individualizing discourses of the World Bank, Hloni and Thatho's vision of entrepreneurship – or 'be[ing] your own boss' – did not rest upon ideas of self-reliance and individual responsibility. Instead, entrepreneurship was understood to provide them with the flexibility and autonomy necessary to build and extend valued forms of social connection – qualities that were understood to be missing from low-end wage employment.

Conclusion

A woman from the government's National Youth Development Agency (NYDA) stood up to speak at the career exhibition soon after I arrived. "Do you want to see yourself somewhere someday – to move from here to Sandton or Honeydew [upmarket suburbs]?" she asked rhetorically, before admonishing the youth for not making use of government initiatives to help them start their own businesses. Her comments show how the state frames entrepreneurship as an inclusive pathway to social mobility. However, there are good reasons to be critical of this discourse of entrepreneurialism. The notion that jobless youth can and should become self-made entrepreneurs diverts attention from the structures underpinning chronic unemployment and poverty and places responsibility on young people to create their own jobs and improve their own lives. Yet, I have shown that young men's desire to be their own boss does not necessarily imply the internalization of a neoliberal logic of self-reliance. Conversely, self-employment provided these men with the time and space to maintain and extend vital social connections; time and space that was denied to them by low-end wage employment.

At the same time, there is a risk of overemphasizing and romanticizing the aspirational dimension of young men's entrepreneurial activities. Doing so risks downplaying the precarity that pervades most economic activity in South Africa's informal economy. It also overlooks the ways in which the livelihoods of people like Hloni and Thatho have a high chance of running counter to their long-term ambitions. Working in and running enterprises in the informal sector is precarious and earnings are very low for all but a few (Fourie, 2018). So how do we, as researchers, pay attention to both the agency and aspirations of informal entrepreneurs and the degrading structural conditions that underpin them? Here, Tatiana Thieme (2018, 3) reminds us that young men's informal livelihoods can be 'survivalist but aspirational at the same time'. While Hloni's business allowed him to generate money on his own terms and exert greater control over his time, it did not provide him with much economic stability. Similarly, Thatho's work as a 'connector' provided him with a relatively stable source of income while also putting his life in serious danger. His work as a 'connector' limited his chances of one day leaving Zandspruit for a more comfortable life in the suburbs.

Many of the young men I got to know expressed a desire to leave Zandspruit and move into a suburb with a nice house and car – a change that has long represented movement into the middle class, as invoked by the speech of the government official. These men did not want to "just survive" but instead "be successful" or, as Thatho put it, have a "nice thing and a nice living". When I asked Thatho about his future ambitions, he responded, "I just want to get out of Zandspruit. I want to buy myself a house maybe at Randpark [a suburb in the North of Johannesburg]. I just want to be successful, that's all." His definition of success was thus imagined in terms of consumption and a movement out of Zandspruit. However, rather than expanding his work as a connector, he understood this move to be contingent on getting a government job or starting a formally registered business to benefit from government contracts. Consequently, while Thatho welcomed (and even celebrated) Sandile and his escape from the very bottom of the waged labour market, they were nonetheless anxious about being permanently locked out of the formal economy and excluded from the nostalgically invoked realm of the 'proper job' (Barchiesi, 2011; Ferguson and Li, 2018). The autonomy Thatho and Hloni prized from having found some success in the informal economy must then be seen in relation to the enduring power of the idea of wage employment as a vehicle to class mobility.

By documenting the work histories of Thatho and Hloni, I have attempted to draw attention to the social, relational and reciprocal dimensions of self-employment that are often overlooked in the literature on entrepreneurship. I have argued that low-end waged work disrupts the rhythms of socio-economic life in Zandspruit where having time "to communicate with people" and maintain and extend relations is critical to socio-economic advancement. Contrastingly, informal self-employment enabled my interlocutors to blur the lines between work and life in ways that enabled them to pursue multiple economic opportunities and cultivate desirable forms of inter-dependency. 'Being your own boss' thus opened up spaces for experimental forms of identity, agency and association that were unavailable in a racialized and degrading formal employment market.

Acknowledgements

I wish to thank William Monteith, Liz Fouksman and an anonymous reviewer for comments, criticisms and suggestions. Special acknowledgements go to the Commonwealth Scholarship Commission and the National Research Foundation of South Africa (grant number: 116768) which funded the research and writing of the broader project, from which this chapter is drawn. Finally, a special thanks go to my interlocutors who allowed me into their lives and tolerated my endless questions.

Note

[1] *I'khothane* is primarily known for its performances of 'destructive consumption' that involve poor, predominantly male, township youth burning designer clothes and shoes worth thousands of rands (Jones, 2013). These modes of consumption are seen to raise the status of those engaged in them while also critiquing the culture of consumption that surrounds them.

References

Barchiesi, F. (2011) *Precarious Liberation Workers, the State, and Contested Social Citizenship in Postapartheid South Africa*, New York, NY: State University of New York Press.

Barchiesi, F. (2012) 'Liberation of, through, or from work? Postcolonial Africa and the problem with "job creation" in the global crisis', *Interface: A Journal For and About Social Movements*, 4(2): 230–253.

Bourgois, P.I. (2003) *In Search of Respect: Selling Crack in El Barrio*, Cambridge: Cambridge University Press.

Callebert, R. (2014) 'Transcending dual economies: Reflections on "popular economies in South Africa"', *Africa*, 84(1): 119–134.

Dawson, H.J. (2014) 'Youth politics: Waiting and envy in a South African informal settlement', *Journal of Southern African Studies*, 40(4): 861–882.

Dawson, H.J. (2019) 'The productivity of unemployment: Emerging forms of work and life in urban South Africa', unpublished PhD thesis, Oxford University.

Di Nunzio, M. (2012) '"We are good at surviving": Street hustling in Addis Ababa's inner city', *Urban Forum*, 23(4): 433–447.

Dithupe, I. (2016) *Be The Boss of Your Future*, South Africa: Self-published.

Dolan, C. and Gordon, C. (2019) 'Worker, businessman, entrepreneur?: Kenya's shifting labouring subject', *Critical African Studies*, 11(3): 301–321.

Dolan, C. and Rajak, D. (2016) 'Remaking Africa's informal economies: Youth, entrepreneurship and the promise of inclusion at the bottom of the pyramid', *The Journal of Development Studies*, 52(4): 514–529.

Dolan, C. and Rajak, D. (2018) 'Speculative futures at the bottom of the pyramid', *Journal of the Royal Anthropological Institute*, 24(2): 233–255.

du Toit, A. and Neves, D. (2007) 'In search of South Africa's "second economy"', *Africanus: Journal of Development Studies*, 37(2): 145–174.

Ferguson, J. (2015) *Give a Man a Fish: Reflections on the New Politics of Distribution*, Durham, NC: Duke University Press.

Ferguson, J. and Murray Li, T. (2018) 'Beyond the "proper job: Political-economic analysis after the century of labouring man', Working Paper 51. Bellville: Institute for Poverty, Land And Agrarian Studies, University of the Western Cape.

Fourie, F.C.v.N. (2018) 'Creating Jobs, Reducing Poverty I: Why the Informal Sector Should Be Taken Seriously and Enabled Properly', Econ3x3, available at http://www.econ3x3.org/sites/default/files/articles/Informal%20sector%20series%201.pdf

Glaser, C. (2000) *Bo-Tsotsi: The Youth Gangs of Soweto, 1935–1976*, Oxford: James Currey.

Govender, M. (2017) 'Township Economy Plan Needs to Tackle Skills Deficit', *Business Day Live*, 2 March, https://www.businesslive.co.za/bd/opinion/2017-03-02-township-economy-plan-needs-to-tackle-skills-deficit/

Hart, K. (1973) 'Informal income opportunities and urban employment in Ghana', *Journal of Modern African Studies*, 11(1): 61–89.

Hull, E. and James, D. (2012) 'Introduction: Popular Economies in South Africa', *Africa*, 82(1): 1–19.

Hunter, M. (2010) *Love in the Time of AIDS: Inequality, Gender, and Rights in South Africa*, Bloomington, IN: Indiana University Press.

Jones, J.L. (2010) ' "Nothing is straight in Zimbabwe": The rise of the Kukiya-Kiya economy 2000–2008', *Journal of Southern African Studies*, 36(2): 285–299.

Jones, M. (2013) 'Conspicuous destruction, aspiration and motion in the South African township', *Safundi*, 14(2): 209–224.

Kenny, B. and Webster, E. (1998) 'Eroding the core: Flexibility and the resegmentation of the South African labour market', *Critical Sociology*, 24(3): 216–243.

Langevang, T., Namatovu, R. and Dawa, S. (2012) 'Beyond necessity and opportunity entrepreneurship: Motivations and aspirations of young entrepreneurs in Uganda', *International Development Planning Review*, 34(4): 439–459.

Li, T.M. (2010) 'To make live or let die? Rural dispossession and the protection of surplus populations', *Antipode*, 41(1): 66–93.

Li, T.M. (2017) 'After development: Surplus population and the politics of entitlement', *Development and Change*, 48(6): 1247–1261.

Mains, D. (2012) *Hope Is Cut: Youth, Unemployment, and the Future in Urban Ethiopia*, Global Youth, Philadelphia, PA: Temple University Press.

Mains, D. (2013) 'Friends and money: Balancing affection and reciprocity among young men in urban Ethiopia', *American Ethnologist*, 40(2): 335–346.

Maloney, W.F. (2004) 'Informality revisited', *World Development*, 32(7): 1159–1178.

Masquelier, A. (2013) 'Teatime: Boredom and the temporalities of young men in Niger', *Africa*, 83(3): 470–491.

Mbembe, A. (2001) *On the Postcolony*, Berkeley, CA: University of California Press.

Millar, K.M. (2014) 'The precarious present: Wageless labor and disrupted life in Rio de Janeiro, Brazil', *Cultural Anthropology*, 29(1): 32–53.

Millar, K.M. (2018) *Reclaiming the Discarded: Life and Labor on Rio's Garbage Dump*, Durham, NC: Duke University Press.

Paola, M.D. and Pons-Vignon, N. (2013) 'Labour market restructuring in South Africa: Low wages, high insecurity', *Review of African Political Economy*, 40(138): 628–638.

Patel, L., Khan, Z., Graham, L., Baldry, K. and Mqehe, T. (2016) 'Qualitative analysis of how a national minimum wage might affect young people's labour market outcomes', Investigating the Feasibility of a National Minimum Wage for South Africa (Part 2 of Larger Report). Johannesburg: Centre for Social Development in Africa, University of Johannesburg.

Rakodi, C. (1995) 'The household strategies of the urban poor: Coping with poverty and recession in Gweru, Zimbabwe', *Habitat International*, 19(4): 447–471.

Roy, A. (2010) *Poverty Capital: Microfinance and the Making of Development*, New York, NY and London: Routledge.

Seekings, J. and Nattrass, N. (2005) *Class, Race, and Inequality in South Africa*, New Haven, CT: Yale University Press.

StatsSA (2011) 'Census 2011', Pretoria, South Africa: Statistics South Africa.

Thieme, T.A. (2013) 'The "hustle" among youth entrepreneurs in Mathare's informal waste economy', *Journal of Eastern African Studies*, 7(3): 389–412.

Thieme, T.A. (2018) 'The hustle economy', *Progress in Human Geography*, 42(4): 529–548.

Weeks, K. (2011) *The Problem with Work: Feminist, Marxist, Antiwork Politics, and Postmark Imaginaries*, Durham, NC: Duke University Press.

Zizzamia, R. (2020) 'Is employment a panacea for poverty? A mixed-methods investigation of employment decisions in South Africa', *World Development*, 130 (104938): 1–15.

6

Work Outside the Hamster's Cage: Precarity and the Pursuit of a Life Worth Living in Catalonia

Vinzenz Bäumer Escobar

An increasing number of initiatives, organizations and networks are challenging the hegemony of capitalism in Catalonia. Going beyond the familiar slogan 'another world is possible' (Ponniah and Fisher, 2003), the people involved in these projects are trying to show that 'another world is already in existence' (*un altre món ya existeix*). Within the context of this edited volume, I would like to draw attention to the fact that many contemporary alternative economic projects revolve around generating the conditions necessary for people to pursue a worthy existence, often alongside or even entirely outside of wage employment (Gibson-Graham, 1996; Jonas, 2010; Zademach and Hillebrand, 2013). I seek to understand why many of my interlocutors explicitly rejected, as they called it, 'el món assalariat' ('the world of wages') and sought instead a 'life worth living' (Nartozky and Besnier, 2014, S5).

In this chapter I draw on 14 months of fieldwork in 2016–2017 with an eco-network (*ecoxarxa*) and an affiliated cooperative-cum-social movement based in Barcelona in order to examine various articulations of 'alternative' work that fell outside of the wage labour relation. In particular, I will show that the members of the Cooperative and eco-network[1] actively sought to minimize their dependence on waged labour out of a desire to pursue a life lived outside of a routinized, 'capitalist' work rhythm. I will argue that the literature on precarious work is ill-equipped to analyse cases such as this, where people eschew waged labour and the supposed existential stability this kind of work is thought to bring. Instead, I will draw on recent ethnographic studies from Latin America which examine how people fashion a meaningful existence through different kinds of work that are often characterized as precarious or informal (Gandolfo, 2010; Millar, 2018; O'Hare, 2020).[2] In this way, this chapter contributes to the 'decentering' (Ferguson and Li, 2018) of waged labour by examining experiences of work in Catalonia in relation to perspectives from wage-scarce economies in other regions of the world.

In particular, I will show that the literature on precarious work tends to direct our analytic gaze solely towards the material insecurity of 'wageless lives' (Denning, 2010). I argue that this leaves us with limited conceptual tools for discussing forms of life and relations which do not derive from material insecurity but develop in defiance of it. Bernat, a member of the eco-network, invoked this idea of defiance by comparing life within "the System" to that of "a hamster trapped in a cage". While there was certainly a recognition that life outside of the hamster's cage may be precarious, a degree of material and emotional discomfort was understood to be necessary in order to be able to take ownership over one's existence (*autogestió*),[3] engage in meaningful forms of work, and form non-capitalist modes of living together. Or, as Bernat put it: "I'm precarious [*precario*], but I don't have a boss." In this chapter I therefore show how members of the Cooperative and eco-network created alternative lives outside the wage that were simultaneously precarious, tiring and rewarding.

This chapter is structured as follows. I begin with a description of the context within which the Cooperative and eco-network operate, focusing on the histories of grassroots political mobilization and the more recent decline of wage employment. I then seek to situate this discussion within broader debates on precarious work and life. The remainder of this chapter explores the ways in which the members of the Cooperative and eco-network attempted to minimize their dependence on wage labour in order to pursue alternative value-generating activities. I show how an alternative life was experienced as both empowering and fulfilling, as well draining and precarious.[4] Moreover, I show that my interlocutors' vision of an alternative economic system was still centred on work, and that the idea and practice of 'alternative work' was utilized as a mechanism of inclusion and exclusion. In the conclusion I argue that the literature on precarious work needs to be broadened through an engagement with the plurality of life projects that develop in spite of material insecurity, and suggest that we need to go beyond the severing of work from the wage in order to unsettle the ties between work and *community*.

Economic alterity and work outside the wage in Catalonia: a short history

Catalonia is one of 12 autonomous communities (*communidades autónomas*) that were created during the establishment of the Spanish constitution in 1978 after the death of Francisco Franco, when Spain transitioned from a dictatorship to a democratic state. Catalonia has a long history of left-wing politics, popular labour movements, and anti-capitalist collective action (Dolgoff, 1974). Perhaps the most famous event in this history is what is known as the Social Revolution. In July 1936 the Spanish right started a military insurrection under Franco against the Second Republic in what was to be the start of the Spanish Civil War. In Barcelona, Franco's forces were successfully held off through the combined effort of republicans, socialists, communists and militant anarcho-syndicalists (Seidman, 2002, 416). After the initial defeat of Franco's forces, a large portion of Catalan industry was collectivized and everyday economic and social life came under the control of workers and labour unions rather than the capitalist class (Souchy et al, 1974; Mintz, 2006). After the end of the civil war in 1939 and the subsequent instalment of the Francoist dictatorship, the Second Republic was disbanded, the powerful anarchist and communist labour movements from the civil war era were crippled, and Catalan was prohibited as a spoken language (Narotzky, 2019, 39). This act of repression, it should be said, was felt most acutely by those on the left (Narotzky, 2019, 39). According to Jeffrey Juris, this eventually resulted in the fusion of Catalan nationalism and Catholic and Marxist traditions and would ultimately result in a 'counterhegemonic frame around anti-Francoism and democracy, reinforced by an oppositional culture based on Catalan language, symbols and identity' (2008, 66). Moreover, it was in these spaces that ideas and practices from the civil war era, such as self-management (*autogestió*), collective decision making in assembly, autonomy (*autonomia*) and decentralized organization were preserved. New social movements that sprang up in the 1980s in Catalonia, such as the squatter movement, and the Conscious Objector Movement (MOC), as well as the more recent social movements that grew to prominence in the early 2000s drew heavily from this cultural archive (Juris, 2008, 64–68). Both the Cooperative and eco-networks can be placed within this tradition of grassroots political organizing insofar as they are based on the same principles of horizontality, self-governance and collective decision making.

However, rather than displacing the idea of the unionized, male, wage worker, the Social Revolution contributed to its reification through an emphasis on organized labour. In contrast, contemporary movements have placed the subversion of wage labour at the centre of their political projects. Indeed, work outside of the wage is proliferating in Catalonia for a number of reasons, including the erosion of the standard employment relationship (see the Introduction to this volume) and the fallout of the 2008 financial crisis. While the history described earlier shows that we need to be wary of overly causal and functionalist arguments in which political and economic crises somehow organically lead to the appearance of alternatives (Castells et al, 2012; Narotzky, 2013; Spyridakis, 2016; Knight and Stewart, 2016), it is true that the 2008 financial crisis has had far-reaching consequences for many people from different classes across Spain (Narotzky, 2012; Molina and Godino, 2013). The austerity measures adopted in 2009 in the wake of the crisis, for instance, have made healthcare more expensive (Navarro, 2012), housing less accessible (Palomera, 2014) and work less stable (Riesco-Sanz, 2012).

Over the past three decades, self-employment rates in Spain have declined from 30 per cent to 17 per cent of the working population (just above the EU average of 15 per cent) (Riesco-Sanz, 2016, 4). At 16 per cent, the self-employment rate in Catalonia is only slightly lower than the national figure, though Catalonia does hold the most self-employed people in terms of absolute numbers (Idescat, 2019). Notwithstanding this decline in self-employment, it should be noted that in 2007 the central Spanish government passed the *Ley para el Fomento del Trabajo Autónomo y la Economía Social* ('Law for the Promotion of Autonomous Work and Social Economy'). This entailed a series of labour reforms that encouraged self-employment, including a reduced fee for people registering as self-employed for the first time (Riesco-Sanz, 2016). This development can be seen as part of the broader decline of lifelong employment and the 'flexibilization' of labour in the global North, forcing an increasing amount of people to take up jobs that fall outside of the standard employment contract (Beck, 2000; Davis, 2006; Standing, 2011). In the Spanish context, the decline of wage employment has been understood as the result of the neoliberal reforms of the past 40 years, including the retreat of the welfare state and attack on organized labour (Fraser, 2003; Barbiere and Scherer, 2009; Hewison and Kalleberg, 2013). Passed in

2012, the *Real Decreto de Ley* labour reform incentivized the creation of temporary and flexible positions, and has resulted in workers, in general, enjoying a lesser degree of protection than before (López and Rodríguez, 2010, 2011; Martínez-Pastor and Bernardi, 2011; Petmesidou and Guillén, 2017).

However, these reforms were not passively received by the Spanish population. In 2011 anti-austerity protesters gathered in Madrid to voice their objections to the austerity policies that were implemented by the government in 2009. The demands expressed during the protests, also known as the *indignadas* or 15-M movement, symbolized a growing social discontent with both political Spanish elites and the global financial system (Castells, 2011; Fominaya, 2017). Anywhere between 5 and 8 million citizens took to the streets over the course of several weeks to call for changes in the political and economic system (FnF Europe, 2013). In Catalonia, meanwhile, the struggle for independence has highlighted the political crisis of Spain, with both the Catalan left and right questioning the sovereignty of the central Spanish government and expressing a desire for self-determination (Rübner Hansen, 2017). A growing sense of disenchantment with 'business as usual' has made people more receptive to the idea of constructing alternatives to formal political and economic institutions (Conill et al, 2012; Hughes, 2015; Narotzky, 2012).

What is at stake here is therefore not just a concern for material security and the loss of financial stability in the wake of the financial crisis, but also the pursuit of what Narotzky and Besnier call a 'life worth living' (2014, S5). They argue that people strive for a 'life worth living' in times of crisis by mobilizing 'increasingly elusive resources' through strategies that involve 'not only waged labour but also structures of provisioning, investments in social relations, relations of trust and care, and a multitude of other forms of social action that mainstream economic models generally consider trivial, marginal, and often counterproductive' (2014, S1). This approach draws attention to the generative capacity of life, and work can develop alongside – or in defiance of – material insecurity. In the following sections I will draw on these insights and offer an examination of the reasons why the members of the Cooperative and eco-network actively looked for ways to transcend the confines of the wage contract. I will show that my interlocutors were willing to endure economic hardship in order to take ownership of the economy through forms of work that provided space for self-actualization and the achievement of an alternative 'life worth living' (2014, S5).

Escaping the hamster's cage

My first encounter with an 'alternative economy' was with an eco-network located in a *comarca* (county), north of Barcelona near the Pre-Pyrenees in the spring of 2016. I lived in an old rural estate (*masia*) with three members of the *ecoxarxa* who were renting the *masia* from a local landlord, who had agreed to give them a good deal on the rent while they converted the *masia* into a rural tourism project. A two-hour trip by car from Barcelona, the area was known for its lush forests and hiking trails and was a popular tourist destination for city dwellers looking to unwind from the hustle and bustle of the Catalonian capital. It was here that the members of the eco-network sought to 'create a system of economic relations at the margins of capitalism' (*al marge del capitalisme*), as stated on their website.

Eco-networks are constituted by groups of people who use a social currency to exchange goods and services among each other. Generally, the members (*ecoxarxeires*) traded goods that they themselves had produced, which were mostly though not exclusively food related. In the eco-network where I did my fieldwork, there were beer brewers and bakers, soap makers and cow herders, but also massage therapists and even an eco-village owner who would organize workshops and host people at the village in exchange for social currency. At the time of my research [in 2016–2017], there were between 20 and 30 eco-networks spread throughout Catalonia, located mostly in more rural areas. The size of the networks varied greatly; from groups as small as five people to larger ones, like the one where I did my fieldwork, consisting of roughly 140 members. The *ecoxarxeires* lived at different sites throughout the *comarca* and would meet on a regular basis at the *rebost* (storage) where they would exchange goods, socialize and discuss matters related to the organization of economic life. In the case of the eco-network I encountered, the *rebost* was located in the *masia* where I lived for a period of five months during my research. Far from being self-contained, the network maintained connections with other networks, interacted with socially oriented projects in the region such as consumer groups and time banks, and were affiliated to the anti-capitalist Cooperative in Barcelona that I will discuss later.

Most of the members of the eco-network belonged to a group of neo-rurals, between 45 and 55 years of age. These were men and women who grew up in urban areas, but came to the north of Catalonia at the beginning of the 1990s in search of a rural lifestyle (Robertson, 2012). Practically all of my interlocutors were very aware of their urban backgrounds (and social positionality in general) and often referred to themselves as *neorural*. They mostly hailed from lower middle class or working class backgrounds, generally did not have any university education, and expressed strong distrust towards the state. Moreover, many had been in other social movements before. In addition to this core, there was a slightly younger group of neo-rurals, aged between 30 and 35, with a university education. This group was part of a younger generation of Spaniards who find themselves marginalized by the formal employment market even though they have all the necessary qualifications. Both older and younger members of the eco-network worked in temporary low-paid jobs or received welfare benefits. In this sense, their lives were economically insecure.

However, when I asked my interlocutors about their living situations, they often recognized and rejected precarity in the same breath. For example, Alícia and Edmon were two of the most active members in the eco-network and were in charge of managing the online social currency platform. Outside of their responsibilities in the eco-network, they both had part-time, rather low-paying jobs. However, similar to my housemates, they also had struck a deal with the owner of an abandoned *masia* who was looking for people to rent the estate to. As Alícia said in an interview, "We don't earn a lot, but we also only pay 100 euros worth of rent for this *masia*." Indeed, the members of the eco-network actively sought to decrease their dependency on wage labour and sought out ways of living that enabled them to dedicate themselves to alternative value-generating practices. This observation draws parallels with ethnographic studies of work in the global South, which have documented the attempts of workers to resist wage labour (Millar, 2014; Barchiesi, 2011). For example, Franco Barchiesi (2011, 20) writes of post-Apartheid South Africa: 'informality, self-employment, multiple intermittent jobs offered ... alternatives to the relentless and ferocious regularity of the mines and the factories'. In a similar way, my interlocutors strived to work outside the wage in order to engage in life-sustaining practices that were understood to be more fulfilling than labour in *el capitalismo*; even if these practices came at the cost of increased material insecurity.

The contradictory nature of life outside the wage – simultaneously empowering and materially insecure – became evident to me during an interview with Bernat. One of the youngest members of the eco-network, he too hailed from Barcelona and spent much of his adolescence in alternative and, as he would say, *punki* circles. Like so many Spanish young adults, Bernat was unable to find employment even though he had attended university, received a degree in agricultural engineering, and had all the necessary qualifications.

Through a combination of personal ideological convictions and structural developments in the Spanish economy, then, he was now in a situation where he was working in the informal sector – *todo en negro* – uninsured, and without a pension plan.

When I asked whether or not he thought this was a precarious situation, he paused, took a breath and answered, "Yes ... but for me it isn't." He continued:

> 'Objectively speaking it's a precarious life (*una vida precaria*), it's *una vida de mierda* (a shitty life). But we're happy because we don't want all this bullshit that they're selling us ... The hamster who lives in a cage lives like a king (*de puta madre*), he's got food, a television, but at the end of the day he's still a hamster.'

Here Bernat made a critique of consumerism and emphasized that while life on the margins, or outside of the hamster's cage, may be precarious, at least he could determine the conditions of his own life. Or, in his words, "I'm precarious (*precario*), but I don't have a boss." Outside of the cage, moreover, he did not labour like a hamster, but instead did work as a free man: "In fact, I don't *treballar* [labour], I do *feinas* [work/ tasks]. The origin in Latin is different, *trebalare* comes from when they took slaves and forced them to labour, whereas the free man did *feinas*, from *faenare*." Here Bernat provincializes wage labour by returning us to a broader, pre-industrial understanding of work as artisanship and self-mastery (Arendt, 1958). Only by eschewing the hamster's cage of wage labour were he and the other members of the eco-network able to engage in *feinas* that offered a sense of ownership and self-mastery.

In practice, however, the members of the eco-network often straddled waged and unwaged work. Álicia and Edmon, for instance, worked part-time jobs as a teacher and youth camp guide respectively, but spent a great deal of their non-waged time farming livestock and selling [beef] in social currency under the name *Vakunin* (a contraction of the Spanish word for cow, *vaca*, and the anarchist thinker Bakunin). My housemates, similarly, all worked part-time or seasonal jobs outside of the house. Ínes worked as a part-time teacher, Álex as a guide in a youth camp during the summer, and Vicenc occasionally worked in maintenance at the nearby natural park. Their goal, however, was to transform the *masia* into a self-sustaining rural tourism project. They also cultivated a home garden and held livestock in order to be as self-sufficient as possible. Similarly, Alba worked on a temporary contract as a postal worker and spent her non-waged time doing various tasks for the eco-network and producing apple juice that she later sold in social currency. They were all, moreover, highly aware of this duality of work. After helping her transport some of her juice to a nearby eco-village, Alba said, "It feels like I'm in two worlds ... I've got one foot planted securely in *el capitalismo*, and the other foot is trying to land in *el alternativo*."

This dualistic conception of the economy was mapped onto a moral distinction between 'capitalist' labour, which was seen as alienating and exploitative, and 'alternative' work (*feina*). This distinction, moreover, is also found in social scientific writings on work where labour is the 'human effort which pertains to capitalist relations of production', which is contrasted to work understood as 'the rest of human energy expenditure in relation to non-capitalist realms' (Narotzky, 2018, 31). Narotzky is right to be critical of this distinction at an analytical level, as it implies that these forms of energy expenditure are inherently different, that is, that labour is somehow devoid of affect, emotion and existential fulfilment and that work is never alienating, exploitative and degrading. Later in this chapter we will indeed see how the experience of alternative work was also expressed in terms of fatigue and embedded in relational conflicts and power relations. Yet here I would like to emphasize that my interlocutors mobilized this distinction in order to erect a space where (alternative) work or *feina* was valued and presented as morally superior to conventional wage labour (*treball*).

In response to a system that was perceived to have, in the words of Bernat, 'taken away our structures of sovereignty', the *ecoxarxeires* actively sought to make a living by pursuing activities that fell outside of the wage relation. There are interesting parallels here with informal workers in the global South who '[turn] away from the employment contract' in order to lead a life that does not conform to the routinized work rhythm that is characteristic of waged labour (Millar, 2014, 48). My interlocutors invested their time and energy into developing new skills and carving out spaces in which feelings of sovereignty, self-worth and wealth could be cultivated. For example, Alba contrasted her meagre earnings as a postal worker in the wage economy with the social currency she had earned through the eco-network: "In *moneda social* (social currency)? Uff, I've got so much social money, I'm rich!"

However, some were more reliant on wage employment than others. Sam was a part-time beer brewer who supplied the eco-network with craft beer. Yet this was not his primary source of income. As he told me, "Right now I'm working at a multinational [telecommunications] company, which for me is a contradiction, but ... what I'm doing with this job is using the capital it gives me to do things that help make my surroundings better." He recognized that the wage acquired from this job gave him the peace of mind (*tranquilidad*) to not worry about whether he would be able to pay off his mortgage and provide for his family. He had thought about quitting a number of times but never saw it through due to his responsibilities towards his children: "My daughters were living with me and my life was kind of, well not kind of, entirely devoted to them ... I did not want to take a gamble [by becoming a full time beer brewer]." Realizing alternative forms of work and life, then, was always contingent upon existential deliberations and the responsibility of keeping up with daily living expenses and providing for dependants.

Scholars have conceptualized precarity in different ways. As Kathleen Millar (2017, 3) shows, one influential line of thinking, born out of Bourdieu's writings, views it primarily as a labour condition. In this view, precarity refers to job insecurity, low wages, poverty and unpredictable income flows (Castel, 2003; Vosko, 2006; Hacker, 2008; Ross, 2009; Kalleberg, 2009, 2013; Standing, 2011; Vallas and Prenner, 2012; Pugh, 2015). The focus of this scholarship is therefore primarily on documenting material insecurity and showing the precarity of contemporary labour regimes. Material security was clearly a source of concern to my interlocutors. However, by focusing on material insecurity alone, we lose sight of the deliberate life projects that people pursue, which may not be informed solely by material concerns. That is, rather than struggling to improve the material conditions of their wage work, my interlocutors sought to transcend these conditions by engaging in forms of work outside of the capitalist wage contract. In other words, the solution to precarity was not understood to reside in the reform of waged employment but in its transcendence. Participation in the eco-network enabled my interlocutors to gain a sense of collective ownership and mastery that was not understood to be possible through wage employment; though, as we have seen in the case of Sam, not everyone had the same ability to loosen their ties to the wage. Moving from the eco-network to the Cooperative, however, we find a strategy of eliminating this tension between the need for waged labour and the desire for an alternative way of living. In the following sections I will explore the significance of the cooperative model in mediating the relation between work and life in Catalonia.

Work outside the *assalariat*

My first encounter with the Cooperative contrasted quite starkly with my experience in the eco-network. After some exchanges via email, I was able to schedule an appointment at the Cooperative's headquarters: a squatted luxury spa centre in downtown Barcelona. During my first visit, I entered through a sliding glass door and approached a large, curved, gleaming reception desk. The receptionist told me to take a seat and wait until Niko, who was going to introduce me to the Cooperative, would arrive. As I sat there waiting, perhaps belying my own assumptions of what the 'office' of an alternative economic project should look like, I was surprised by the size, style and overall aura of the Cooperative's squat. Adjacent to the reception desk were two office spaces, decked out with glass tables and a veritable torrent of drawers and cupboards that housed years' worth of paperwork. The reception desk gave way to a labyrinth of hallways and doors that led to windowless yet air-conditioned offices used mostly for meetings. In addition to these smaller rooms, there was a larger rehearsal room that was perhaps originally intended for gym or yoga classes but was now used for the general assemblies of the Cooperative. Upon his arrival, I followed Niko into one of the rooms, where he explained the history and workings of the Cooperative to me.

The Cooperative was officially established in 2010 and was an ambitious project that resulted from the coming together of various activists from a variety of networks active in Catalonia at the time, such as the anti-corporate globalization movements, squatter movements, De-Growth networks and also some of the first eco-networks. As discussed earlier, these movements draw on a rich history of grassroots political mobilization in Catalonia. Similar to the eco-network, the goal of the Cooperative was to create an economic system at 'the margins of capitalism' (al marge del capitalsme). Though different members articulated different variations of what the 'margins' meant, this was generally envisioned to be a space where people could be free from the yoke of the state and capital (that is el Sistema), and construct an economy that was controlled by local actors instead of transnational elites (for example bankers and politicians), and based on values that were seen to be lacking in 'the System'. In the discourse of the Cooperative, this was a space that 'allows for overcoming our dependence on the structures of the System and ... [reconstructing] society from the bottom up by recovering affective human relations based on proximity (proximitat) and trust (confiança)'.

During the first years of the Cooperative's existence, the core group of members consisted of highly educated, young (in their 20s to mid-30s at that time), predominantly middle class Catalan speakers. As the Cooperative grew in the aftermath of anti-austerity protests beginning in 2011 and attracted more people, however, its profile became more diverse. Whenever I asked my interlocutors how many people were members of the cooperative and eco-network, I heard estimates up to and exceeding 15,000 people. However, they often included people who made use of their services, as well as those of affiliated groups and projects. The truth was that there was no reliable statistical data about the membership, and members were still trying to map the scope of the organization during the time of my research. At this time, there were approximately 40 people receiving a regular remuneration from the Cooperative. These remunerated activists were spread throughout Catalonia but had their base of operations in the aforementioned downtown squat.

The youngest member of the Cooperative was 24, and the oldest was close to 60. So while some had experienced Spain's transition to democracy (1975–1978) and were even active in some social movements during the dictatorship, most of the people involved in the Cooperative came of age during the 1980s and 1990s. Most had enjoyed a university education, and the majority hailed from middle class backgrounds, although some proudly identified as working class. In fact, many members of the Cooperative previously enjoyed comfortable, salaried positions which they gave up in order to join the Cooperative. There were roughly as many women as men, and at least two people who did not identify according to this binary. In general, Catalan speakers outnumbered non-Catalan speakers and there were a few non-Spanish members.

The Cooperative provided remuneration in order to facilitate an alternative employment system that enabled people to be self-employed outside of the state's legal framework for self-employment. In Spain, being self-employed comes at a high financial cost. A self-employed person (*autónoma*) is required to pay a monthly fee of 278 euros a month, consisting mostly of social security fees. While recent reforms have made self-employment cheaper for certain groups,[5] being self-employed in Spain is still expensive when compared to other European countries. The Cooperative, however, offered an alternative to this system by making use of the cooperative legal form which allowed people to become *socis* (members). This enabled people to pursue economic activities without paying the monthly self-employment fees to the state. Instead, a trimestral contribution of 75 monetary units was required, of which a percentage could be paid in social currency. These monetary resources were subsequently pooled by the members of the Cooperative and used for a variety of purposes.

The amount of *socis* fluctuated during my research, but at any point in time there were roughly 400 users of this system. This amounted to a yearly revenue stream of around 400,000 euros that was used to remunerate a group of activists called the *liberadas*.[6] The name of this group was understood to convey the fact that they had been liberated from wage labour. Instead, they were now free to dedicate their time to alternative forms of work and economy. In practice, they were required to manage the various projects of the Cooperative, including the alternative employment system, an interest free bank, a telecommunications service and a food distribution network. All these projects were designed to loosen people's dependency on 'the System', which referred to globalized, state-sanctioned political and financial institutions (that is the state and capitalism). The social currency, for instance, was thought to make people less reliant on what was seen to be volatile fiat currency controlled by banks and the state. It was the responsibility of the *liberadas* to create and manage these (semi-) public goods.

But did the remunerations received by *liberadas* not represent a salary? This question was addressed by Roc in an interview. When I asked him how much he earned, he quickly corrected me by saying: "I don't talk about 'earning'. I might be mistaken but earning is … in my mind I've linked earning (*cobrar*) conceptually to a salary (*sueldo*). But it's not a salary. It's a compensation, for the time I dedicate, for the energy I spend." The distinction between a salary and a compensation reflects an intentional choice to pursue a 'wageless life' (Denning, 2010) that we also saw among the members of the eco-network. Indeed, before joining the Cooperative, Roc had studied chemistry and worked at a number of companies in "el mundo de empresas [the world of companies]". However, he was always critical of capitalist wage labour and the capitalist system more generally and sought ways he could go beyond this system: "I was always looking, what's going wrong here, and particularly I was interested in finding out about money: what is it exactly and why do we use it?" The Cooperative became well known throughout Catalonia in the wake of the 15-M movement. Roc saw a video clip of a renowned activist of the Cooperative and "within two minutes I said 'that's where I'm going'." He attended an assembly of the Cooperative and after a while started to work in its food distribution committee and received a remuneration for his work. Now, he said, "I don't have any desire of returning to *el món assalariat* (the world of wages). In fact I reject it, entirely." This rejection of a salaried life was a broadly shared sentiment among my interlocutors, who, as we have seen, attempted to minimize their dependence on wage labour.

By rejecting *el món assalariat*, however, the *liberadas* did not access a more comfortable material existence. The maximum remuneration was based on a 30-hour working week and set at 900 monetary units a month, of which 15 per cent had to be in social currency. Only a few *liberadas*, moreover, received the maximum remuneration. Others worked part time or had their own projects on the side. In fact, the *liberadas* were encouraged not just to depend on the Cooperative for money, but instead also to set up their own value-generating projects (*projecte productiu*). Yet, particularly in an urban area such as Barcelona, 900 monetary units was often only barely enough to get by. This was a frequent topic of debate in the Cooperative. Some argued that the remuneration needed to be raised. Others, such as Roc, however, argued that this would be detrimental to the revolutionary spirit of the Cooperative: "If we were to earn 1500 a month and if we'd have a high standard of living, we'd conform a lot [to the system]." He continued, "It's important to just barely cover one's necessities, so that people will continue to work for the project [the Cooperative]." Indeed, cooperative meetings often involved a performance of material precarity. For example, Iker, another *liberado* would often emphasize, "We don't even have a dime (*no tenemos ni un duro*)" during his long orations at the general assemblies. Using the plural form, he invoked a shared sense of material poverty supposedly felt by all members that was understood to be symbolic of their refusal of capitalist wage labour and dedication to the Cooperative. In this way, material security was understood to be subordinate – and even inimical – to the activity of bringing about alternative modes of socio-economic life.

The experience of life in a Catalonian cooperative complicates conventional accounts of precarious work in several ways. I have shown that members of the eco-network and the cooperative sought to escape what they saw as the drudgery of capitalist wage labour by engaging in alternative socio-economic practices. While material insecurity was very much part of the lives of my interlocutors, I have shown that their experiences of work cannot be understood through a singular focus on the material. Instead, I have suggested the importance of paying attention to the broad range of activities they engage in in pursuit of a 'life worth living', in which wage employment often plays only a minor role (Narotzky and Besnier, 2014, S5). The case of the *liberadas* complicates the idea that people in precarious positions necessarily desire material comfort. As is evident from Bernat's and Roc's statements, members thought it important not to live comfortably 'in the hamster's cage', but rather to experience a degree of material hardship and insecurity in pursuit of alternative socio-economic projects.

However, while my interlocutors challenged the hegemony of wage labour, work in the form of *feina* still featured centrally in the imagination of a post-capitalist way of living. Chamberlain (2018) has argued that visions of post-capitalist societies are often still built on the assumption that a community is formed on the basis of work. That is, he shows how many influential critical accounts of a society based on wage labour still work under the assumption that full inclusion in a political community and the creation of social bonds rests on the ability to engage in some kind of productive and cooperative action with people who take part in common (voluntary) associations (2018, 112–114). He further argues, however, that this means that it is likely that 'the type of productive or reproductive activities that a person performs will continue to function as a mechanism of inclusion/exclusion' (2018, 103). In the following section, I will analyse how the idea of work as formative of an alternative community did indeed feature in the politics of exclusion in the Cooperative, paying particular attention to the experience of fatigue and the collapse of work into life.

Fatigue, frustration and exit

Earlier we saw how Bernat conceived of his activities not as labour (*treball*) but *feina*, with the former being perceived as alienating, capitalist wage labour carried out by people trapped within the standard employment contract and the latter referring to freely taken-up work done outside of the confines of the hamster's cage. In a similar way, the *liberados* attempted to avoid terms such as 'salary' and 'labour'. They used *assignació* instead of salary and *activista* instead of *treballador* (labourer), mimicking Bernat's distinction between *treballar* and *feina*. Work in the cooperative was valued and performed in terms that were intentionally distinguished from wage labour. In fact, going one step further, *feina* was at times seen as inseparable from life. This became evident as I visited the assemblies of the Cooperative.

Decisions regarding the planning of activities and distribution of resources were taken at the general assembly each month. The assemblies were spaces of debate where people tried to convince others to pursue certain actions, and where members of the Cooperative performed their activism through carefully formulated discourses and negotiations. It was not uncommon for these assemblies to take several hours, sometimes lasting from the morning until well into the evening. I and other members of the Cooperative found the meetings to be physically and emotionally exhausting. I recall one instance during an assembly where there was a dispute about certain tasks that had not been done. Aida, who was thought to be in charge of carrying out these tasks, felt that there had been some miscommunication. Lena, however, responded curtly and reminded Aida that "This isn't just some job, it is a calling, a life project (*projecte de vida*)." Indeed, the core nucleus of activists at the Cooperative often emphasized that the work of the Cooperative was a life project, not just some kind of job to be taken up or left whenever one pleased. *Feina* was seen as an integral part of life.

Studies of informal economies in the global South have shown that the conceptual distinction between work and life often breaks down in practice. For example, Millar argues that waste pickers in Rio de Janeiro find it difficult to distinguish between activities that are part of life and those that can be categorized as work. Instead, work is understood to sustain life through acts of care and 'work on the self' (2014, 48). In the context of the Cooperative, however, this association is not the organic result of the blurring of various life-sustaining practices. Rather, we see a more deliberate, conscious effort to collapse work into life, making work in the Cooperative an activity that required full dedication.

When one member of the Cooperative informed the assembly that she had decided to leave the organization after a few months of being a *liberada*, she was told by another, "You've only been here a couple of months and to me it gives off the impression that you came, had a bit of a tough time, didn't like what you saw, and then left. ... whereas for me this is my life project." Turning work into a "life project" therefore allowed for a separation to be made between the truly dedicated who were in it for the long haul and those who did not have the endurance to be part of the collective. Work/life in the Cooperative was a taxing affair and many members left during the time of my fieldwork due to physical and emotional fatigue.

Such experiences of fatigue often gave way to frustration, as Federico de Musso has shown in the case of alternative provisioning networks in Italy (de Musso, 2017). Indeed, the figure of the burned-out activist (*quemat*) is common in activist networks across the world. A former member of the IT committee put it this way: "I realized that it [the Cooperative] is a *quema-activistas*, un *quemagente* (it burns through activists and people) because of the intensity and energy drain (*desgaste de energia*) it requires." A number of former members told me that they left as a result of physical fatigue. They also often talked of a kind of relational fatigue, through which personal conflicts grew too much to bear. For example, a former member of the communication committee recounted, "I'm very tired of how things have been going here [the

Cooperative] in the past two years ... so many uncomfortable situations, so many fights ... it's been very tiresome, both physically as well as mentally." Those who left felt drained, exhausted and disillusioned. The former member of the IT committee I interviewed said he had only recently deleted all his files related to the Cooperative and was only just now starting to be able to talk about his experience. Significantly, material discomfort or financial insecurity rarely played a role in people's decision to leave. Rather, it was the continuous criticism of one's work and the questioning of whether one was really committed to the Cooperative that ultimately made people exit the Cooperative. This echoes Chamberlain's (2018, 113) hypothesis that

> when [a] person fails to conform to the norm of participating more actively in associational activities and thus to prove his or her worth to the community, there is the real possibility that he or she will suffer disrespect and a lack of consideration from others. In this respect, the multiactivity society carries forward one of the chief problems of the existing work society.

Conclusion

Scholarly reflections on the changing nature of work in the global North have tended to sketch a transition from a situation of relative stability wherein workers enjoyed stable employment and their rights were protected by the welfare state, towards a situation of insecurity wherein the state no longer safeguards those privileges and rights that were secured in the post-war era. As such, these analyses have tended to foreground precarity, both as a labour condition (precarious work) and an ontological experience (precarious life), in their descriptions of contemporary work. They are underpinned by a sense of loss and wage work-related melancholia (Barchiesi, 2011) which forecloses the possibility that people might actively seek to escape the confines of wage employment in pursuit of more fulfilling and liberating forms of work.

In this chapter I have shown that members of a Catalonian eco-network and Cooperative often struggled to balance their desire for a life outside of the *assalariat* with their need to secure a basic level of economic security, creating a sense of fatigue and frustration. Their experiences of alternative work, then, oscillated between affirmations of liberty and autonomy on the one hand, and, fatigue and insecurity on the other. I have argued that the literature on precarious work, with its normative emphasis on the standard employment relationship, is ill-equipped to explain why people under certain circumstances might pursue life and labour trajectories outside of wage labour. A life 'outside of the hamster's cage' may be insecure in material terms, but it enabled members of the Cooperative and eco-network to obtain a sense of ownership and mastery over their economic lives, providing them with a sense of fulfilment that was often missing from their experiences of formal employment.

As I have shown earlier, the *liberados* collapsed the distinction between work and life through the concept of the 'life project' (*projecte de vida*). Yet while this conceptualization was successful in reclaiming work from the confines of the wage, it reified the connections between work and community, reproducing particular forms of inclusion and exclusion. I have shown that the association between work, life and community placed heavy expectations on members that left many feeling physically, emotionally and financially drained. Work was a continuous topic of debate and was often invoked to question people's dedication to the Cooperative and the project of realizing an alternative non-capitalist economy more broadly. In this way, the spectre of work society continues to haunt post-capitalist imaginaries and practices, inviting us to move beyond the wage in order to further disentangle the relationship between work and community.

Acknowledgements

This chapter grew out of a conference on the Post-Wage Economy at Queen Mary University in London. I am grateful to all the participants and the organizers of the conference in particular for their helpful comments and discussions.

Notes

1   In order to preserve the anonymity of the organization where I did my fieldwork, I will refer to it simply as 'the Cooperative'. Similarly, I do not disclose the specific location of the eco-network.

2   Earlier work in feminist economics has also shown how practices that would appear to fall outside of what is generally considered to be 'the economy' are in fact crucial to the (re-)production of social life (Collins and Gimenez, 1990; Molyneux, 1979; Beasley, 1994.

3   While I understood Catalan, I carried out my research in Spanish. If I have left certain words untranslated in direct quotes they will therefore mostly be in Spanish. However, emic terms such as *eina*, *autogestió*, and *feina* circulated more widely among my interlocutors. In the running text these are therefore left in Catalan as much as possible (though in many spaces people also spoke Spanish in addition to Catalan, meaning that many of these terms also circulated in Spanish).

4   In this chapter I join in a growing critique of the notion of precarity. However, precarity is not just an analytic concept and my interlocutors did use this

term – *precario/precariat* – to express their lived experience of work. As such I will continue to use this term sparingly, but mostly when it is used as such by my interlocutors.

5   Recent changes in the law have amended this system slightly. For those becoming self-employed for the first time there is a reduced fee – 52 euros – that is applicable during the first six months of being self-employed. After that the base fee of 278 euros applies. For people under 30 years of age, a reduced fee can be maintained for up to 30 months, although the maximum reduction only applies for the first six months.

6   I more often heard the Spanish term *liberada* than the Catalan translation, which would be *alliberat*.

References

Arendt, H. (1958 [1998]). *The Human Condition*, Chicago, IL: Chicago University Press.

Barbieri, P. and Schererm, S. (2009) 'Labour market flexibilization and its consequences in Italy', *European Sociological Review*, 25(6): 677–692.

Barchiesi, F. (2011) *Precarious Liberation: Workers, the State, and Contested Social Citizenship in Postapartheid South Africa*, Albany, NY: SUNY.

Beasley, C. (1994) *Sexual Economyths: Conceiving a Feminist Economics*, Sydney: Allen & Unwin.

Beck, U. (2000) *The Brave New World of Work*, Cambridge: Polity.

Castel, R. (2003) *From Manual Workers to Wage Laborers: Transformation of the Social Question*, trans. Richard Boyd, New Brunswick, NJ: Transaction Publishers.

Castells, M. (2011) *Networks of Outrage and Hope. Social Movements in the Internet Age*, Cambridge: Polity.

Castells, M., Caraça, J. and Cardoso, G. (2012) 'The cultures of the economic crisis: An introduction', in Castells, M., Caraça, J. and Cardoso, G. (eds) *Aftermath: The Cultures of the Economic Crisis*, Oxford: Oxford University Press, pp 1–16.

Chamberlain, J. A. (2018) *Undoing Work, Rethinking Community: A Critique of the Social Function of Work*, Ithaca, NY: Cornell University Press.

Collins, J. and Gimenez, M. (1990) *Work Without Wages: Comparative Studies of Domestic Labour and Self-Employment*, Albany, NY: Suny Press.

Conill, J., Castells, M., Cardenas, A. and Servon, L. (2012) 'Beyond the crisis: The emergence of alternative economic practices', in Castells, M., Caraça, J. and Cardoso, G. (eds) *Aftermath: The Cultures of the Economic Crisis*, Oxford: Oxford University Press, pp 210–250.

Davis, M. (2006) *Planet of Slums*, London: Verso.

de Musso, F. (2017) 'Distance, fatigue, and presence. An approach to livelihood from the network of solidarity economy of the Italian south', unpublished paper presented at the second international conference of the research group Sovereignty and Social Contestation 'Sovereignty, Contestation, and "The Economy"'.

Denning, M. (2010) 'Wageless life', *New Left Review*, 66: 79–97.

Dolgoff, S. (1974) 'The Spanish Revolution', in Dolgoff, S, (ed) *The Anarchist Collectives: Workers' Self-management in the Spanish Revolution, 1936–1939*, New York, NY: Rose Books, pp 5–18.

Edelman (2020) 'Edelman Trust Barometer 2020', available at https://edl.mn/2NOwltm.

Ferguson, J. and Li, T. (2018) 'Beyond the "proper job": Political-economic analysis after the century of labouring man', Working Paper 51. PLAAS UWC: Cape Town.

FnfEurope (2013) 'The Spanish Slump – Political Crisis and the Need for Institutional Reform', available at http://fnf-europe.org/2013/06/17/the-spanish-slump-

Fominaya, C.F. (2015) 'Debunking spontaneity: Spain's 15-M/*Indignados* as autonomous movement', *Social Movement Studies*, 14(2): 142–163.

Fominaya, C.F. (2017) 'European anti-austerity and pro-democracy protests in the wake of the global financial crisis', *Social Movement Studies*, 16(1): 1–20.

Fraser, N. (2003) 'From discipline to flexibilization? Rereading Foucault in the shadow of globalization', *Constellations*, 10(2): 160–171.

Gandolfo, D. (2013) 'Formless: A day at Lima's Office of Formalization', *Cultural Anthropology*, 28(2): 278–298.

Gibson-Graham, J.K. (1996) *The End of Capitalism (As We Knew It). A Feminist Critique of Political Economy*, Minneapolis, MN: University of Minnesota Press.

Hacker J.S. (2008) *The Great Risk Shift: The New Economic Insecurity and the Decline of the American Dream* (2nd edn), New Haven, CT: Yale University Press.

Hewison, K. and Kalleberg, A.L. (2013) 'Precarious work and flexibilization in South and Southeast Asia', *American Behavioral Scientist*, 57(4): 395–402.

Hughes, N. (2015) 'The community currency scene in Spain', *International Journal of Community Currency Research*, 19: 1–11.

Institut d'Estadística de Catalunya (Idescat) (2019) 'Evolució i perfil del treball autònom, last updated 6 February 2020, available at http://observatoritreball.gencat.cat/web/.content/generic/documents/treball/estudis/Evolucio_i_perfil_del_treball_autonom/2019/arxius/Evolucio_i_perfil_treb_autonom_des_2019.pdf

Jonas, A. (2010) ' "Alternative" this, "alternative" that …: Interrogating alterity and diversity', in Fuller, D., Jonas, A. and Lee, R. (eds) *Interrogating Alterity. Alternative Economic and Political Spaces*, Farnham: Ashgate, pp 3–30.

Juris, J.S. (2008) *Networking Futures. The Movements Against Corporate Globalization*, Durham, NC: Duke University Press.

Kalleberg, A.L. (2009) 'Precarious work, insecure workers: Employment relations in transition', *American Sociological Review*, 74(1): 1–22.

Kalleberg, A.L. (2013) *Good Jobs, Bad Jobs: The Rise of Polarized and Precarious Employment Systems in the United States, 1970s to 2000s*, New York, NY: Russell Sage Foundation.

Knight, D. and Stewart, C. (2016) 'Ethnographies of austerity: Temporality, crisis and affect in Southern Europe', *History and Anthropology*, 27(1): 1–18.

Leyshon, A. and Lee, R. (2003) 'Introduction', in Leyshon, A., Lee, R. and Williams, C. (eds) *Alternative Economic Spaces*, London: Sage, pp 1–26.

López, I. and Rodríguez, E. (2010) *Fin de ciclo. Financiarización, territorio, y sociedad de propietarios en la onda larga del capitalismo Hispano (1959–2010)*, Madrid: Traficantes de Sueños.

López, I. and Rodríguez, E. (2011) 'The Spanish model', *New Left Review*, 69(3): 5–29.

Martínez-Pastor, J.-I. and Bernardi, F. (2011) 'The flexibilization of the Spanish labour market: Meaning and consequences for inequality from a life-course perspective', in Blossfeld, H.-P., Buchholz, S., Hofäcker, D. and Kolb, K. (eds) *Globalised Labour Markets and Social Inequality in Europe*, New York, NY: Palgrave Macmillan, pp 79–107.

Millar, K. (2014) 'The precarious present: Wageless labour and disrupted life in Rio de Janeiro, Brazil', *Cultural Anthropology*, 29(1): 32–53.

Millar, K. (2017) 'Toward a critical politics of precarity', *Sociology Compass*, 11(6): 1–11.

Millar, K. (2018) *Reclaiming the Discarded: Life and Labour on Rio's Garbage Dump*, Durham, NC: Duke University Press.

Mintz, F. (2006) *Autogestión y anarcosindicalismo en la España revolucionaria*, Madrid: Traficantes de Sueños.

Molina, Ó. and Godino, A. (2013) 'Economic reforms and the labour market: Zapatero's endless period in the wilderness', in Field, B.N. and Botti, A. (eds) *Politics and Society in Contemporary Spain From Zapatero to Rajoy*, New York, NY: Palgrave Macmillan, pp 101–122.

Molyneux, M. (1979) 'Beyond the domestic labour debate', *New Left Review*, 116(3).

Narotzky, S. (2012) 'Alternatives to expanded accumulation and the anthropological imagination. Turning necessity into a challenge to capitalism', in Pauline Gardiner, P., Leach Barber, B. and Lem, W. (eds) *Confronting Capital Critique and Engagement in Anthropology*, New York, NY: Routledge, pp 293–252.

Narotzky, S. (2013) 'Economías cotidianas, economías sociales, economías sostenibles', in Narotzky, S. (ed) *Economías cotidianas, economías sociales, economías sostenibles*, Barcelona: Icaria, pp 7–26.

Narotzky, S. (2018) 'Rethinking the concept of labour', *Journal of the Royal Anthropological Institute*, 24(S1): 29–43.

Narotzky, S. (2019) 'Evidence struggles: Legality, legitimacy, and social mobilizations in the Catalan political conflict', *Indiana Journal of Global Legal Studies*, 26(1): 31–60.

Narotzky, S. and Besnier, N. (2014) 'Crisis, value, hope. Rethinking the economy', *Current Anthropology*, 55(S9): S4–S16.

Navarro, V. (2012) 'El error de las políticas de austeridad, recortes incluidos, en la Sanidad Pública', *Gaceta Sanitaria*, 26(2), available at http://scielo.isciii.es/scielo.php?script=sci_arttext&pid=S0213-91112012000200014

O'Hare, P. (2020) '"We looked after people better when we were informal": The "quasi-formalization" of Montevideo's waste-pickers', *Bulletin of Latin American Research*, 39(1): 53–68.

Palomera, J. (2014) 'How did finance capital infiltrate the world of the urban poor? Home ownership and social fragmentation in a Spanish neighborhood', *International Journal of Urban and Regional Research*, 38(1): 218–235.

Petmesidou, M. and Guillén, M. (2017) 'Can the welfare state as we know it survive? A view from the crisis-ridden southern European periphery', in Petmesidou, M. and Guillén, M. (eds) *Economic Crisis and Austerity in Southern Europe: Threat or Opportunity for a Sustainable Welfare State*, New York, NY: Routledge, pp 1–14.

Picot, G. and Tassinari, A. (2017) 'All of one kind? Labour market reforms under austerity in Italy and Spain', *Socio-Economic Review*, 15(2): 461–482.

Ponniah, T. and Fisher, W.F. (2003) 'Introduction: The World Social Forum and the reinvention of democracy' in Ponniah, T. and Fisher, W.F. (eds) *Another World is Possible: Popular Alternatives to Globalization at the World Social Forum*, Chicago, IL: University of Chicago Press, pp 1–20.

Pugh A. (2015) *Tumbleweed Society: Working and Caring in an Age of Insecurity*, Oxford: Oxford University Press.

Riesco-Sanz, A. (2012) 'Empresas sin asalariados y asalariados sin empresas. Apuntes sobre la crisis y transformación del empleo', *Revista de Relaciones Laborales*, 27(2): 134–148.

Riesco-Sanz, A. (2016) 'Trabajo, independencia y subordinación. La regulación del trabajo autónomo en España', *Revista Internacional de Sociologia*, 74(1): 1–16.

Roberston, A.F. (2012) *Mieres Reborn: The Reinvention of a Catalan Community*, Tuscaloosa, AL: University of Alabama Press.

Ross, A. (2009) *Nice Work if you can get it: Life and Labor in Precarious Times,* New York: New York University Press.

Rübner Hansen, B. (2017) 'Winter in Catalonia', *Viewpoint Magazine*, December 19, available at https://www.viewpointmag.com/2017/12/19/winter-in-catalonia/

Seidman, M. (2002) *A Republic of Egos: A Social History of the Spanish Civil War*, Madison, WI: University of Wisconsin Press.

Souchy A., Rochford B, Worden S. and Benford R. (1974) 'Workers' self-management in industry' in Dolgoff, S. (ed) *The Anarchist Collectives: Workers' Self-Management in the Spanish Revolution, 1936–1939*, New York, NY: Rose Books, pp 65–77.

Spyridakis, M. (2016) *The Liminal Worker. An Ethnography of Work, Unemployment and Precariousness in Contemporary Greece*, Oxford: Routledge.

Standing, G. (2011) *The Precariat: The New Dangerous Class*, London: Bloomsbury.

Vallas, S. and Prener, C. (2012) 'Dualism, job polarization, and the social construction of precarious work', *Work Occupation*, 39(4): 331–353.

Vosko, L.F. (ed) (2006) *Precarious Employment: Understanding Labour Market Insecurity in Canada*, Montreal: McGill-Queens University Press.

Zademach, H.-M. and Lillebrand, S. (2013) 'Alternative economies and spaces: Introductory remarks', in Zademach, H.M. and Lillebrand, S. (eds) *Alternative Economies and Spaces: New Perspectives for a Sustainable Economy*, Bielefeld: Transcript Global Studies, pp 9–22.

7

Choosing to Be Unfree? The Aspirations and Constraints of Debt-bonded Brick Workers in Cambodia

Nithya Natarajan, Katherine Brickell and Laurie Parsons

'Because my parents were sick, I sold our land and our house to treat them. After they died, I came to work at the brick kiln. If the boss shuts down the brick kiln, I don't know where I'd go.'

Roumjoung, female debt-bonded brick kiln worker

Almost three decades after Cambodia first embraced neoliberalism, the plight of its working poor offers a stark picture of the impact that untrammelled growth has had upon the lives of the most vulnerable. The country has undergone a rapid transformation since 1991, from a largely agrarian to industrial and services sector-led economy (Hughes, 2003). Contrary to the promise of 'decent work' advocated by proponents of growth-led development (see for example, Goal 8, UN, 2015), the country's labour market exemplifies the tethering of low-waged and insecure work to burgeoning growth (Natarajan et al, 2019a; Lawreniuk and Parsons, 2020).

This chapter explores the case of labour exploitation in Cambodia's brick kilns, focusing on the *unfreedom* of their debt-bonded brick workers. Cambodia has seen a construction boom in recent decades, as part of its broader shift to neoliberal growth from 1991 (Hughes,

2003). Yet the country's sustained GDP growth has been accompanied by poor levels of job creation, with the majority of what limited jobs there are remaining informal, low paid and precarious (ILO, 2018a). Brick work in the construction sector is exemplary of this, involving physically exhausting and unsafe work, long hours, no protective equipment, and noted instances of child labour; and the majority of work in this sector is debt bonded. Development thinkers have acknowledged the centrality of low-waged work and insecure livelihoods to neoliberal transformation across the global South (Davis, 2006; Breman and van der Linden, 2014). Yet there remains some debate as to whether such structuralist views risk obscuring the agency and generative potential of such livelihoods (Gibson–Graham, 2008; Roy, 2011; Thieme, 2017).

We build on work which highlights the increasing centrality of debt as a focal point from which to understand evolving relations of work. As Lazzarato has argued (2012, 30), 'indebted man' offers a new form of '*homo economicus*' under neoliberalism, where the labour–capital relation characterized by 'effort-reward' is compounded by creditors' subjective control over debtors through guilt, and a morality of promising to repay. For LeBaron (2014), this form of control belies how debt has become a new form of class-based discipline against labour. Yet as Pettinger (2019) suggests, the generalized foregrounding of waged work as 'work' conceals the continued significance of unfree labour, thus foreclosing a broader discussion of how capital commodifies the human body through work. Our chapter aims to bring to the fore an analysis of unfree labour within broader debates on informal work by conceptualizing the forging and maintaining of unfreedom on Cambodian brick kilns as a form of work connected to broader structures of exploitation.

We draw on the Marxist framework of unfree labour relations to reassert the structural oppression experienced by brick workers in Cambodia, conceptualizing debt bondage on brick kilns as part of a continuum of *unfree labour relations* in Cambodia's economy (Lerche, 2011), and highlighting the role of debt in disciplining workers into kiln work, and on the kiln itself. In building on the challenge for theory to 'enact and construct rather than resist (or succumb to) economic realities' (Gibson–Graham, 2008, 619), this chapter considers how such unfreedom is a path carved out by workers as a proactive response to the lack of alternative financial options open to them in rural areas. Yet, it also highlights how such a choice reveals wider, structural constraints, as labourers are unable to choose the conditions of their work and are compelled to remain on brick kilns in unsafe working conditions until debts are paid off. The insights of Roumjoung, introduced at the start of this chapter, provide a glimpse into the *choices* which led her to the kiln as well as the paternalistic relationship with the kiln owner who continues to bond her. Unlike dominant accounts of debt bondage as a coerced form of labour, where direct employers are held up as perpetrators (Bales, 2002), our research with brick workers foregrounds bondage as relief from coercive forces of rural over-indebtedness. In other words, unfree labour is compelled by wider forces of structural constraint beyond the wage relation.

The research we share in this chapter was generated as part of the 'Blood Bricks' project, which examines the nexus between climate change and modern slavery in Cambodia. Specifically, the project focuses on how climate change-induced rural indebtedness leads small farmers from villages across Cambodia to urban, insecure work as debt-bonded labour in brick kilns around Phnom Penh. Our findings are based on mixed-method data collected in several stages between 2017 and 2018. First, we conducted semi-structured interviews with 51 brick kiln workers, supplemented by a further 31 interviews with other actors such as kiln owners, union leaders, former kiln workers, residents around the kilns and Buddhist monks. Second, we carried out 308 quantitative surveys in three villages that comprise high levels of out-migration to brick kilns. These surveys were accompanied by interviews with a sample of labour-sending households and other figures in the three villages. All interviews were conducted by Dr Laurie Parsons and/or a long-standing Cambodian research assistant (who prefers to remain anonymous), and interviews were conducted in Khmer and later transcribed and then translated into English. Interviewees' names have been changed to protect their identities.

In the following section we explore debates about labour and unfreedom to develop a theoretical approach which challenges the dominant focus on direct coercion in the scholarship on modern slavery and debt bondage to instead emphasize the role of constrained choice. We then explore the structural drivers that lead households to leave their rural villages to work in brick kilns. We show how kiln work itself forecloses the possibility of material uplift, before finally arguing that aspiration and resistance in work need to be understood within the broader sets of constraints we set out.

Choosing unfreedom? Unfree labour as oppression and choice

A growing literature documents the transformation of 'work' under neoliberalism. This literature has foregrounded the apparently novel phenomenon of insecure, informal, precarious work that has emerged through the fragmentation of labour regulation and social safety nets that formed the basis of the 'standard employment relationship' in the mid-twentieth century (see, for example, Standing, 2011). Yet this view has been challenged by scholars of the global South, who point to the historical ubiquity of informal and insecure labour relations in the majority of the world (Munck, 2013). This is not to say that the global turn towards neoliberalism has not materially transformed the livelihoods of the working poor in countries such as Cambodia – rather it is only by decentring waged work that we can begin to appreciate the complexity of actually existing labour relations. For example, Bernstein (2006) has argued that contrary to patterns of transformation in parts of the global North, where the emergence of agrarian capitalism saw former peasants transformed into waged workers and to some extent absorbed by industrial services sector growth, the South has seen rural dispossession without labour absorption. Furthermore, the globalization of capital under neoliberalism has seen nation states cede controls over the most vulnerable – through regulation of foreign investment, labour regulation and even social safety nets – to market vagaries (Breman and Agarwal, 2002; Bernstein, 2006). As such, burgeoning 'classes of labour' have emerged, characterized by their day-to-day reproduction through fragmented and precarious waged work, combined with petty enterprise, as well as complex and evolving livelihood strategies to simply make ends meet (Bernstein, 2006).

In a similar vein, Davis (2006) highlights that the world's urban population continues to supersede the rural, with the delinking of industrial growth from urbanization creating a phenomenon of underemployed urban 'slum' dwellers. Alongside those settled in rural areas are the many who live between both rural and urban settings, sending back remitted wages to natal village households, where possible, to make ends meet (Brickell and Datta, 2011; Lawreniuk and Parsons, 2020). These classes of labour arguably exist outside the classical Marxist notion of a reserve army of labour – a section of the population kept under- or unemployed in order to reduce workers' bargaining power within waged work. Instead, given their breadth and resilience, they are surplus to the requirements of capital, an argument echoed in the context of Southeast Asia (see Li, 2009). Certainly in Cambodia, work in the informal economy is the norm, with an estimated 93.1 per cent of Cambodian workers classified as informal (ILO, 2018b). Such surplus labourers characteristically lack relative bargaining power vis-à-vis the labour market. As Li argues (2009, 67), 'no one has a market incentive to pay the costs of keeping them alive from day to day, or from one generation to the next'. As such, surplus labourers often undertake the most insecure, low-waged and unsafe forms of work, with little recourse to upward mobility.

The concept of 'surplus labour' offers a relatively bleak view of working lives in Southeast Asia. Conversely, a different conceptualization of informality as a space of creativity, potential and even an alternative path to betterment was popularized in the 1980s. For De Soto (1989), the informal economy represents a form of petty entrepreneurialism among those choosing to operate outside the bounds of a restrictive, regulated market. The solution to addressing informality thus appears to be market deregulation, and the extension of private property rights to the most marginal, to ensure greater access to markets. Gibson-Graham (2008) echoes De Soto's valorization of informal economies as generative spaces, while crucially advocating an anti-capitalist approach, seeing the informal sector as a space which gives rise to alternative economic possibilities. Drawing on such work Thieme (2017, 542) develops her account of the 'hustle economy' in Nairobi as 'a set of working practices in the face of uncertainty, and place-based performative politics of style that potentially speaks to multiple elsewheres'. She argues that structuralist approaches to informal work too often view it as 'pathologies of despair and deviance to be fixed, or as enhanced flexibility and innovation' (2017, 530). Thieme's critique therefore argues for greater emphasis on the creative potential of those within the informal economy to assert agency and creativity in making their realities, while remaining wedded to a critique of structuralist approaches which sees capitalism everywhere. While acknowledging the key challenge set out by Thieme to recognize the complex realities that are made outside of the limitations imposed by capitalism, this chapter remains rooted in a more broadly structuralist understanding of work. This recognizes that any approach seeking to broaden our understanding of work beyond the wage relation, and rooted in a grounded episteme, must acknowledge both agency and constraint in people's narratives, and both generative and restrictive forms of economic opportunity, rooted in particular contexts. To that end, while foregrounding the structural constraints of kiln work, we also consider such work as offering livelihood opportunities.

In order to explore debt bondage within a capitalist framework, we conceptualize it as a form of *unfree labour*. This theorization emerges from Marxist thinking and offers a robust set of analytical tools from which to understand the interplay of obstruction and aspiration characterizing brick workers' move to the kiln in Cambodia. For Marx, the distinction between unfree and so-called 'free' labour stemmed from relations of exploitation that were pre-capitalist and capitalist respectively. Feudal relations of exploitation relied upon peasant workers being *unfree* in two distinct ways: from choosing their own conditions of work, and from having to undertake subsistence production to reproduce themselves (Marx, 1976; Lerche, 2011). The transition to capitalist waged work following the penetration of capitalism in the countryside would therefore see peasants divorced from owning their means of production in the form of land, and free to choose waged work in a wider labour market. Yet the reality of transition across much of the global South highlights the messy realities of actually existing labour relations. In Laos, for example, Brown (2019) charts how semi-subsistence producers continue to produce their own food while also undertaking low-paid waged work, with wages remaining too low to allow for food purchasing. Additionally in India, Breman's work (2007) has highlighted the proliferation of new types of bondage under neoliberal restructuring of the countryside, as historical patterns of caste and class-based discrimination are reproduced to (re) engender exploitative labour relations, albeit for profit-driven motives.

In an attempt to make sense of this complex picture, Banaji (1977, 2003) has argued that unfree labour relations exist as part of exploitation under *capitalist* accumulation. Viewing Marx's mode of capitalist production at an abstracted level rather than at the concrete, micro-level of labour relations, Banaji suggests that unfree labour is one among a number of methods through which capital exploits labour beyond the wage relation, rather than a residual form of oppression that will disappear with deeper capitalist penetration (see, for example, Rao, 2014). In thinking about this specifically with regard to debt bondage, LeBaron (2014) has argued that debt under neoliberal capitalism represents a class-based form of labour discipline, both in terms of unregulated private debts driving poor households into low-paid, precarious work, and more directly through debt-bonded labour relations. Banaji (2003) suggests the very notion of *free* labour as an oppositional category to *unfree* labour appears irrelevant, given that all labour is subject to class-based oppression. In this regard, LeBaron's work highlights the particular ways in which debt can discipline and thus oppress the unfree working poor. In exploring the contours of labour unfreedom Lerche (2011, 7) has argued for a 'continuum' approach, suggesting that 'most of the labour relations which today are classified as unfree labour share characteristics with a wider set of [labour] relations, both with regard to the underlying processes which lead to their creation by capital and concerning conditions of work and pay for labour'. This recasting of debt bondage within a wider context of labour exploitation leads us to explore *how* and *why* workers become unfree and to demonstrate how such unfreedom is engendered beyond the immediate labour–employer relation through debt discipline.

Responding to Thieme's challenge to uncover the generative possibilities of informal work, we argue that viewing unfree labour as part of a wider set of labour relations offers scope to understand how workers may conceive of such labour as offering potential for material uplift. For example, Guérin's work on debt bondage in Tamil Nadu, India, (2013, 419) illuminates the fact that in less severe instances of seasonal bondage in the brick sector, 'rising aspirations for equality and integration, as exemplified by the desire for consumption' drive workers to seek out such unfree labour relations. Similarly, in her study of seasonal brick workers migrating from the Indian state of Jharkhand to difficult conditions on kilns in other states, Shah (2006) flags the need to look beyond the confines of economic imperatives in explaining migrant choices. Young Jharkhandi migrants are shown to opt for seasonal migration as 'a temporary escape from a problem at home and an opportunity to explore a new country, gain independence from parents, and live out prohibited amorous relationships' in the context of broader structures of capitalist exploitation (Shah, 2006, 93). This latter point is key. While the decision to engage in unfree and exploitative labour may be driven by such aspirations, both Guérin and Shah remain pessimistic about the potential for uplift within such work. This chapter foregrounds both the oppression experienced at Cambodia's brick kilns and the hope that led workers to them. In the process, we stress the importance of looking beyond structural drivers alone for understanding the move to unfree labour, while remaining cautious about the generative possibilities of such work.

Agency and constraint: the journey from village to kiln in Cambodia

In exploring how and why workers came to be debt bonded on brick kilns in Cambodia, we were surprised to find that Cambodian workers *chose* to move to kilns. This is contrary to wider accounts of forced or trafficked labour, under the aegis of 'modern slavery', which stress that coercion is implicit in debt bondage (see, for example, Antislavery, 2018). The majority of brick workers we interviewed were previously rural labourers, or small or marginal farmers in villages across Cambodia. The central driver that brought the majority of these former farmers and farm workers into the kiln was debt incurred outside of the kiln.

Respondents repeatedly indicated that they had become over-indebted to microfinance institutions and local money lenders in villages, and had sold their whole debt to the brick kiln owner, in exchange for a consolidated debt bond which saw them, and usually their immediate family, compelled to move to a brick kiln to pay this off (Brickell et al, 2018). There were certainly variations among different kiln workers as to the levels of debt, with an average of US $712[1] of debt among the 51 brick workers interviewed. However, a key trope repeated among workers in explaining their decision to swap their debts for a debt bond was the feeling of being *over-indebted*.

> 'After borrowing, I had no money to repay. Then, I went to borrow more from others to repay my first debt. Therefore, my debts increased and I paid only the interest ... I have sold my land to repay the debt but it is still not enough, so to fully repay that debt I have borrowed more from the owner at the brick kiln.' (Kunthea, debt-bonded brick kiln worker)

As Schicks has indicated (2010, 2013), the issue of what constitutes over-indebtedness remains thorny, with the majority of accepted definitions prioritizing risk avoidance for lenders as opposed to borrowers. Schicks develops what she terms a 'customer protection'-led definition to define a debtor as over-indebted 'if he/she is continuously struggling to meet repayment deadlines and structurally has to make unduly high sacrifices related to his/her loan obligations' (2013, 1239). As Kunthea highlights, her initial debt leads her to take on further debts to service it, and this eventually results in a debt bond, in lieu of further indebtedness to microfinance institutions and informal lenders. The swapping of a debt for debt-bonded labour certainly warrants the definition 'unduly high sacrifices', thus the majority of brick workers that we interviewed fit within Schicks' notion.

While Kunthea made a choice to enter into unfree labour relations, we argue that in this context choice needs to be understood as a form of 'constrained agency' (Coe and Jordhus-Lier, 2011). Surveys and interviews conducted in three villages with high levels of out-migration to brick kilns (see Brickell et al, 2018) reveal that the confluence of rural marketization – in particular land redistribution policies and the shift to more commercial cropping, combined with the impacts of climate change, the lack of available healthcare and social protection, and the rise in unsustainable microfinance lending – culminated in the decision by certain families to swap debt for debt bondage.

The shifts in land tenure and land distribution in the last half-century have played a significant role in shaping structural insecurity and precarity among rural households. Following the end of the genocidal Khmer Rouge era in 1979, the Vietnamese-backed 'People's Republic of Kampuchea' government was installed and remained in place until the early 1990s. In this period, the refusal of the US and other key international allies to back this government, instead pumping aid into the fragmented remnants of the Khmer Rouge, saw Cambodia undergo a period of political isolation and economic decline (Hughes, 2003). In the aftermath of the Khmer Rouge (2003), the new government instigated a system of land redistribution, whereby each family member of a given family was given approximately one third of an acre to farm in the region where the three study villages were located. Interviews with brick-sending households highlighted the difficulties in cultivating such land in a situation where households had no income or capital, and research highlighted a period of semi-subsistence farming, petty business, and land sales in the 1980s. Poorer households, in particular, sold land and opted to rely on waged work in the village on other people's farms, as well as foraging and fishing in communal lands. A process of class differentiation was thus under way, whereby a class of rural landless working households was forged, alongside small and marginal farming households that relied on both waged work and agricultural production, and a smaller elite of rural capitalists.

Aside from intra-village land transfers, the process of land titling that began in the late 1980s and continues to the present day has had profound impacts on rural livelihoods (Beban and Gorman, 2017; Schoenberger, 2017; Diepart et al, 2019) and has led to deepening class differentiation in our three study villages. This differentiation emerged as part of Cambodia's broader shift towards a neoliberal growth trajectory from the early 1990s onwards, with governance under Prime Minister Hun Sen's Cambodian People's Party (CPP) since 1997, leading the country to be heavily reliant both on foreign aid and foreign direct investment. Since the 1980s, and strengthened under CPP rule, the World Bank and partner multilateral agencies have ushered in a process of land titling that has seen communal grazing, fishing and foraging lands placed into private hands, and the seizure of millions of hectares of land from rural people to private entities

(LICADHO, 2012). Female brick workers Kolab and Phary have experienced the impacts of such land policies first hand:

Kolab: '[People began to work on this kiln] because they had no land to grow rice anymore ... They had land in the forest, but now they sold all of it to the owner of the brick kiln ... Some sold their land, so others followed them to do so one after another.'

Phary: 'We had to follow them when our land was in the middle of others' land. We had to make the last decision.'

Kolab: 'All people sold off their land, why we still kept ours in the middle? It was impossible.'

Phary: 'People sold their land in order, one after another.'

A minority of kiln workers interviewed were not debt bonded and had come to work on kilns following the sale of land to a kiln owner. For example, a kiln owner purchased large parcels of communal and private land in Kolab and Phary's village, leaving their landholding stranded in a sea of privatized land, leading them to *choose* to sell. The wider move towards titling and land sales enabled such instances of large-scale land appropriation, and again emphasizes how choices made by Kolab and Phary are both emblematic of their resilience to the broader workings of capitalist accumulation in Cambodia (Katz, 2004; Natarajan et al, 2019b), while also being entangled in evolving processes of labour exploitation.

The impacts of land privatization upon the rural poor are also manifest in the three study villages. Landless households in particular reported that the loss of access to communal lands had a negative impact on food security. Land titling formed part of a broader shift towards agricultural commercialization, as neoliberal governance placed an onus upon commercial farming in rice and other cash crops (World Bank, 2015; Parsons, 2017).

'My rice land is too small, so by just cultivating rice I was unable to feed my family members. That's why we found this job ... The sales from rice production were not enough to pay off debts, because we spent a lot of money before farming on fertiliser and labour costs.' (Malis, female debt-bonded brick worker)

Malis highlights how the financial costs of commercial agricultural production – requiring chemical inputs and waged labour – were drivers of debt taking and debt bondage. He was thus resigned to abandoning agricultural work. The vagaries of climate change, in particular floods and droughts, were also a key factor affecting agricultural production in Cambodia. As Leakeana, a bonded brick kiln worker and former farmer highlighted, "I rented 3.4 hectares of rice fields, but they were all destroyed by flood, so I decided to borrow money from PRASAC."[2] The impacts of climate were unquestioningly felt most profoundly within the wider conditions of precarity faced by aspiring commercial smallholders (Natarajan et al, 2019a).

Another key reason for debt taking was ill-health, as Roumjoung's words highlighted at the start of this chapter. Other workers also noted this: "Four years ago, I got sick and went to borrow money from micro finance. Since I was not able to repay, I decided to work at brick kiln" (Makara, debt-bonded brick worker). Cambodia's poor social safety net and patchy healthcare coverage, reliant in large part on NGO presence (Kwon et al, 2015), meant that just one illness could tip a family into a livelihood crisis (Krishna, 2010). Crucially, rural respondents repeatedly indicated that they took on loans, and associated debt, as a means of coping.

'We do farming which we need the capital to buy the fertiliser, if we do not have money, we have to borrow from them. And I sold my land to pay off to them.' (Sangha, female debt-bonded brick worker)

'My kid was getting sick, and I borrowed money for treatment ... After that, my kid was dead, and I had to pay for loan interest. Because I could not effort to repay the loan, I had decided to sell my agricultural land. To earn money for daily spending, I was hired for transplanting and harvesting.' (Samrin, male debt-bonded brick worker)

The proliferation of credit options flooding the market in the past decade in particular have offered poor rural households a means of accessing immediate liquidity, both for coping and for more aspirational endeavours, and almost entirely under the aegis of 'microfinance'. The commercialization and deregulation of microfinance in Cambodia has seen it move from a developmental to profit-oriented scheme, seeking out increasingly vulnerable borrowers in its bid to expand (Bateman, 2017; Bateman et al, 2019). Crucially, microfinance institutions increasingly take homestead land titles as collateral and place borrowers on stringent monthly repayment schedules, with late payments resulting in seizure of homeland. The stakes are thus worryingly high and place immense pressure on families to keep up repayments.

The most vulnerable borrowers are among those that chose to swap multiple debts for debt bondage on kilns. Research among our study villages highlighted that debt levels between households with brick kiln workers and households without varied significantly. The former held an average debt of US $1,380.93, and the latter US $814.72. To contextualize, gross national income per capita in Cambodia in 2016 was US $1,140 (World Bank, 2016). Thus higher levels of debt compelled over-indebtedness, and led individuals to sacrifice themselves through debt bondage. Villagers sought out kiln owners, in most cases through regional ties between particular villages and kilns, and asked for a single advance sum to pay off local debts, agreeing in return to move to the kiln, often with whole families in tow.

In the context of such over-indebtedness, and returning to the notion of generative capacity, our research demonstrates that the move onto brick kilns was an active choice and a relief for many. Yet workers varied in their depiction of the kiln and kiln owner.

'We have to work here because of debt; it not we decided to leave this place long ago. This is our unsolved problem, but the loan from the boss is without interest. If the boss allows us, all of us will go back home because of our hard work. People prefer to rent land for growing rice or vegetables; as for us, we're in debt so we couldn't do this. If we had enough money we would repay him the loan.' (Kosal, male debt-bonded brick worker)

Kosal makes clear that the 'sacrifice' of over-indebtedness is reproduced on the kiln, as bondage represents a compulsion and not a clear choice. He was thus resigned to working in the kiln. Nonetheless, kiln work did offer respite from debt repayments for many, as indicated by Roumjoung at the start of this chapter, and by Sokhanya, a female debt-bonded brick worker: "We were jobless. We came here so we could borrow money to pay back the debt at home, and we've continued living here since then ... Beside growing rice, people are jobless. And my village has water shortage."

In the context of limited and precarious livelihood opportunities in rural Cambodia, debt-bonded work on the brick kilns represents an alternative avenue for survival. In this context brick kiln workers are part of a broader labour migration in Southeast Asia that moves to urban and peri-urban areas in the hope of realizing some of the benefits of the urbanization boom. However, more often, those hopes are unrealized. The next section explores the generative capacities of brick work for those that have chosen debt bondage.

The contours of unfreedom in Cambodian brick kilns

Cambodian brick workers labour in conditions of severe unfreedom. The contours of unfreedom are forged both by the broader structural forces driving the rise in such exploitative work, and by the immediate conditions of work on brick kilns. We have argued that the move to the kiln is largely a constrained *choice*. In this section we turn to the question of how capitalist accumulation in the current era is forged through engendering unfreedoms for workers, and the concomitant foreclosure of generative capacities that this entails.

Kiln work is difficult and unsafe, Workers are required to first move wet clay from trucks onto piles, then to clean it. Cleaned clay is placed by hand into a brick moulding machine, with reported incidents of limb amputation from this piece of machinery. Moulded bricks are then carried into the sun and left to dry, before being placed in a kin and fired over up to ten days. Workers stoke kiln fires for 12-hour shifts or longer, with little to no protective equipment, and fumes from fires are often highly unsafe, with garment off-cuts often burned in lieu of wood (see Crang et al, 2020). As Achariya, a female debt-bonded brick worker, explained, "The work in the brick factory is so difficult nowadays. If only I had other choices. If I wasn't still in debt, I would have let all my children go elsewhere." The nature of kiln labour is thus *severely unfree*, where unfree labour is understood to be part of a continuum of relations comprising increasingly severe restrictions upon workers, representing techniques to 'discipline and cheapen labour' (Lerche, 2011, 23). For Achariya, work itself was difficult, and the ability to move beyond it and choose something else was curtailed by the bonds of debt to the kiln owner. In practice, kiln wages were too low to enable workers to make ends meet: "We can work only here. We can work somewhere else after the loan is repaid ... we just earn 10,000 riels or 20,000 riels [US $2.4 –$4.90] per day. It is not even enough to make a living." The reality is that brick kiln workers could barely cover their daily expenses, let alone repay their bonded loans and quit the kiln in the longer term.

The low-paid, piece-rate structure of brick kiln wages compelled kiln workers to maximize their productivity, which meant children were often pushed into kiln work to increase the family income. Entire families were left without sufficient recompense to enable them to both repay their debts and pay for daily expenses.

> 'No matter how much I try to work every day, I can only make ends meet. I can't find the money to pay him [the brick kiln owner] back even 200,000 riels or 300,000 riels [US $50 or $73]. I don't even have 100,000 riels [US $25] ... I have to try my best to work for the boss and pay him bit by bit. I have no other way because I have nothing.' (Davuth, male debt-bonded brick worker)

As Davuth says, debt therefore becomes a material bond between worker and owner, and the basis for exploitative working relations. The bond compels workers to remain in low-paid work with poor conditions, thus curtailing their relative freedoms vis-à-vis others in the labour market. Low wages further lead some families to incur further debts on the kiln, particularly in the 'low season', when rains place a halt on production. As Piseth, a male debt-bonded brick worker, explained, "We're just sitting here waiting for the rain to pass. We can break up (clay) soil and collect it to be crushed. This is our hardship. Even though we want to leave, we're not permitted." Many workers, like Piseth, were prevented from leaving in the low season and were therefore forced to borrow from kiln owners, and increase their debt.

The full-time nature of this work contrasts with debt bondage in south India's brick kilns, where labour advance systems are seasonal and temporarily bind workers to the kiln for a period of months (see Guérin, 2013). Conditions on Cambodian kilns are also dangerous. While a national survey (Parsons and Ly Vouch, 2019) revealed unevenness in terms of the technological advancement of kilns, a number of kilns in our study continued to use hazardous equipment such as manual brick moulding machines, which reduce costs but risk limb amputations among adults and children. In general, a large component of kiln work involves being exposed to unremitting heat in the form of kiln fires, often for days on end. Workers complain of dizziness, vomiting, headaches and longer-term issues such as organ failure and even unexplained deaths. Kilns burn a range of substances, including rice husks and garment fragments that emit noxious gases (see Crang et al, 2020 for more information from our study). Malis, a female debt-bonded brick worker, highlighted the occupational health effects of kiln work: "The more I'm sick the more debt I take on. And my wage is just enough for daily spending only." In instances of ill-health, kiln owners forced workers to take on increased debts in order to access medical treatments. Labour exploitation thus degrades workers' bodies, and kiln owners deepen their corporeal exploitation through financializing the costs of addressing this.

These narratives lay bare the unfree conditions of kiln work and the contours of unfreedom on the kiln itself. They highlight the material constraints on workers' ability to find safety, dignity and material ascension in their work, and to look beyond the bonds of debt. When workers *were* able to move off the kilns, they did so not through their own wages, but often through wages from a family member in a unionized sector of the economy, such as garment work. Certainly life was lived on the kiln – families came together to help one another, children played together amidst the brick piles and kiln fumes, friendships were forged among workers, fights broke out, and forms of religious worship were sustained and even strengthened (Parsons and Brickell, 2020). Yet this is not, we argue, evidence of the kiln being *generative* in terms of livelihood opportunities. A repeated refrain was the conceptualization of kiln life as temporary and transitory. We have written elsewhere (see Natarajan et al, 2019b) that workers aspire to move beyond the kiln and back to rural life. They conceptualize this aspiration as a form of *resilience* – 'restorative and strengthening acts' – that are early on the path to structural resistance (Katz, 2004, 242). In this regard, imaginaries of life beyond the kiln speak to the lack of generative capacities on it. In fact, the recasting of kiln life as temporary highlights how aspiration for life beyond the kiln drives exploitation on it, as workers desperate to repay debts push themselves and their children to over-work.

Yet in addressing the challenge from Gibson–Graham (2008) to examine the generative potential of work outside the capitalist wage relation, we have shown that for the case of kiln workers, generative capacities at the individual level are embedded in, and constrained by, broader structures of exploitation and appropriation, which devalue and disempower people's aspirations. Furthermore, the disempowerment of workers into unfree labour conditions is part of a wider strategy on the part of capital to discipline workers, and through this, increase exploitation in late capitalist contexts. As LeBaron argues (2014, 765), 'there is a need to understand debt bondage as a profitable strategy of labor discipline that appears to be accelerating within advanced capitalist countries'.

Debt-bonded brick workers in Cambodia produce incredibly cheap bricks to fuel the country's urban construction boom, which, driven by domestic and foreign investment, represents one of the top three most profitable sectors in the country, vying for the top spot year on year with the garments and services sectors (World Bank, 2019). Rather than representing a unique or exceptional case, we argue that the brick kiln sector's practices of debt bondage and its profits are at the heart of Cambodia's capital accumulation strategy. Research from one kiln suggested that labour costs constituted 21.1 per cent of production costs, totalling USD $3,316 (including labour, materials and transport) for 200,000 bricks, and 8.8 per cent of sale costs, with one load of 20,000 bricks selling for USD $8,000 (Brickell et al, 2018). A cursory glance at these figures tells us that labour costs could be raised considerably while still ensuring profits for kiln owners, yet as our research highlights, it is the system of debt bondage, comprising piece-rate low wages, discipline on mobility and bodily exploitation that underpins such high returns. Thus, in paying heed to workers' aspirations and the forms of resilience without a clear understanding of how and why these processes are curtailed, we risk fetishizing the possibilities for resistance in a context where systemic exploitation prevents it. Furthermore, in thinking through the possibilities for progressive politics in wageless contexts such as the one we document here, we argue that analysis of the creative and generative capacities of those engaged in informal work needs to begin by asking *how* such capacities can be empowered through structural reform, thus focusing on systemic rather than individual conceptualizations of poverty and vulnerability (Hickey and du Toit, 2007).

Conclusion

In this chapter, we have sought to analyse the narratives of debt-bonded brick workers in and around Cambodia's capital city, Phnom Penh, in order to document experiences of unfree labour. We have argued that workers' unfreedom was forged and chosen by individuals and families, and simultaneously delimited the capacity for generative aspirations. A confluence of climate change, rural marketization and deregulated microfinance created the conditions for over-indebtedness, consigning rural households to an exit from subsistence agriculture and an entry into debt bondage. We have further highlighted how the exploitative relations of debt bondage and forms of labour discipline on the kiln, enacted through the bonds of debt, foreclosed the generative capacity of kiln work. The profits generated through such work drive GDP growth in Cambodia, and thus the debt-disciplined exploitation of workers through severe unfree labour is at the heart of the country's capitalist growth.

In thinking through the broader questions of unfree labour and the generative capacity of informal work, we have illustrated the agency of rural households in *choosing* to take on debt bondage, while asking: what does this choice tell us about the wider choices available to such households? In her analysis of debt as a form of class-based discipline, LeBaron (2014, 772) suggests that such discipline manifests both in a direct sense, in debt-bonded labour relations, and more structurally through 'debt-fuelled labor discipline', compelling over-indebted workers into precarious and exploitative jobs. Thus, in understanding how debt indirectly and directly forges unfree labour relations; what appears as a choice on the part of workers is recast into a form of labour control, with rural households moving to kilns as a means of avoiding deeper crisis.

This chapter ultimately argues that exploring both the contours of and constraints upon choices, aspirations and resistance among workers in severely exploitative labour relations is central to analysis of work beyond the wage, and how it both opens and forecloses opportunities for social uplift. By bringing unfree labour to the fore within wider discussions of non-waged work (Pettinger, 2019), we are able to emphasize the constraining forces of work, alongside more optimistic accounts, with a particular focus on the disciplining force of debt upon aspiration (LeBaron, 2014). Placing the locus of analysis simultaneously within worker narratives and structural political economy, our multiscalar analysis has thus foregrounded how individual aspirations viewed through wider structures of oppression recast our understanding of aspiration, and through this, our understanding of the generative potential of work beyond the wage.

Acknowledgements

We are grateful to the many respondents who were part of our research and who enabled us to develop our analysis in this chapter, and to the Cambodian research assistants who were central to our work. We also thank the editors for their insightful comments. The research in this study was funded by the ESRC and the former UK Department for International Development (ref: ES/R00238X/1). Katherine Brickell would like to express her gratitude to the Leverhulme Trust for her Philip Leverhulme Prize (PLP-2016–127), which supported her during the writing of this chapter, and Laurie Parsons is grateful to the British Academy for his Postdoctoral Fellowship (ref: pf170152). Access requests to underlying research materials should be addressed to rdm@royalholloway.ac.uk.

Notes

[1] To put this in context, gross national income per capita in Cambodia in 2017 was US $3770 (World Bank, 2018).

[2] This is one of the largest commercial Microfinance Institutions in Cambodia.

References

Antislavery (2018) What is modern slavery? *Antislavery.org*, available at https://www.antislavery.org/slavery-today/modern-slavery/

Bales, K. (2002) 'The social psychology of modern slavery', *Scientific American*, 286(4): 80–88.

Banaji, J. (1977) 'Capitalist domination and the small peasantry: Deccan districts in the late nineteenth century', *Economic and Political Weekly*, 12(33/34): 1375–1404.

Banaji, J. (2003) 'The fictions of free labour: Contract, coercion, and so-called unfree labour', *Historical Materialism*, 11(3): 69–95.

Bateman, M. (2017) 'Post-War reconstruction and development in Cambodia and the destructive role of microcredit', presented at the 8th International Scientific Conference 'Future World by 2050', Pula, Croatia.

Bateman, M., Natarajan, N., Brickell, K. and Parsons, L. (2019) Descending into Debt in Cambodia, *Made in China*, available at: https://madeinchinajournal.com/2019/04/18/descending-into-debt-in-cambodia

Beban, A. and Gorman, T. (2017) 'From land grab to agrarian transition? Hybrid trajectories of accumulation and environmental change on the Cambodia–Vietnam border', *The Journal of Peasant Studies*, 44(4): 748–768.

Bernstein, H. (2006) 'Once were/still are peasants? Farming in a globalising "south"', *New Political Economy*, 11(3): 399–406.

Breman, J. (2007) *Labour Bondage in West India: From Past to Present*, New Delhi: Oxford University Press.

Breman, J. and Agarwal, R. (2002) 'Down and out: Laboring under global capitalism', *Critical Asian Studies*, 34(1): 116–128.

Breman, J. and van der Linden, M. (2014) 'Informalizing the economy: The return of the social question at a global level', *Development and Change*, 45(5): 920–490.

Brickell, K. and Datta, A. (2011) L'Introduction: Translocal geographies', in Brickell, K. and Datta, A. (eds) *Translocal Geographies: Spaces, Places, Connections*, Abingdon: Routledge.

Brickell, K., Parsons, L., Natarajan, N. and Chann, S. (2018) *Blood Bricks: Untold Stories of Modern Slavery and Climate Change in Cambodia*, London: Royal Holloway, University of London.

Brown, J.A. (2019) 'Territorial (in) coherence: Labour and special economic zones in Laos's border manufacturing', *Antipode*, 51(2): 438–457.

Coe, N.M. and Jordhus-Lier, D.C. (2011) 'Constrained agency? Re-evaluating the geographies of labour', *Progress in Human Geography*, 35(2): 211–233.

Crang, P., Brickell, K., Parsons, L., Natarajan, N., Cristofoletti, T. and Graham, N. (2020) 'Discardscapes of fashion: Commodity biography, patch geographies, and preconsumer garment waste in Cambodia', *Social & Cultural Geography*, 1–20.

Davis, M. (2006) *Planet of Slums*, London: Verso.

De Soto, H. (1989) *The Other Path: The Economic Answer to Terrorism*, New York, NY: Harper Collins.

Diepart, J.-C., Ngin, C. and Oeur, I. (2019) 'Struggles for life: Smallholder farmers' resistance and state land relations in contemporary Cambodia', *Journal of Current Southeast Asian Affairs*, 38(1): 10–32.

Gibson-Graham, J.K. (2008) 'Diverse economies: Performative practices for "other worlds"', *Progress in Human Geography*, 32(5): 613–632.

Guérin, I. (2013) 'Bonded labour, agrarian changes and capitalism: Emerging patterns in South India', *Journal of Agrarian Change*, 13(3): 405–423.

Hickey, S. and du Toit, A. (2007) *Adverse Incorporation, Social Exclusion and Chronic Poverty*, Manchester: Chronic Poverty Research Centre, No. 81.

Hughes, C. (2003) *The Political Economy of Cambodia's Transition 1991–2001*, London: RoutledgeCurzon.

ILO (2018a) *World Employment Social Outlook: Trends*, Geneva: International Labour Organization.

ILO (2018b) *Women and Men in the Informal Economy: A Statistical Picture*, Geneva: International Labour Office.

Katz, C. (2004) *Growing Up Global: Economic Restructuring and Children's Everyday Lives*, Minneapolis, MN: University of Minnesota Press.

Krishna, A. (2010) *One Illness Away: Why People Become Poor and How they Escape Poverty*, Oxford: Oxford University Press.

Kwon, H., Cook, S. and Kim, Y. (2015) 'Shaping the national social protection strategy in Cambodia: Global influence and national ownership', *Global Social Policy*, 15(2): 125–145.

Lawreniuk, S. and Parsons, L. (2020) *Going Nowhere Fast: Mobile Inequality in the Age of Translocality*, Oxford: Oxford University Press.

Lazzarato, M. (2012) *The Making of the Indebted Man: An Essay on the Neoliberal Condition*, Los Angeles, CA: Semiotext(e).

LeBaron, G. (2014) 'Reconceptualizing debt bondage: Debt as a class-based form of labor discipline', *Critical Sociology*, 40(5): 763–780.

Lerche, J. (2011) 'The unfree labour category and unfree labour estimates: A continuum within low-end labour relations? *Manchester Papers in Political Economy*, (10): 1–45.

Li, T.M. (2009) 'To make live or let die? Rural dispossession and the protection of surplus populations', *Antipode*, 41(s1): 66–93.

LICADHO (2012) *The Great Cambodian Giveaway: Visualizing Land Concessions over Time*, Phnom Penh: LICADHO.

Marx, K. (1976) *Capital: Critique of Political Economy, Volume I*, London: Penguin.

Munck, R. (2013) 'The precariat: A view from the South', *Third World Quarterly*, 34(5): 747–762.

Natarajan, N., Brickell, K. and Parsons, L. (2019a) 'Climate change adaptation and precarity across the rural–urban divide in Cambodia: Towards a "climate precarity" approach', *Environment and Planning E: Nature and Space*, 2514848619858155.

Natarajan, N., Parsons, L. and Brickell, K. (2019b) 'Debt-bonded brick kiln workers and their intent to return: Towards a labour geography of smallholder farming persistence in Cambodia', *Antipode*, 51(5): 1581–1599.

Parsons, L. (2017) 'Under pressure: Environmental risk and contemporary resilience strategies in rural Cambodia', in Brickell, K. and Springer, S. (eds) *The Handbook of Contemporary Cambodia*, Abingdon: Routledge, pp 146–156.

Parsons, L. and Brickell K. (2020) 'The spirit in the machine: Towards a spiritual geography of debt bondage and labour (im)mobility in Cambodian brick kilns', *Transactions of the Institute of British Geographers*.

Parsons, L. and Ly Vouch L. (2019) *A Census of the Cambodian Brick Industry: Population, Geography, Practice [DRAFT]*, Phnom Penh: Solidarity Centre.

Pettinger, L. (2019) *What's Wrong with Work?* Bristol: Policy Press.

Rao, J.M. (2014) 'Unfree labour under capitalism: A contradiction in (useful) terms', *Agrarian South: Journal of Political Economy*, 3(2): 151–178.

Roy, A. (2019) 'Slumdog cities: Rethinking subaltern urbanism', *International Journal of Urban and Regional Research*, 35(2): 223–238.

Schicks, J. (2010) *Microfinance Over-Indebtedness: Understanding Its Drivers and Challenging the Common Myths*, Brussels: Solvay Brussels School, Economics and Management, No. 10/048.

Schicks, J. (2013) 'The sacrifices of micro-borrowers in Ghana – A customer-protection perspective on measuring over-indebtedness', *The Journal of Development Studies*, 49(9): 1238–1255.

Schoenberger, L. (2017) 'Struggling against excuses: Winning back land in Cambodia', *The Journal of Peasant Studies*, 44(4): 870–890.

Shah, A. (2006) 'The labour of love: Seasonal migration from Jharkhand to the brick kilns of other states in India', *Contributions to Indian Sociology*, 40(1): 91–118.

Standing, G. (2011) *The Precariat: The New Dangerous Class*, London: Bloomsbury Academic.

Thieme, T.A. (2017) 'The hustle economy: Informality, uncertainty and the geographies of getting by', *Progress in Human Geography*, 42(4): 529–548.

UN (2015) Sustainable Development Goals: 17 Goals to Transform our World, *United Nations*, available from https://www.un.org/sustainabledevelopment/sustainable-development-goals/

World Bank (2015) *Cambodian Agriculture in Transition: Opportunities and Risks*, Washington, DC: World Bank Group: Agriculture.

World Bank (2016) *Cambodia Gross National Income per Capita*, Washington, DC: World Bank.

World Bank., (2018) *Cambodia Gross National Income per Capita*, Washington, DC: World Bank.

World Bank (2019) *Cambodia Economic Update: Recent Economic Developments and Outlook*, Phnom Penh: World Bank.

PART III

Struggles

8

"Earning Money as the Wheels Turn Around": Cycle-rickshaw Drivers and Wageless Work in Dhaka

Annemiek Prins

Jamal[1] had just arrived in Dhaka when I met him at a rickshaw garage on the outskirts of the city. It was the summer of 2017 and the ongoing monsoon rains were causing excessive flooding all over Bangladesh. Jamal told me that the floods had compelled him to leave behind his home village in the coastal area of Satkhira. As our conversation unfolded, it became clear that such rural–urban journeys had been common throughout his working life. Jamal first came to Dhaka in 2004 to sell fish at one of the city's wholesale markets. After four years he fell into trouble as the growing number of *hartals* (political strikes),[2] exploding petrol bombs and street fires that heralded Bangladesh's national election made it impossible to operate a business in Dhaka city. The political mayhem resulted in deliveries being held up and fresh fish going bad. Jamal decided to change strategies and started working as a vendor, selling cheap jewellery and cosmetics on the streets of Dhaka for over a year. However, the political turmoil persisted and after a while Jamal was forced to move back to the countryside. For some time, he could not bring himself to work at all. His lost investments and failed entrepreneurial endeavours had left him depressed and broke. With time, Jamal managed to pull himself back together and established a fish farm in his home village. However, the heavy monsoon rains and ensuing floods dealt him another blow by damaging part of his fish stock. To make up for his losses, he decided to spend four months in Dhaka to earn some extra cash as a cycle-rickshaw driver. His brother, a former rickshaw puller himself, introduced Jamal to the garage from where he rented his rickshaw. Feeling ashamed about his temporary job, Jamal spent his days avoiding the parts of the city where he might run into distant relatives or acquaintances and spent his nights at the makeshift attic above the garage where he slept in the company of 25 or so other rural–urban migrants.

There are hundreds of thousands of men like Jamal in Dhaka, ranging from energetic teenage boys to slow-pedalling senior drivers, who move in and out of the city's rickshaw industry as the seasons change, the rivers swell, investments are lost and political unrest builds. No one knows exactly how many cycle-rickshaws – let alone drivers – are operating in the crowded and rapidly growing capital of Bangladesh. Hardly any official licences have been awarded since the 1980s and estimates fluctuate between 500,000 and 1.1 million (RAJUK, 2015, chap. 5, 9; Hasan and Dávila, 2018, 247). These figures, moreover, do not correspond neatly with the number of rickshaw pullers in the city, considering that different men often take shifts driving the same vehicle. Furthermore, in the dry winter months quite a few rickshaw carts are left unused as temporary drivers like Jamal move back to the countryside to cultivate the different crops – rice, cauliflower, peanuts, carrot, lentils – that need tending to. The summer rains, on the other hand, instigate a small exodus from the countryside to the city as fields are submerged in water and opportunities for piecemeal agricultural work, with the exception of jute cutting, dry up. The same goes for the weeks that precede the two main Eid celebrations, when many rural labourers venture into the city to earn some extra cash to spend on the festivities.

This chapter highlights the nodal role that Dhaka's rickshaw industry plays amidst such rural–urban comings and goings and explores the significance of unwaged rickshaw labour in offering people like Jamal something to fall back on in times of economic and ecological crisis. Dhaka's rickshaw garages provide an accessible avenue for work that requires few formal skills and no investment capital and allows rural–urban migrants to come and go according to their needs and wishes. Rickshaws can be rented on a *per diem* basis and the only real requirement for prospective rickshaw pullers, in order to gain access to a vehicle, is that they have a neighbour or family member who can introduce and vouch for them with a rickshaw *malik* (owner). However, rickshaw driving is also seen as a physically demanding, and at times hazardous, profession. When I asked drivers about their motivations for joining the rickshaw industry, the default response was "We are helpless (*nirupay*)" or "We are bound to do this job." At the same time, this was never the full story, for rickshaw labour was understood to hold a significant advantage over low-end wage employment, such as factory work or agricultural day-labouring, which were understood to entail either waiting for money or waiting for work. Indeed, the rickshaw pullers I spoke with throughout my fieldwork consistently stressed that the work brought them "instant cash" (*nogod poysa*), "independence" (*nij sadhin*) and allowed them to "earn money as the wheels turn around" (*chaka ghurle taka*).

By analysing the nuanced narratives through which cycle-rickshaw pullers make sense of their strenuous labour, I join the efforts of other scholars to decentre wage labour as the inevitable starting point for making sense of work and work-related vulnerabilities (Denning, 2010; Millar, 2014; Ferguson and Li, 2018; Narotzky, 2018; Millar, 2019). The experiences of rickshaw drivers significantly blur intuitive distinctions between precarious self-employment and stable wage labour. Furthermore, drivers' insistence on the need for "instant cash" suggests that workers might have good reason to pursue forms of work that offer them cash-in-hand rather than regular wages. The work biographies of rickshaw drivers thus complicate universalist, class-based analyses that argue that precaritization results from people being 'pushed out' of stable wage employment (Standing, 2011). Indeed, the fact that their efforts to make a living often consist of multiple labour trajectories that intersect or overlap with one another makes it difficult to differentiate 'work' from other spheres of life.

The entanglement of waged work and 'nonwage, self-employed, homebased, piece-rate, and contract work' (Gidwani and Maringanti, 2016, 122) has been well documented by scholars working on South Asia and Bengal.[3] Ethnographers and historians have emphasized the long-standing coexistence and interpenetration of different livelihood strategies, including: family production, factory work, subsistence farming, day-labouring, sharecropping, entrepreneurship, tenancy, cottage industry work, and migration (De Haan, 1997a, 1997b; Sen, 1997; Bhattacharya, 1998; Van Schendel, 2006). The histories and realities of work in South Asia and Bengal therefore do not warrant the privileging of wage labour as an analytical category. In fact, wage workers in the so-called 'organized sector' have never formed more than one tenth of the working population of South Asia (Van Schendel, 2006, 231). Still, South Asian labour historiography has been significantly influenced by the emphasis that traditional Marxist theory has placed on the revolutionary potential of the industrial workforce. Indeed, Bhattacharya (2006, 10) observes that the field has long been characterized by a 'myopic concentration on the industrial wage-worker'.

The powerful image of the industrial wage worker has not only overshadowed histories and realities of work in South Asia. The tendency to consider wage labour and the employment contract as a near-universal norm also continues to misguide our understanding of life under capitalism (Denning, 2010; Narotzky, 2018), urban poverty (Das and Randeria, 2015), class politics (Millar, 2008; Gidwani and Maringanti, 2016), decent work (Munck, 2013; Barchiesi, 2016) and precarious labour conditions (Munck, 2013; Scully, 2016; Millar, 2017). Indeed, precarious work has commonly been conceptualized in relation to post-Fordist capitalism and the dismantling of full-time, lifelong, waged employment under neoliberal regimes (Millar, 2017, 3). However, for many low-income workers outside of Europe and North America, this kind of stability – or the promise thereof (Muehlebach and Shoshan, 2012) – has never been a reality. Moving beyond such a 'Northern' bias requires a clearer understanding of the ways in which work-related vulnerabilities differ across historical moments, geographic sites, and social positions (Neilson and Rossiter, 2008, 64).

In what follows, I aim to expand the vocabularies and imaginaries concerning work and work-related vulnerabilities by drawing on the emic categorizations that rickshaw drivers use to describe and contrast their work with other avenues of employment. In doing so, I respond to Van Schendel's (2006, 254) call for scholars to further unpack the great variety of Bengali expressions that signal labour, work, toil and income. In the first section of this chapter, I analyse what it means to "earn money as the wheels turn around". I show that the ability to earn "instant cash" stands in productive tension with what rickshaw drivers described as "*betone chakri kore*" (working for wages). In drawing this comparison, I push back against the idea that people do not take up forms of wageless work unless they are pushed out of stable waged employment. In the second section, I further substantiate this point by arguing that, although far from offering a secure or safe mode of employment, rickshaw labour offers workers a relatively 'stable refuge' (Millar, 2014, 39) in the context of ongoing ecological, economic and entrepreneurial emergencies.

Finally, in the last section of the chapter, I examine the ways in which this avenue of refuge is increasingly undermined by the implementation of rickshaw bans and restrictions in Dhaka city. I challenge the idea – which stems from the tendency to treat wageless work as a residual category (Denning, 2010) – that wageless or informal work is always already inherently precarious. Instead, I show that rickshaw labour is also subject to processes of precaritization. Rather than employer–employee relations, I highlight the role of the state and urban regulation in deepening work-related vulnerabilities. In analysing the effects of a specific set of rickshaw restrictions and regulations that were implemented in 2016, I show that what rickshaw drivers stand to lose is not the stability of a fixed-term contract, but a place to return to when faced with losses of various kinds.

The accounts presented here are the product of 11 months of ethnographic fieldwork in Dhaka between 2015 and 2018. The bulk of this fieldwork was spent at so-called 'rickshaw garages' in different parts of the city. Rickshaw garages are improvised, half-open storage spaces where rickshaw drivers either rent or park their vehicles,[4] and which function as makeshift hostels for the drivers who do not have a permanent place to stay in the city. Throughout my fieldwork I visited approximately 75 of these spaces and, with the help of a local research assistant, conducted semi-structured group discussions and individual interviews with both drivers and rickshaw owners.

Instant cash or waiting for wages?

Wageless work, including informal work, has often been interpreted as a 'situation of lack' or 'the space of exclusion' (Denning, 2010, 80). Denning (2010, 79) attributes this bias to the fact that classic Marxist readings of labour leave little conceptual room for the activities of people conducting wageless work, other than the residual categories of the 'reserve army of labour' and the 'lumpenproletariat'. Pettinger (2019, 115) has similarly argued that early modernization discourses of organizations such as the International Labour Organization (ILO) have turned informal work into a residual category by assuming that economic development would eventually get rid of informal work through formal sector absorption. This line of argument, however, glosses over the fact that people are not 'permanently quarantined within the informal economy' (Samson, 2015, 815). Indeed, there is much evidence to suggest that workers – especially in the South Asian context – constantly traverse the porous line between wage labour and wageless work (Gidwani and Maringanti, 2016, 122).

In more rigid, class-based analyses of precaritization such boundary crossing is frequently presented as evidence of what both Engels and Marx have described as the 'reserve army of labour' (Magdoff and Magdoff, 2004, 14; Wilson, 2019, 8). This notion entails that 'Both precarious and informalized workers constitute a "disposable" labor force that can be hired during periods of economic expansion and discarded during recession and economic contraction' (Wilson, 2019, 8). Such an understanding of the global labour market thus perpetuates the idea that wageless and informal workers constitute 'an amorphous labour force, hidden and informal, that is used flexibly to meet labour demand' (Pettinger, 2019, 116). The recurring assumption throughout such universalist, class-based approaches (see also Standing, 2011) is that people are actively excluded from waged employment by larger-than-life economic processes and would not voluntarily choose to take up forms of wageless work.

Ethnographic studies of unwaged work have challenged this tendency to approach wageless workers as a residual group of not-yet-absorbed or recently-pushed-out waged workers who can always be drawn back into the formal sector on a whim. Instead, such studies have shed light on the reasons why poor workers might prefer forms of informal work over the rigidity of waged employment (Millar, 2014; Sopranzetti 2017). Throughout my fieldwork I similarly found that many cycle-rickshaw drivers, although hesitant to label any aspect of their job as even remotely positive, were nonetheless convinced that driving a rickshaw held certain advantages over the forms of waged work available to them. This is illustrated by the story of Zubair, an older rickshaw puller in his sixties who had worked as a rickshaw driver for 15 years. When we met him he had been running his own rickshaw business for eight years and only occasionally drove a rickshaw himself.

Zubair first came to Dhaka in 1968; three years before the Bangladesh Independence War would engulf the country in nine months of bloodshed. He initially ran a small eatery, selling tea and rice, but his earnings dropped when the Pakistani army pitched a camp in front of his shop in 1971 and started demanding food for free. He retreated to the countryside and after Bangladesh had gained independence from Pakistan he returned to Dhaka to find his shop in ashes. For a while he worked as a cook in another restaurant, but gradually his lungs started to fail him as a result of working near smoke and fire all day long. His doctor urged him to quit and he started driving a rickshaw. He carefully weighed his words while reflecting on the nature of the job he had done for more than a decade: "It is not good that we cannot get a different job. But although the work is not good, we have some independence (*sadhinota*). We can get a bit more money than we would earn at a factory." He went on to elaborate that when he did not feel well or when his body was aching, he could decide to take some rest; an advantage that set the rickshaw industry apart from other low-skilled work. Zubair explained, "When you do a salaried job (*chakri*) you have to stay the entire day from eight in the morning till eight in the evening."

Zubair was not the only person to compare rickshaw labour with forms of factory work which required employees to be present during fixed hours and report to an ever-present boss. Indeed, many rickshaw drivers had worked in factories before getting married and starting a family. However, low-skilled factory work was regarded as a form of employment that did not generate a sufficient income for those who had to take care of their families and children. The contrast between factory work and driving a rickshaw was perhaps best explained by Jamila, one of the very few female rickshaw drivers in Dhaka. Jamila worked and lived in one of the city's peripheral neighbourhoods where, in contrast to the rest of the capital, battery-run rickshaws were tolerated by the police.[5] Operating an electric rickshaw, which is essentially a cycle-rickshaw with an added battery, is physically less demanding than driving a regular pedal rickshaw. As a consequence, it had begun to attract a few women to the industry. Jamila was a divorced single mother and like many of her male colleagues, she was the rice-winner of her family. She used to work in a shoe factory to provide for her two children, but now proudly operated a battery-run rickshaw and rode around the city wearing a sporty cap over her colourful headscarf. Jamila explained her decision to change occupations:

'In the past I used to work in a factory. At the factory they paid me 1100 *taka*[6] (US$12.98) per week, about 4000 taka (US$47.19) per four weeks. But 4000 taka per month is not enough. My rent is 3000 taka (US$35.39) per month … It takes a lot of effort. You have a "time-to-time duty"[7] from the moment you wake up. I could not give time to my children. I have one son and one daughter. Then I thought: "What can be done?" I was used to working like a man, because I agreed to face hard work for my children's future. … Then I thought: I will drive a rickshaw.'

During a focus group discussion with a group of male rickshaw drivers very similar remarks were made. Faisal, for example, complained that "working for wages" (*betone chakri kore*) was not worth the effort. Not only did waged work come with the risk of being abused by a superior, but salaries were also often insufficient and unreliable. He emphasized that they needed "instant cash" (*nogod poysa*), echoing a common refrain among rickshaw drivers. Yet another rickshaw puller recalled his days working as a cook. He used to work as part of a team of caterers who offered their services for weddings and celebrations. What made this work difficult, however, was the fact that the supervisor would often only distribute the money after two or three days. The 32-year-old Rahat summarized their predicament as follows: "We are poor people (*gorib manus*), we cannot wait for money." He added that the work was very hard (*kosto besi*), but at least offered them instant cash. Hence, whereas factory work involved "waiting for wages", rickshaw labour enabled workers to "earn money as the wheels turn around".

This strong preference for work that did not require "waiting for money" was born out of necessity rather than principle and did not necessarily coincide with an objection to all forms of waged employment. The jobs that rickshaw pullers considered stable or desirable, namely so-called "government jobs", however, were often out of reach. In Bangladesh, working in a public institution is associated with lifelong employment, pensions and other benefits. Moreover, even low-level salaried government jobs are considered to be a gateway to becoming middle class (Kibria, 1995, 296). Rickshaw drivers were always quick to point out that one needed *ghush* (bribe money) in order to be able to land a government job. Kibria (1995) also alludes to this point in her work among Bangladeshi garment workers. She describes how one woman told her 'that she was saving her wages to pay the bribe that was necessary for her husband to get a salaried government job' (Kibria, 1995, 301). These commonplace practices of bribery meant that even for rickshaw drivers who had gone through secondary education, finding a "government job" was far from easy.

The difficulties of acquiring a job in the public sector are perhaps best exemplified by the story of Ravi, a young, unmarried rickshaw driver who had just completed his secondary school education when we conducted a short interview with him at a rickshaw garage. Ravi had arrived in Dhaka only five days prior to our conversation. He drove a rickshaw irregularly and lived in Nilphamari, a district in the far northern corner of Bangladesh. Ravi only travelled to Dhaka when he needed some extra cash, either because he could not cover his education costs or because he simply wanted to buy a new item, such as a mobile phone. Although he had successfully obtained his Secondary School Certificate (SCC), Ravi was rather pessimistic about his opportunities for landing a "government job". He had tried to join the police, but this had turned out to be a rather expensive affair. To enter the police force he needed to pay nine *lakh*[8] taka (US\$10,617) in bribe money but Ravi could only afford seven lakh. Such payments were not unique to government jobs. In fact, many of the long-term strategies that rickshaw drivers pursued in the hope of escaping poverty, such as starting a business, migrating abroad or acquiring a piece of land, were both cost intensive and financially risky. Rickshaw work is thus entangled with various other livelihood activities and projects, for, as we will see in the next section, the rickshaw industry provides workers with a relatively stable refuge when other labour projects are sidetracked or unsustainable.

A stable site of return

In the previous section I have shown that one of the main reasons why rickshaw pullers turn to wageless work and, in particular, to the rickshaw industry is that it offers them instant cash where other available jobs leave them waiting for wages. In addition, pedalling a rickshaw was also seen as a more gainful form of employment than low-skilled work in the industrial or service sector. The experiences of rickshaw drivers thus complicate the idea that wageless work is ultimately a residual category that workers turn to after they have been pushed out of waged employment. Millar (2014, 2018) makes a similar point in her ethnographic work on garbage collectors or *catadores* in Rio de Janeiro. She describes how many of her interlocutors had worked for wages at some point during their lives but found it difficult to adapt to the rigidity and regularity of a fixed-hours contract (Millar, 2014, 48). Short episodes of waged labour were therefore interrupted by frequent returns to the garbage dump. This has prompted Millar (2014, 33) to present the ever-present, always-available garbage dump not as a last resort, but as a site of 'continual return'.

From what follows it will become clear that the rickshaw industry similarly functions as a site of return, although not entirely in the same way as the Rio de Janeiro garbage dump in Millar's example. Millar (2014, 2018) argues that people's frequent returns to the dump should be understood in terms of the everyday emergencies – prompted by disease, eviction or accidents – that inevitably coincide with life in poverty. She argues that the destabilizing effects of precarious living made it difficult for workers to adjust to the regularity of fixed-hours contracts. The garbage dump, on the other hand, offered *catadores* a degree of autonomy that enabled them to 'sustain relationships, fulfil social obligations, and pursue life projects in an uncertain everyday' (Millar, 2014, 36). The rickshaw industry similarly affords such experiences of autonomy, as becomes clear from the emphasis that rickshaw drivers put on the independent (*sadhinota, nij sadhin*) nature of the work. However, the rickshaw industry not only makes it possible for workers to cope with everyday emergencies and familial obligations, but also, crucially, offers them an avenue of refuge when other labour projects fail. In fact, rickshaw labour should be understood as part of a wider web of agricultural, entrepreneurial, migrational and familial strategies that rickshaw drivers pursue in order to escape poverty.

The relative appeal of the rickshaw sector can be interpreted as part of a wider trend towards the diversification of livelihood strategies by poor rural families in the face of landlessness or agricultural stagnation (Van Schendel, 1986; Toufique and Turton, 2002; Gardner, 2012). People's decisions to take up rickshaw labour therefore cannot be analysed in isolation from rural realities and vulnerabilities. Indeed, the most important reason why the rickshaw industry functions as a continual site of return for rickshaw drivers is because many of them lead multi-local lives across city and countryside. In fact, the Bangladesh Institute of Labour Studies (BILS) found, based on a survey of 200 participants, that although 94 per cent of rickshaw pullers were married, only 45 per cent rented a room in the city with their family (Karim and Salam, 2019, 38). Furthermore, over 80 per cent of the rickshaw pullers that were interviewed spent at least some time, eight days on average, at their rural home every six months, while two thirds of them travelled home once every three months (Karim and Salam, 2019, 46).

I first became aware of this profoundly multi-local lifestyle during a group discussion with five rickshaw drivers at a dilapidated workers' hostel in Old Dhaka. The men explained to us that it would be common for them to return to their home villages after six weeks of work in the city and to stay with their wives and families in the countryside for approximately two weeks. In the dry winter months these rural stays sometimes extended to two or three months, as opportunities for agricultural day-labouring opened up. None of the men, however, considered this form of day-labouring to be a sustainable avenue for long-term employment. In a clear and calm voice, a rickshaw driver called Jiyad started to explain their situation: "At present the living costs in Bangladesh are too high. If I did a different job, I would not be able to maintain my family." He added the Bengali word *to* for emphasis, underlining that his choice to operate a rickshaw for a living was mostly a negative one. "I would prefer to do a different job. I would rather work the fields in the countryside, but the salary is 300 taka (US$3.54) [per day]. With 300 taka I cannot run my family." Fahim, who entertained the idea of leaving Bangladesh altogether to try his luck as a labourer in one of the Gulf States, further elaborated, "When you earn 500 taka (US$5.90) or more it is possible to maintain your family." He went on to specify that driving a rickshaw for a full day could earn them as much as 700 or 800 taka (US$8.26–9.44).

Agricultural labour, on the other hand, usually entailed "waiting for work" as employment opportunities fluctuated with the seasons. Or in the words of Khadim, "Every day of work is followed by five days without work. How can you maintain your family in this way?"

Rickshaw pullers' meagre employment opportunities in the countryside were compounded by varying degrees of landlessness, as most of them did not own a substantial piece of land themselves and therefore relied on day-labouring (see also Begum and Sen, 2005). Gardner (2012, 99) has succinctly summarized the rural labour hierarchy in Bangladesh: 'Those who didn't own land sharecropped it; those who were unable to negotiate sharecropping arrangements worked as agricultural labourers.' These inequitable land relations have been shaped profoundly by the trend towards de-peasantization that was set in motion by the advent of colonial capitalism and the rise of commercial agriculture. Van Schendel and Faraizi (1984) have shown that this process, which achieved momentum in the late nineteenth century, did not necessarily result in outright expropriation or full dispossession, but rather created a system of rural production and accumulation that relied on an increase in indebtedness, sharecropping and agricultural day-labouring. Although de-peasantization often did not result in absolute landlessness – indeed, many rural labourers held on to tiny, scattered plots of land – it did prompt workers to diversify and expand their income-earning activities beyond the scope of agriculture (Van Schendel and Faraizi, 1984).

Today, this process is increasingly intensified, not only by population growth, but also by ecological and climate related vulnerabilities. Riverbank erosion, in particular, is an enormous driver behind landlessness and people's search for alternative employment opportunities (FAO, 2011, 5). For instance, the occupants of the previously discussed informal hostel in Old Dhaka almost all came from the northern, riverine part of Bangladesh, where riverbank erosion is particularly widespread. Many of them lived on *chars*, sandbanks in the middle of the river that disappear and re-emerge as the river shifts and changes course. A rickshaw driver called Abdul elaborated on the unpredictability of living in the floodplains of one of Bangladesh's largest rivers. Initially he had lost his land to river erosion, but after seven years the land had reappeared as a *char* in the middle of the river. However, his newly gained land was not yet suitable for cropping because the soil was comprised almost entirely out of loose sand.

Ecological vulnerabilities such as river erosion, flooding and cyclones were often deepened by processes of financialization, as is exemplified by the story of Fahim. During the same group discussion mentioned earlier, Fahim told us that he had tried to start a small farming business back home. He had taken out a substantial loan from an NGO to cultivate some potatoes, chillies and lentils. However, as a consequence of heavy rainfall all his crops had been washed away, thereby pulling the plug on his business plans. Fahim was far from the only rickshaw driver who had taken out a substantial loan at some point in his life, whether to start a business, buy a rickshaw, migrate abroad, buy a piece of land or bribe an official to land a "government job". Indeed, many of the more long-term labour projects that rickshaw drivers aspired to required some kind of investment capital and therefore led to debt accumulation.

Whereas in the past access to credit was predominantly controlled by powerful landholders and local moneylenders, this role has now increasingly been taken over by Micro Finance Institutions (MFIs) (Paprocki, 2016, 31). The premise of such organizations is that they provide the poor with access to credit and enable them to become 'entrepreneurs'. The rickshaw drivers I spoke to throughout my research, however, explained that there were many MFIs that handed out loans for all kinds of purposes, even when people were not in a position to repay them.[9] In fact, Kar (2013) has shown that MFIs are often instrumental in incorporating the poor in processes of financialization. Banerjee and Jackson (2017), moreover, found that the issuance of microfinance in rural Bangladesh often failed to generate meaningful employment opportunities and, instead, led to increasing levels of indebtedness among already impoverished communities. Moreover, even when MFIs are working in the best interest of their clients, the question can be raised to what extent the promotion of entrepreneurial activity provides a way out of poverty.

Stories of failed business attempts and lost investments were a recurring theme throughout my research and often one of the reasons why people would turn to the rickshaw industry in the first place. Jamal had started pulling a rickshaw after losing his fish stock. Fahim had lost his crops to heavy rainfall. Khadim, now a rickshaw driver, used to run his own rickshaw business until four of them were stolen. Ajmul had worked as a street vendor, selling fresh orange juice at a busy traffic junction, until hawking was banned from the street where he had his little stand. Zubair had lost his small restaurant during the Liberation War, and Sadiq had come to Dhaka to escape the burden of a loan that he could not pay back. He had used the money, approximately 1.5 lakh taka (US$1,770), to start a poultry farm but a large number of fowl died as the result of a virus infection. Unable to pay back the investment he owed, Sadiq had decided to hide out in Dhaka with his family while working as a rickshaw puller.

These different examples all underscore the profound risks – ecological, political, economic – that coincide with starting a business and highlight why poor workers might need a 'stable refuge' (Millar, 2014, 39). This is perhaps even more true for those who are willing to take the costly risk of migrating abroad. Raihan, for instance, had come to Dhaka with the hope of eventually travelling onwards to Italy. To achieve this, he had spent 8.5 lakh taka (US$10,027) on an immigration broker who was supposed to help him with a ticket and visa. Yet after waiting for 11 months, Raihan realized that he had wasted his money on a journey that was not going to happen. With the help of a rickshaw mechanic he had bought a battery-run rickshaw, which he now operated on a daily basis. Hakim had initially been more successful in his migration attempts. He had spent three years in Dubai working as a construction worker and a year in Singapore. However, after making a return visit to Bangladesh to see his family he had been unable to renew his work visa. Instead, he had tried to migrate to Malaysia but to no avail. Hakim had lost 6 lakh taka (US$7,078) to an immigration broker in the process and the urgent need for "instant cash" had driven him to the rickshaw industry.

Examples like these all highlight the accessibility and availability of rickshaw labour. This accessibility is aided by the fact that drivers can rent a rickshaw on a daily basis, without having to commit to long-term obligations. Such flexible arrangements make it possible for rickshaw pullers to lead multi-local lives in-between the city and countryside. These working conditions also allow for the continual return of agricultural labourers who do not have access to year-round employment. Moreover, the fact that driving a rickshaw requires little prior training and no financial assets makes the rickshaw industry a safeguard to fall back on in times of scarcity and crisis. As we have seen, poor households have long dealt with conditions of landlessness and scarcity by diversifying their livelihood strategies; often by exploiting multiple sources of income at the same time (Van Schendel, 1986; Toufique and Turton, 2002). Rickshaw labour should therefore be understood as one of several strategies to manage risks and spread income, which had the explicit advantage of being less cost intensive and financially risky than many of the alternative strategies available to rickshaw drivers, such as starting a business, migrating abroad or acquiring land. In the context of these alternatives, the rickshaw industry functioned as a stable refuge. However, as we will see in the next section, this 'stability' is increasingly under threat from municipal regulation and urban regeneration.

When the wheels stop turning

The majority of the drivers I spoke with in Dhaka were adamant about their dislike of rickshaw work. It would therefore be amiss to imply that rickshaw labour provides a secure and unproblematic mode of employment. On the contrary, the work itself is physically demanding, unhealthy and hazardous. Yet although rickshaw labour does not offer long-term economic stability or even the prospect thereof, we have seen that it does function as a relatively stable safeguard from broader political, economic and ecological crises. This function is premised on the accessibility of the rickshaw industry and the fact that it enables drivers to "earn money as the wheels turn around". This particular description of the work, however, also implies that the generation of "instant cash" is very much dependent on the ability to "keep the wheels turning". Indeed, for many older rickshaw drivers this eventually proved to be a problem, as they were no longer able to pedal a rickshaw for long periods of time. Their experiences thus hint at the ways in which the functioning of urban infrastructure relies on the degradation of human lives and bodies (Doherty, 2017). At the same time, it was not just the physical toll of the work that prevented the wheels from turning and the money from coming in. The implementation of state-led regulations also significantly undermined the relative flexibility and security afforded by rickshaw work.

In the previous sections I have pushed back against the notion of wageless work as a 'residual category'. The tendency to approach wageless life solely as a 'situation of lack' (Denning, 2010) leaves little room for the different reasons – other than sheer destitution – that people might have for taking up informal or wageless forms of work. Moreover, such a perspective also assumes that wageless work is always already inherently precarious. This takes away from the fact that many informal workers, including rickshaw drivers, are subject to regulations and restrictions that actively intervene in making their labour precarious. The fact that the state plays an important role in fuelling these processes complicates the idea that precaritization primarily constitutes a shift in employer–employee relations and functions as 'a means for employers to shift risks and responsibilities on to workers' (ILO, 2012, 27). Indeed, the work-related vulnerabilities that rickshaw drivers experience are not necessarily the result of exploitative employer–employee relations, but instead, the outcome of attempts to regulate access to urban space. In the South Asian context, moreover, such attempts at urban regulation are increasingly shaped by aspirations of world-class city making (Anand, 2006; Baviskar, 2006; Schindler, 2014; Ghertner, 2015).

The rickshaw plays a contentious role within the larger, aesthetic framework of the world-class city and is often framed as antithetical to these powerful aspirations (Baviskar, 2011). In the specific context of Dhaka, the widespread presence of rickshaws has been perceived as an obstacle to urban regulation almost since its introduction. The cycle-rickshaw is not only blamed for the city's incessant traffic jams, but also 'often seen as inefficient and backward; an impediment to progress; and inconsistent with a modern urban image' (Rahman, D'Este and Bunker, 2009, 1). Talk of banning and replacing the vehicle started as early as 1944, only six years after the rickshaw was first introduced to the city. The first restrictions on the allocation of rickshaw licences followed shortly thereafter and were implemented from the early 1950s onwards (Hasan, 2013, 19). In 1979 Dhaka City Corporation stopped providing licences to rickshaws altogether and the number of officially licensed rickshaws was capped at 79,554 (Hasan, 2013, 27). Some additional licences were released in 1986 as part of a general amnesty, raising the number of licensed rickshaws and rickshaw-vans to 90,000 (Gallagher, 1992, 93). This is less than a tenth of the 1.1 million rickshaws that, according to the most recent estimates, are operating in Dhaka city (Hasan and Dávila, 2018, 247).

Increasingly, such efforts to restrict the presence of the rickshaw have taken on an aesthetic and spatial dimension as well. In July 2019 the mayor of north Dhaka, Mohammed Atiqul Islam, vowed that 'all of Dhaka will be "rickshaw-free" within two years'.[10] His comments came in the wake of a new set of rickshaw restrictions that had been implemented that same month. Under the new rules, the cycle-rickshaw was banned from three major thoroughfares in the city.[11] Efforts to ban cycle-rickshaws from major routes and intersections first started in 2002, when Dhaka City Corporation initiated a 'Phased Implementation Plan'. The plan was part of the Dhaka Urban Transport Project (DUTP), funded by the World Bank, and proposed the phased withdrawal of rickshaws from 11 major roads, constituting a total of 120 km (Efroymson and Bari, 2005; Rahman, D'Este and Bunker, 2009; Hasan and Dávila, 2018). The aim was to ease traffic congestion by separating fast, motorized traffic from slow-moving, non-motorized traffic. In reality, however, this translated into a one-sided rickshaw ban on a number of routes that are now commonly referred to as VIP roads.

The repercussions of these rickshaw restrictions were aptly summarized by a 30-year-old rickshaw puller named Arif: "The rickshaw is very important for slum dwellers. If we have no rickshaws in Dhaka city we fall into trouble. But nowadays there are many roads in Dhaka where the rickshaw is no longer allowed." I met with Arif at a rickshaw garage in Korail *bosti* (slum), one of the largest informal settlements in Dhaka. The area was located on a low-lying peninsula and separated by garbage and water from the expensive high-rise blocks that towered over Dhaka's exclusive diplomatic neighbourhood. Arif had stayed at, and worked from, this particular garage since he first came to Dhaka at the age of 14. The implementation of a new set of rickshaw restrictions in the area, however, had prompted him to re-evaluate his stay in Dhaka. The new regulations severely restricted his daily rickshaw journeys and reduced his income from 500 (US$5.90) to 300 taka (US$3.54) per day. This was roughly the same amount as he would be able to earn as an agricultural day-labourer in his home village in Mymensingh. Arif emphasized that these changes were recent. Whereas in the past he used to travel all over the city – southwards in the direction of Old Dhaka and then on to peripheral areas like Shonir Akhra and Duniya – he now simply moved back and forth down the same stretch of road every day; a journey of about 1 km.

This drastic restriction of Arif's mobility can only be partly explained by the expansion of VIP roads. An additional factor that complicated Arif's efforts to make a living concerned the local restructuring of the rickshaw system in the area. In August 2016, the upscale, diplomatic neighbourhood that bordered the slum settlement where Arif lived had introduced a localized, restructured neighbourhood-based rickshaw system in response to security fears. The housing associations of the four residential areas that constituted the 'diplomatic zone' – Gulshan, Baridhara, Banani and Niketan – had successfully pushed for the restructuring of the local rickshaw system in the aftermath of a deadly terrorist attack at the local Holey Artisan Bakery cafe.[12] The new system was supposed to guarantee the safety of (expatriate) residents by allowing for a limited number of fully licensed and colour-coded 'community rickshaws' to operate in the area.[13] As a result, the total number of rickshaws in the area had plummeted from an estimated 10,000 to a mere 1,230.[14] Like many other rickshaw drivers in the vicinity, Arif had not managed to access a licensed rickshaw and so the majority of his journeys were now confined to the same 1 km stretch of road. His journeys started at the nearest VIP road in the area and ended at 'Gate number 5', a police checkpoint that marked the border with the diplomatic zone.

Such restrictions on the mobility of rickshaws have had a direct bearing on rickshaw drivers' ability to earn an income. In a way, these measures have undermined the model of "earning money as the wheels turn around", with many local drivers now accumulating debt rather than "instant cash". During an informal group discussion at a local rickshaw garage near the diplomatic zone, one vocal rickshaw driver summarized their predicament as follows: "*Ekhon sobar rin ache* [Now everyone is in debt!]" Several of the rickshaw drivers present had taken out additional loans from local MFIs to cover their children's education fees, unforeseen medical costs or to simply supplement their income. However, they now struggled to pay back their weekly instalments. Hence, the careful balancing act of "earning money as the wheels turn around" had been tipped in the wrong direction and rendered drivers vulnerable to moneylenders and MFIs.

The forms of displacement and indebtedness that have resulted from recent restrictions on rickshaw drivers represent a form of precaritization. Yet, rather than being the result of the dismantling of workers' rights and securities, this process was facilitated by tightening municipal regulations, reflecting unequal urban agendas and priorities. What is more, the exploitative employer–employee relationship characteristic of waged work cannot be easily mapped onto the personalized and reciprocal relation between rickshaw operators and rickshaw owners. The recent restrictions, moreover, generally had debilitating consequences for both operators and owners. This becomes particularly clear from the attempt at rickshaw reform in the diplomatic zone. At first sight, the heavily regulated 'community rickshaw system' could be interpreted as gainful for rickshaw owners, especially when taking into account that the rent for a licensed community rickshaw amounts to four times the daily rent for a regular rickshaw.[15] Still, none of the local rickshaw owners I spoke to throughout my research had been remotely happy about the new system. In fact, many of them had obtained only a handful of licences and feared losing their business altogether as most of their rickshaws were rusting away unused.

The situation of rickshaw owners who are based near the diplomatic area is best exemplified by the case of Mahfuz. When we met Mahfuz in Korail *bosti* he owned a total of 20 rickshaws, having already sold eight of his regular vehicles in the wake of the new localized restrictions. He explained that only local owners with political connections had been successful in obtaining a sufficient number of licences. Mahfuz himself had only managed to get two community rickshaw licences. The first licence was granted to him by Dhaka North City Corporation. The second one he bought from another *malik* for the exorbitant amount of 90,000 taka (US$1,062) – more than four times the price of a rickshaw. Both of Mahfuz's licensed rickshaws were now shared among three drivers each, who divided their time between operating a yellow-coloured, community rickshaw and a regular rickshaw. Mahfuz explained that some of his drivers still managed to enter the diplomatic area with a regular rickshaw by paying a bribe to the local traffic police that guarded the entrance gate. However, such practices of bribery only offered limited protection and on some occasions the rickshaw would still end up being seized by a different police officer. When that happened Mahfuz would split the total fine of 600 taka (US$7.08) with the driver. In fact, on the day we ran into him, three of his rickshaws had been taken into police custody.

Examples like these illustrate the ways in which work-related vulnerabilities result not from a change in employer–employee relations but from municipal policies which shape the regulation of urban space, including the policy of VIP roads. Anjaria's (2006, 2011) work on street vendors in Mumbai also hints at the importance of the municipal state in fuelling processes of precaritization. In this work, he argues that it is not spatial restrictions per se that subject hawkers to processes of precaritization, but the fact that their legal status is deliberately kept 'in a constant state of flux' (Anjaria 2006, 2145). Although rickshaw drivers in Dhaka do suffer in fairly direct ways from the implementation of VIP roads, these forms of spatial exclusion are also intimately connected to issues of legality. Indeed, their spatial exclusion is in many ways exacerbated by the limited distribution of licences and the inevitable legal vacuum that this has created.

Gallagher (1992, 72) has long warned that 'Imposing an artificial ceiling on rickshaw licenses is a certain recipe for corruption'. This is not just the case for the diplomatic zone, where the new rickshaw system has coincided with the implementation of a neighbourhood-based licence ceiling. In fact, ever since Dhaka City Corporation definitively capped the number of licences in 1986, all kinds of political associations – often misleadingly referred to as 'unions' – have stepped in to provide unofficial licences (see Suykens, 2018). Indeed, despite the large numbers of unregistered rickshaws that operate in Dhaka, it is almost impossible to find a rickshaw that does not have some sort of licence plate attached to its back. The so-called 'unions' that profit from the sale of these unofficial licences, far from being engaged in mobilizing 'proletarian workers', tend to have fairly direct links with the ruling party (Suykens, 2018, 432). Hence, the legal vacuum that has been created by the institution of licence ceilings, does not reflect so much the absence of the state as its power 'to construct and reconstruct categories of legitimacy and illegitimacy' (Roy, 2005, 149). More than anything, the example of the diplomatic zone exemplifies how certain spatial restrictions – legitimized in the name of order, safety and modernity – coincide with such a reconfiguration of what can be considered (il)legitimate. It is the redrawing of this boundary, rather than a shift in employer–employee relations, that fuels the forms of precaritization experienced by rickshaw drivers.

Conclusion

In this chapter I have attempted to diversify the vocabularies and imaginaries through which scholars make sense of work-related vulnerabilities. Whereas such vulnerabilities are bound to differ across historical moments, geographic sites, and social positions (Neilson and Rossiter, 2008), they are often intuitively interpreted as the absence or casualization of wage labour. This analytical privileging of wage labour easily feeds into the assumption that wageless or informal work is always already inherently precarious. Such an assumption averts attention away from the ways in which politics and situated policy efforts actually intervene in making informal work precarious. Throughout this chapter I have shown that the vulnerabilities that rickshaw drivers face are not the result of casualization or a change in employment relations, but of regulations that limit rickshaw drivers' mobility and, consequently, their income-earning abilities. The specific example of the 'community rickshaw system' that was implemented in the diplomatic zone of Dhaka highlights that such spatial interventions, far from denoting a straightforward attempt at regulation, reflect a reconfiguration of what can be considered (il)legitimate. It is the redrawing of this boundary between legitimacy and illegitimacy, specifically through the implementation of a neighbourhood-based licence ceiling, that has rendered rickshaw drivers vulnerable to employment displacement and debt accumulation.

Throughout this chapter I have emphasized that such processes of precaritization have not necessarily deprived rickshaw drivers of a stable, secure or safe job, as none of the rickshaw pullers I spoke with perceived their work along those lines. However, these processes have undermined the rickshaw industry's function as a relatively stable site of return amidst ecological and financial emergencies. For, as we have seen, rickshaw labour provides poor workers with access to "instant cash" when other, more cost-intensive labour projects fail. This appeal of instant cash, coupled with the degree of independence that the work offers, also explains why many workers would rather pedal a rickshaw than work for wages in a factory. None of this is to imply that rickshaw labour somehow comes with an infinite ability to "earn money as the wheels turn around". Indeed, the wheels inevitably stop or slow down when drivers get sick or become older. What I have attempted to demonstrate, however, is that the rickshaw industry plays a vital role in people's monumental and often costly efforts to transcend poverty, by providing a space in which they are able to cope with ecological emergencies and lost investments. Municipal restrictions on mobility obstruct these efforts and, ultimately, throw a proverbial stick in the wheels that have kept rickshaw drivers going for so long.

Acknowledgements

This research project would not have been possible without the efforts and hard work of Yasin Kazi, who accompanied me as a research assistant to different rickshaw garages in Dhaka. I am also grateful for the support and affiliation of Work for Better Bangladesh (WBB), who generously hosted me throughout my fieldwork.

Notes

[1] I use pseudonyms throughout this chapter.

[2] In the context of Bangladesh, such political strikes or shutdowns are usually orchestrated by one of the country's political (opposition) parties.

[3] Bengal consists of the Indian state West Bengal and contemporary Bangladesh, which was known as East Bengal before the Partition of the Indian subcontinent in 1947.

[4] The overwhelming majority of rickshaw pullers rent their vehicles. Begum and Sen (2005) found that only 13 per cent of rickshaw drivers owned their vehicle. The Bangladesh Institute of Labour Studies (BILS) reported an even lower percentage of rickshaw ownership and detailed that 96 per cent rented their vehicle (Karim and Salam 2019, 51)

[5] In 2015 the Bangladesh High Court ruled in favour of banning the improvised electric rickshaw from Dhaka City Corporation. 'HC Bans Battery-Run Rickshaw', *The Daily Star*, 8 March 2015, https://www.thedailystar.net/hc-bans-battery-run-rickshaw-31617

[6] Officially, Bangladeshi Taka (BDT).

[7] Jamila used the English phrase 'time-to-time duty' here to describe fixed-hour work arrangements.

[8] One *lakh* is a measuring unit that equals 100,000.

[9] The BILS study found that 53.5 per cent of the interviewed rickshaw pullers had a loan at the time of the survey. In 85.8 per cent of the cases these loans were handed out by NGOs or similar organizations (Karim and Salam, 2019, 37).

[10] The mayor was cited in an article in the *The Economist*: 'Three Wheels v Four. Bangladesh's Biggest City Plans to Ban Cycle Rickshaws', 7 November 2019, https://www.economist.com/asia/2019/11/07/bangladeshs-biggest-city-plans-to-ban-cycle-rickshaws

11 Mizanur Rahman, '3 Major Routes to Ban Rickshaws From Sunday', *The Dhaka Tribune*, 6 July 2019, https://www.dhakatribune.com/bangladesh/dhaka/2019/07/06/3-major-routes-to-ban-rickshaws-from-sunday

12 On 2 July 2016 gunmen stormed the Holey Artisan Bakery cafe in Gulshan. After a 10-hour siege Bangladeshi commandos freed the building, but by that time already 20 hostages, predominantly of foreign nationality, had been killed. The attack was later claimed by Islamic State of Iraq and the Levant (ISIL).

13 The *Dhaka Tribune* has also reported on some of these changes to the rickshaw system: Sohel Mamum, 'Diplomatic Zone gets Special Rickshaws, Buses', 10 August 2016, https://www.dhakatribune.com/uncategorized/2016/08/10/diplomatic-zone-gets-special-rickshaws-buses

14 During a visit to the Banani Housing association on 22 September 2017 I was informed that Banani was awarded 560 licensed rickshaws, Gulshan 470, Baridhara 100 and Niketan 100. This included a total of 230 licences for disabled pullers.

15 Whereas the rent for a regular rickshaw amounts to 100 taka (US$1.18) for a full day, the rent for a community rickshaw is 400 taka (US$4.72). Due to this increase in rent most community rickshaws are shared among two or three drivers who operate the vehicle in shifts.

References

Anand, N. (2006) 'Disconnecting experience: Making world-class Roads in Mumbai', *Economic and Political Weekly*, 41(31): 3422–3429.

Anjaria, J.S. (2006) 'Street hawkers and public space in Mumbai', *Economic and Political Weekly*, 41(21): 2140–2146.

Anjaria, J.S. (2011) 'Ordinary states: Everyday corruption and the politics of space in Mumbai', *American Ethnologist*, 38(1): 58–72.

Banerjee, S.B. and Jackson, L. (2017) 'Microfinance and the business of poverty reduction: Critical perspectives from rural Bangladesh', *Human Relations*, 70(1): 63–91.

Barchiesi, F. (2016) 'The violence of work: Revisiting South Africa's "labour question" through precarity and anti-Blackness', *Journal of Southern African Studies*, 42(5): 875–891.

Baviskar, A. (2006) 'Demolishing Delhi: World-class city in the making', *Mute,* 2(3): 88–95.

Baviskar, A. (2011) 'Cows, cars and cycle-rickshaws: Bourgeois environmentalists and the battle for Delhi's streets', in Baviskar, A. and Ray, R. (eds) *Elites and Everyman: The Cultural Politics of the Indian Middle Classes*, New Delhi: Routledge, pp 391–418.

Begum, S. and Sen, B. (2005) 'Pulling rickshaws in the city of Dhaka: A way out of poverty?, *Environment and Urbanization*, 17(2): 11–25.

Bhattacharya, S. (1998) 'Famine and the labouring poor: An unpublished manuscript of a Folk-Poet of Mid-19th Century Bengal', *Proceedings of the Indian History Congress*, 59: 561–565.

Bhattacharya, S. (2006) 'Introduction', in Behal, R.P. and van der Linden, M. (eds) *Coolies, Capital and Colonialism: Studies in Indian Labour History*, Cambridge: Cambridge University Press, pp 7–20.

Das, V. and Randeria, S. (2015) 'Politics of the urban poor: Aesthetics, ethics, volatility, precarity. An introduction to Supplement 11', *Current Anthropology*, 56(S11): S3–S14.

De Haan, A. (1997a) 'Migration as family strategy: Rural–urban labor migration in India during the twentieth century', *The History of the Family*, 2(4): 481–505.

De Haan, A. (1997b) 'Unsettled settlers: Migrant workers and industrial capitalism in Calcutta', *Modern Asian Studies*, 31(4): 919–949.

Denning, M. (2010) 'Wageless life', *New Left Review*, 66: 79–97.

Doherty, J. (2017) 'Life (and limb) in the fast-lane: Disposable people as infrastructure in Kampala's boda boda industry', *Critical African Studies*, 9(2): 192–209.

Efroymson, D. and Bari, M.M. (2005) 'Improving Dhaka's traffic situation: Lessons from Mirpur Road', Prepared by WBB Trust, Dhaka.

FAO (2011) 'On Solid Ground: Addressing Land Tenure Issues Following Natural Disasters (Bangladesh)', http://www.fao.org/3/i1255b/i1255b03.pdf

Ferguson, J. and Li, T. (2018) 'Beyond the "proper job": Political-economic analysis after the century of labouring man', *Working Paper 51*. PLAAS, UWC: Cape Town.

Gallagher, R. (1992) *The Rickshaws of Bangladesh*, Dhaka: University Press Limited.

Gardner, K. (2012) *Discordant Development: Global Capitalism and the Struggle for Connection in Bangladesh*, London: Pluto Press.

Ghertner, D.A. (2015) *Rule by Aesthetics: World-class City Making in Delhi*, Oxford: Oxford University Press.

Gidwani, V. and Maringanti, A. (2016) 'The Waste-value dialectic: Lumpen urbanization in contemporary India', *Comparative Studies of South Asia, Africa and the Middle East*, 36(1): 112–133.

Hasan, M.M.U. (2013) 'Unjust mobilities: The case of rickshaw bans and restrictions in Dhaka', PhD Dissertation, Development Planning Unit, University College London.

Hasan, M.M.U. and Dávila, J.D. (2018) 'The politics of (im) mobility: Rickshaw bans in Dhaka, Bangladesh', *Journal of Transport Geography*, 70: 246–255.

ILO (2012) 'From precarious work to decent work', Proceedings of the Workers' Symposium on Policies and Regulations to Combat Precarious Employment, Geneva, Switzerland, 4–7 October 2011.

Kar, S. (2013) 'Recovering debts: Microfinance loan officers and the work of "proxy-creditors" in India', *American Ethnologist*, 40(3): 480–493.

Karim, R.M. and Salam, K.A. (2019) 'Organizing the informal economy workers: A study of rickshaw pullers in Dhaka City', prepared for the Bangladesh Institute of Labour Studies-BILS.

Kibria, N. (1995) 'Culture, social class, and income control in the lives of women garment workers in Bangladesh', *Gender and Society*, 9(3): 289–309.

Magdoff, F. and Magdoff, H. (2004) 'Disposable workers', *Monthly Review*, 55(11): 18–35.

Millar, K. (2008) 'Making trash into treasure: Struggles for autonomy on a Brazilian garbage dump', *Anthropology of Work Review*, 29(2): 25–34.

Millar, K. (2014) 'The precarious present: Wageless labor and disrupted life in Rio de Janeiro, Brazil', *Cultural Anthropology*, 29(1): 32–53.

Millar, K. (2017) 'Toward a critical politics of precarity', *Sociology Compass*, 11(6): e12483.

Millar, K. (2018) *Reclaiming the Discarded. Life and Labor on Rio's Garbage Dump*, Durham, NC: Duke University Press.

Millar, K. (2019) 'Decentering wage labor as a new class politics', *Dialectical Anthropology*, 44 (83–85): 1–3.

Muehlebach, A. and Shoshan, N. (2012) 'Post-Fordist affect: Introduction', *Anthropological Quarterly*, 85(2): 317–343.

Munck, R. (2013) 'The precariat: A view from the South', *Third World Quarterly*, 34(5): 747–762.

Narotzky, S. (2018) 'Rethinking the concept of labour', *Journal of the Royal Anthropological Institute*, 24(S1): 29–43.

Neilson, B. and Rossiter, N. (2008) 'Precarity as a political concept, or, Fordism as exception', *Theory, Culture & Society*, 25(7–8): 51–72.

Paprocki, K. (2016) ' "Selling our own skin": Social dispossession through microcredit in rural Bangladesh', *Geoforum*, 74: 29–38.

Pettinger, L. (2019) *What's Wrong With Work?* Bristol: Bristol University Press.

Rahman, M.M, D'Este, G.M. and Bunker, J. (2009) 'Is there a future for non-motorized public transport in Asia?' Proceedings of the 8th International Conference of the Eastern Asia Society for Transportation Studies (EASTS), Surabaya, Indonesia, 16–19 November.

RAJUK (2015) 'Dhaka Structure Plan (2016–2035), Draft', prepared under the City Region Development Project (CRDP) for the Ministry of Housing and Public Works.

Roy, A. (2005) 'Urban informality: Toward an epistemology of planning', *Journal of the American Planning Association*, 71(2): 147–158.

Samson, M. (2015) 'Accumulation by dispossession and the informal economy – Struggles over knowledge, being and waste at a Soweto garbage dump', *Environment and Planning D: Society and Space*, 33(5): 813–830.

Schindler, S. (2014) 'The making of "world-class" Delhi: Relations between street hawkers and the new middle class', *Antipode*, 46(2): 557–573.

Scully, B. (2016) 'Precarity North and South: A Southern Critique of Guy Standing', *Global Labour Journal*, 7(2): 160–173.

Sen, S. (1997) 'Gendered exclusion: Domesticity and dependence in Bengal', *International Review of Social History*, 42(S5): 65–86.

Sopranzetti, C. (2017) 'Framed by freedom: Emancipation and oppression in post-Fordist Thailand', *Cultural Anthropology*, 32(1): 68–92.

Standing, G. (2011) *The Precariat: The New Dangerous Class*, London: Bloomsbury.

Suykens, B. (2018) 'The mimicry of the state as a state practice: The regulation of rickshaw licenses in Dhaka (Bangladesh)', *Critical Asian Studies*, 50(3): 422–441.

Toufique, K.A. and Turton, C. (2002) 'Hands not land: How livelihoods are changing in rural Bangladesh', prepared for the Bangladesh Institute of Development Studies (BIDS) and the Department for International Development (DFID).

Van Schendel, W. (1986) 'Self-rescue and survival: The rural poor in Bangladesh', *South Asia: Journal of South Asian Studies*, 9(1): 41–59.

Van Schendel, W. (2006) 'Stretching labour historiography: Pointers from South Asia', *International Review of Social History*, 51(S14): 229–261.

Van Schendel, W. and Faraizi, A.H. (1984) *Rural Labourers in Bengal, 1880 to 1980*, Rotterdam: Comparative Asian Studies Program (CASP) 12.

Wilson, T.D. (2019) 'Precarization, informalization, and Marx', *Review of Radical Political Economics*, 52(3): 1–17.

9

Going Gojek, or Staying *Ojek*? Competing Visions of Work and Economy in Jakarta's Motorbike Taxi Industry

Mechthild von Vacano

In early 2015 Jakarta's notoriously congested streets became populated by a new road user. Within the space of a few weeks, thousands of green-helmeted motorcyclists in black and green jackets proliferated across the capital. These uniformed drivers marked the entrance of the platform economy into Indonesia's motorbike taxi industry. The Indonesian start-up Gojek was the first business to adapt the global business model of digital 'ride-sharing' platforms to Indonesia's two-wheeled taxi market, closely followed by the Singapore-based company Grab. Enticing consumers with cheap promotion schemes during the fasting month of mid-June to mid-July, Gojek took control of the market. By July of that year, Gojek had become a topic of everyday conversation and the company's name – a play on words combining the vernacular *ojek* (motorbike taxi) with the English verb 'to go' – became synonymous with application-based ride-hailing services in Indonesia, and its bright corporate green a permanent feature of street life in Jakarta.

Conventional *ojek* drivers – drivers operating according to the non-digital, established service model – rallied against the rapid expansion of this new business model and its disruption of their customary system of local ranks (*pangkalan*). They put up banners across the city with slogans that read: 'Gojek and Grab are prohibited from entering this territory'. News media reported several instances of conventional *ojek* drivers violently attacking motorcyclists in Gojek uniforms. Framed as the '*ojek* vs. Gojek' controversy, the conflict triggered a broad public debate. At first glance, this conflict appeared to resemble responses to the forceful expansion of 'ride-hailing' platforms in other metropoles around the globe. Just as taxi drivers from New York to New Delhi were mobilizing against Uber, Jakarta's *ojek* drivers were protesting the advent of a new digital competitor. There was, however, one significant difference: while four-wheeled ride-hailing platforms such as Uber were accused of undercutting the strict regulations of the formal taxi industry (see, for example, Kenney and Zysman, 2016, 67), Gojek was entering a branch of the Indonesian transportation sector which had never been recognized as public transportation, nor regulated under any Indonesian law. In other words, the conflict between conventional motorbike taxi drivers and their digital competitors could not be explained by conventional narratives of secure vs. precarious work, or formal vs. informal economy, but instead represented a clash of two different modes of work outside of 'standard' wage employment.

In this chapter I trace the rise of the Indonesian platform pioneer Gojek, before providing an in-depth comparison with the established system of *pangkalan*-based motorbike taxis. This case study is based on ethnographic fieldwork conducted in a South Jakarta neighbourhood between 2014 and 2015 on the broader topic of subjectivity and work, complemented by an analysis of local media coverage and data from two shorter follow-up visits in 2016 and 2018. The empirical analysis is informed by a deconstructive reading of the in/formality paradigm, which breaks down the blurry, yet normative concept of 'form' by problematizing the hegemonic notions of 'standard' employment, state regulation and bureaucratic procedure. Through this framework, I shift focus from the structural conditions of work to the underlying modes of social and economic organization, and the – mostly implicit – values these modes enact. By examining issues of ride distribution, labour market access and pricing, I seek to identify and distinguish the underlying principles of conventional and platform-based *ojek* services. I then turn to the organization of digital drivers, before closing with a brief synopsis of the comparison. I argue that the conflict between conventional *ojek* and their digital analogues invites us to think about the social logics of work and its distribution, as well as moral understandings of the right to a living.

The informal sector meets platform capitalism: forms of work beyond the wage

Motorbike taxis constitute a common, and often indispensable feature of public transport in many cities across the global South (see, for example, Doherty, 2017; Sopranzetti, 2017; Agbiboa, 2019). In Jakarta, *ojek* began to emerge in the 1970s and exploded in the late 1990s during the Asian financial crisis (Lee, 2018). Offering an inexpensive, yet speedy form of on-demand transportation, motorbike taxis became popular among wide strata of the population. As Jakarta has expanded into a metropolitan area of over 30 million inhabitants, its residents have learned to appreciate the two-wheelers' ability to cut through the capital's infamous traffic gridlock or squeeze their way through the narrow alleyways of urban neighbourhoods. Formally, *ojek* have always operated outside the law, because – unlike regular taxis – the Indonesian Law on Traffic and Land Transportation (No 22/2009) does not recognize motorbike taxis as legitimate forms of 'unscheduled public transportation'. But after early attempts to prohibit *ojek*, local administration and law enforcement began to tolerate them as permanent features of the urban transport economy.

Prior to the emergence of digital platforms, the Indonesian motorbike taxi industry provided a textbook example of the kinds of economic activity which inspired Keith Hart (1973) and the authors of the International Labour Organization's (ILO) Kenya report (1972) to coin the concept of the 'informal sector'. Like commercial motorcyclists elsewhere (see, for example, Doherty, 2017, 195), conventional *ojek* drivers offer a prototypical representation of the self-employed 'urban poor' in the global South creatively engineering a livelihood from an economic activity outside of the purview of government regulation. *Ojek* drivers are organized through a system of local ranks strategically positioned across the city: at train stations, bus stops, footbridges or any fairly significant intersection leading into a residential neighbourhood. These *pangkalan* are easily recognizable as clusters of sun-tanned men in Indonesian-style motorbike gear – open helmets, fingerless gloves and foamed plastic cuirasses to protect against the wind[1] – waiting around for clientele, especially during rush hour. If space permits, the ranks also manifest as physical shelters for drivers to rest and wait. Before Gojek, work as a conventional *ojek* driver could provide a moderate, or even decent income, depending on the location. At the *pangkalan* close to my field site, a lower middle class neighbourhood in South

Jakarta, a driver's average monthly earnings totalled an amount slightly above the regional minimum wage of then IDR2.7 million (roughly US$200) – a statutory minimum that applies only to regular workers, that is wage workers with labour contracts, who represented 21.5 per cent of the country's non-agricultural workforce in the year 2016 (ILO, 2019). Drivers in my field site managed to achieve this standard with their average earnings, whereas drivers operating in the vicinity of business districts or the housing complexes of the new middle class could earn as much as double (Yusuf, 2015). But the livelihoods of these drivers were threatened by the influx of a new flock of green-helmeted motorcyclists into the city.

The rise of application-based *ojek* began with the simple, but powerful idea to adapt the globally expanding business model of ride-hailing platforms to the local transport industry in Indonesia, and therefore to motorbike taxi services. In this sense, Gojek represents a classic example of 'platform capitalism' (Srnicek, 2017). Officially, the company operates as a technological intermediary which provides an online platform to match independent *ojek* drivers and prospective customers. It is formally registered as a tech enterprise, and as such regulated and taxed by the Indonesian state. Yet as a platform provider, Gojek does not employ any of its drivers, but insists on playing a purely mediating function for which it charges a 20 per cent 'service fee'. Instead of a labour contract then, drivers enter a commercial contract which positions them as 'partners' of the platform. Even though they receive their uniforms, clients and every payment from Gojek, they are declared 'self-employed'. Similar to the much-discussed case of Uber (see, for example, Davies et al, 2017), Gojek acts as a 'pseudo-employer' (Ford and Honan, 2017, 283). The drivers find themselves in a position of dependent 'self-employment', which structurally resembles the position of industrial outworkers (see Kenney and Zysman, 2016). They are bound to the conditions the platform unilaterally sets – for example, its service rules and pricing schemes – while carrying the entire economic risk of the operation by themselves.

From an analytical standpoint, we can map these two modes of work onto the historic trajectory of the in/formal work paradigm. The self-organized mode of conventional *ojek* work corresponds with the early notion of 'informal sector' activity, which had been framed as a transitional phase of development in the global South, expected to fade away with industrialization (Breman and van der Linden, 2014). By contrast, the (self-)employment model of Gojek corresponds to the later, broader notion of 'informal employment' characterized by pseudo-self-employment, temporary and subcontracted labour, as well as other 'sub-standard' labour conditions within otherwise registered enterprises (see, for example, ILO, 2002; Breman and van der Linden, 2014). This notion of informal work has been invoked to describe a global phenomenon, inherent in the neoliberal age of capitalism (Sassen, 1994), although neo-Marxist critics have shown how both modes have always coexisted and overlapped in practice (Breman, 1976).

As two variants of informality, the 'informal sector' and the 'informal employment' framing appear to measure the organization of conventional and platform-based *ojek* services in Indonesia against a standardized understanding of formal wage employment derived from industrial Europe. This leaves the 'informal' itself as a wide and underdefined, residual category (Burchardt et al, 2013), which fails to distinguish the self-organized structures of *pangkalan* from the corporate structure of a commercial ride-hailing platform like Gojek, or the extra-legal status of conventional motorbike services from the legal character of the platform economy's effort to circumvent regulation. It thus erases important differences between different modes of work, focusing instead on their deviance from the Fordist ideal of stable and legally protected employment.

My analysis of the 'ojek vs. Gojek' case started with the innocent question of what exactly constitutes 'form', and how we might unravel and decentre the normative assumptions implied in the binary notion of 'in/formal work'. These questions provided a framework to analyse the contested visions of work in the Indonesian motorbike taxi industry. However, they also provide a helpful starting point for the study of work in all its *forms*, inside and outside the wage.

Briefly outlined, it is possible to identify three dominant ways of conceiving 'form' in the literature on 'in/formal work'. The most specific notion of form is perhaps provided by the ILO's (2002) definition of 'informal employment', which defines the formal as a specific labour standard, of regular and socially secured wage protected by official labour laws. Entrenched in a Fordist vision of wage employment, this normative notion of form presents a vision of the future of work under 'tamed' capitalism. It directs our focus to the structural qualities of employment, to the social experience of in/security and in/dependence and to the wider context of relationships of production. A second and most widely shared notion of form identifies formality with (effective) state regulation (Meagher, 2010, 14; Portes, 2010, 133). This notion foregrounds the juridical-regulative aspects of form and perpetuates a state-centric normativity which tends to overlook the regulative role of non-state institutions. Finally, a third understanding is provided by Keith Hart's (2006) emphasis on the bureaucratic qualities of form. Echoing the Weberian thesis of (formal) rationalization, this approach places emphasis on procedural practices and values in recognition of the existence of a plurality of regulative orders and institutions.

So, how should the *form* of conventional and digital *ojek* services be characterized? What are the operating principles and regulative mechanisms of *pangkalan* and platform? And by which rationalities are they informed?

Promises of a unicorn: Gojek's rise and appeal

Although Gojek had been operating a call centre service for motorbike taxis since 2010, the company's real success only began in January 2015 with the launch of its digital *ojek* application for the Greater Jakarta region. This app was the first of its kind in Indonesia and was celebrated for bringing an 'Indonesian-style revolution' to the transport industry (Suryarandika, 2016).

Within months, Gojek was joined by a second player, the Malaysian-founded and Singapore-based platform Grab. These two platforms came to dominate the field, although numerous other, mostly smaller players joined the early scramble for market share. The new platform-based service model resonated exceptionally well with the large crowd of smartphone-savvy Jakartans, whose appetite for digital innovation was stimulated by the platform's promotional offers. Gojek's big breakthrough came with its fasting month promotion in June 2015, which offered an IDR10,000 flat price (approximately 75 US cents) for any destination within a 25 km radius. For comparison, conventional *ojek* drivers would start at IDR5,000 for a short distance trip and often charge IDR50,000 for a 10 km ride. Similar promotional offers followed, spurred by fierce competition between Gojek and Grab over market leadership.

While these offers attracted large customer crowds, they also enticed drivers as Gojek partners were compensated the regular fare of initially IDR4,000 per kilometre. This combination of extremely low consumer prices with high kilometre rates for the drivers generated almost fantastic income figures: drivers reported monthly earnings of up to IDR8 million, roughly triple the amount of a regular minimum wage (see, for example, Al Azhariet al, 2016). These prospects attracted new demographics to the *ojek* business. If *pangkalan*-based services had been an exclusively male activity, mostly serving as a primary source of income (Lee, 2018) and dominated by a middle-to-elderly age group with a lower or lower middle class background, the digitalized version also attracted educated office workers, housewives and students, many of whom started taking up *ojek* driving as a side job.

In a head-to-head race, Gojek and Grab expanded into the urban centres of the Indonesian archipelago; while Gojek pursued a complementary expansion strategy diversifying its service range to include food delivery, as well as courier, shopping, massage, beauty, house cleaning and house moving services. By March 2016, Gojek had registered 210,000 drivers nationwide and its application had been downloaded over 13 million times (Suryarandika, 2016),[2] becoming Indonesia's first 'unicorn' – a tech company with a valuation of over US$1 billion – in August 2016 (Pratama, 2016). With both platforms generating staggering growth rates, the global giant Uber did not want to miss out on this exciting new market and launched its own application-based *ojek* service in April 2016. However, it conceded to the two regional rivals after only two years and retreated from the Southeast Asian market altogether, selling its entire operation to Grab.

As a domestic pioneer in its field, Gojek was predestined to become Indonesia's posterchild for digital innovation. The platform's management was determined to capitalize on this potential by adapting its marketing strategy to the tone of national development. It embraced a discourse of modernity and technological progress, presenting itself as innovative solution for Jakarta's congestion and public transport crises. Yet, it underscored the social motives of this endeavour by introducing itself as 'a socially-oriented technology company which aims at improving the wellbeing of workers in various informal sectors in Indonesia'.[3] Gojek touted a welfare approach towards its 'partners' and advertised that it would provide them with health and other types of social insurance – a claim in line with the nationwide rollout of universal health insurance coverage launched in 2014. In the fine print, however, it transpired that these insurances were only brokered by the platform and had to be purchased on a private basis. But these details were overshadowed by the larger promise of individual economic empowerment – a promise which aligns perfectly with neoliberal discourses of 'development' through (micro-)entrepreneurialism, frequently applied to the platform economy in the global South (Pollio, 2019, 761).

Gojek promised its customers a new and current *ojek* experience, alluding to the service values of speed, reliability and safety, but also comfort and hygiene. With small details, like the provision of free scrunchies for long-haired customers and a disinfection policy for passengers' helmets, the platform tried to clean up and modernize the image of *ojek*. Although these details have been lost over time, they marked a habitual distinction and served to shape the public perception of Gojek as a service-oriented enterprise in contrast to the rough and rude image of *ojek pangkalan*. Yet the platform carefully avoided positioning itself in direct opposition to conventional *ojek* drivers, embracing a rhetoric of inclusion instead. *Ojek* drivers were the primary group of workers whom Gojek claimed to empower, by offering them new ways to effectively find clientele and reduce unproductive 'waiting time'. As company representatives suggested, all *ojek* drivers should simply join the platform in order to enjoy the benefits of the new business model.

This image of technological might softened by social conscience generated broad support among local elites. Policy makers and media outlets celebrated the platform as the flagship for a truly Indonesian digital start-up culture. However, the majority of *pangkalan*-based drivers remained unconvinced and received Gojek's paternalistic rhetoric of empowerment with great scepticism. Many rejected the opportunity to give up their independence to 'partner' with a digital platform, citing a principled refusal to 'work for someone else' and share the fruits of their own labour, even if this meant passing up the increased income opportunities (also see Freischlad, 2015). Furthermore, they interpreted the rapid expansion of the platforms as a substantial threat to their livelihoods. From the standpoint of conventional drivers, the platforms were undermining the established business code among *pangkalan* and flooding the industry with an artificial oversupply of drivers, while distorting it by dumping prices. To fend off the new competition, *pangkalan* across Jakarta put up banners prohibiting Gojek and Grab from "pick[ing] up passengers in this area" or even "enter[ing] this territory". These bans were underscored with threats of violence, and news media reported several occasions of green-uniformed Gojek drivers being attacked by members of a local rank.

On the surface, these confrontations appeared as battles over customers – as the incumbents' last desperate attempt to fend off their powerful new market rivals. However, the conflict went much deeper, as the platform business model did not just challenge the livelihoods of individual drivers, but the entire system of *pangkalan*, and the forms of life and labour it sustained.

Pangkalan vs. platform: contested visions of work in the *ojek* industry

Conventional *ojek* ranks are more than mere physical waiting zones. They are also a prime example of cooperative self-organization among so-called 'informal' transportation workers (Cervero and Golubb, 2007, 449), and commercial motorbike riders in particular (Doherty, 2017; Ibrahim and Bize, 2018; Agbiboa, 2019). What I have generally dubbed the '*pangkalan* system' is a vast web of coexisting *pangkalan*, each of which constitutes a location-bound driver cooperative in its own right. Although these local ranks lack any superordinate body, they are interconnected by a shared business code (CDIA, 2011, 36). This decentralized system regulated the *ojek* industry for decades, based on a logic of neighbourhood organization. However, it was undermined by the arrival of the digital platform.

The conflict between conventional and digital *ojek* drivers came down to the fundamental question of how work in the *ojek* industry should be organized: whether and by whom the industry ought to be regulated, and according to which economic principles it should operate. In public, this contestation revolved around issues of ride distribution, labour market access and pricing. In what follows, I will take these three issues as my starting point for a deeper analysis comparing the *pangkalan* to the platform system as two distinct economic orders, governed by two different sets of values and principles.

Ride distribution

The conflict between *pangkalan* and platform-based drivers ignited issues of ride distribution, as Gojek's novel ordering system was seen to break the rules of coexistence among ranks. Each *pangkalan* covers a specific territory and possesses privileged access to all journeys departing from this area. Thousands of ranks create a dense service net, set up at any strategic transportation hub across the city from the exit doors of big train stations, to the small street corners where the minivan route passes an entry ally into a residential area. If a driver crosses into another territory, the code stipulates, they ought to return to their own *pangkalan* immediately after drop-off, and refrain from picking up new clientele until they have reached their home territory. If a passenger's destination lies close to a different *pangkalan*, drivers should even abstain from offering to wait for the return trip and leave 'their' passenger to arrange her return with a local driver instead. These rules ensure that rides and income opportunities are evenly distributed between territories and ranks. Rides are allocated on a rotating basis among drivers within the same territory. The entire system is thus organized around a principle of income distribution, through which the livelihoods of drivers are prioritized over gross profit and efficiency.

However, this principle is disregarded by the platform system, which allocates orders by its own algorithm. Digital *ojek* can be hailed from any given location, by anyone. Based on GPS tracking, customers can check their application for locally available Gojek drivers and preview a fare and time estimate. The request is then forwarded to registered drivers nearby, who can accept or reject the order through a complementary app. This system replaces the location-based institution of the *pangkalan* with the digital platform as the new impersonal intermediary; it deterritorializes the allocation process, though the service itself remains place bound (Johnston, 2020, 26). At the same time, the platform replaces the cooperative and distributive organization of the *pangkalan* with a competitive structure which allocates orders by the meritocratic measures of proximity and promptness, as well as individual performance scores. The latter appears to privilege more active drivers, though drivers can only develop a heuristic understanding of the actual allocation process, as the exact nature and weighting of the parameters remain obscure. These algorithmic metrics are complemented by complex bonus schemes which incentivize Gojek 'partners' to take as many orders as possible. These incentives highlight the accumulative logic of the platform, which addresses *ojek* drivers as individual entrepreneurs and encourages them to maximize their personal income – and with it the profit of the platform.

Labour market access

By circumventing the *pangkalan*, the Gojek platform undermined not only established systems of passenger distribution, but also labour market access. Before Gojek, the total number of *ojek* drivers had been regulated through a system in which each *pangkalan* limited its membership size in order to sustain a minimum level of income. As *ojek* driving demands not much more than a motorbike and the skill to ride it, it has long provided an important source of employment for the economically disenfranchised. And yet, the economic viability of the job depends on a sufficient volume of orders to yield each driver an adequate income. Both of these facts imply opposite claims – a right to economic participation versus a right of protectionist exclusion – which are rooted in the same moral right to make a living.

To resolve this dilemma, the rank close to my South Jakarta field site had, for example, determined that a fixed membership size of a dozen was sufficient to match local demand. New members were only accepted as a direct replacement for an outgoing member. The outgoing member had the right to nominate their successor so long as this person was a member of their extended family. Since all of the current members have kinship ties to 'old-established' families in the area, the family principle ensured that the *pangkalan* stayed in the hands of men with close ties to the neighbourhood and its informal power structures (see Wilson, 2011, 251). The *pangkalan* system is thus a socially thick model of work organization, regulated through face-to-face interactions with communal connections within distinct territorial boundaries.

These principles tended to discriminate against newcomers and (other) community outsiders – though from the standpoint of *pangkalan* members, their personal ties to the neighbourhood only solidified their sense of territorial entitlement as inscribed in the afore described *pangkalan* code. Registering with Gojek, in contrast, required neither kinship relations nor neighbourhood ties, but a range of bureaucratic documents: an identity card, a proof of local residency, a driver's licence and proof of road tax payment. In the digital business model, registration is a formal, that is, bureaucratic procedure during which drivers enter a contractual relationship with the platform provider – though the official contract stipulates a 'partnering agreement', not an employment relationship. Gojek 'partners' are further required to be in good physical and mental health and possess sufficient literacy to operate the Gojek smartphone. The company originally stipulated a maximum age limit of 55 years, but as of July 2019 this requirement has been eased to allow applicants from ages 17 to 65.[4]

These requirements were designed to standardize the platform's service quality and to increase customer confidence (Langley and Leyshon, 2017, 19–20). At the same time, the bureaucratic quality of the registration process was argued to 'democratize' the *ojek* labour market. The idea was that, as long as all of the requirements were met, everyone had an equal chance to become a Gojek driver, irrespective of their personal connections, gender, age or resident status. Gojek was careful to cultivate this 'democratic' image; for example, its ad campaigns foregrounded images of young women in green corporate uniforms (see also Frey, 2020, 41), representing a spectrum of contemporary beauty standards (long brown hair or functional-fashionable headscarves).

However, despite its claims to democratize the motorbike taxi industry, the platform's requirements effectively rendered vast numbers of *pangkalan* drivers ineligible for registration – a fact that contradicted Gojek's public suggestion that conventional drivers should stop protesting and join the platform. Many *pangkalan* drivers either exceeded the company's age limit or did not meet the health or (digital) literacy standards. Or they failed the company's bureaucratic requirements; some had never acquired a driver's licence, nor paid their vehicle taxes, while a few were unable to produce official identity documents, avoiding the expensive and time-consuming bureaucratic demands that these entailed.

The democratizing effects of the platform were, in this sense, tied to a liberal idea of equality. Invoking the abstract principle of individual rights and opportunity, the enrolment process behind Gojek effectively ignored the existing structural inequalities which made the young, educated, urban drivers eligible to enrol, while excluding the old, the under-documented and the minimally literate. The *ojek* industry provided a space for these groups to make a living, though the space was exclusively male. By contrast, Gojek attracted new demographics, including women, and large numbers of part-time drivers who sought to supplement their main income from other jobs; a trend that has been observed in the platform economy in other parts of the world (Schor and Attwood-Charles, 2017). Conventional drivers found it hard to accept: 'some of the Gojek and Grab Bike drivers work just for additional income on top of their daily office work, while we do this to survive', as one young driver at Kalibata City put it (Budiari, 2015). The idea of newcomers depriving them of their livelihoods in order to top up incomes from other jobs was seen to violate their sense of distributive fairness. It was perceived as an undue accumulation of livelihood opportunities which infringed upon the moral right of everyone to make a living.

These tensions were aggravated by Gojek's aggressive expansion strategy. Especially at the beginning, when the numbers of registered drivers were surging, the company did not seem to have any quantitative limits. For as long as the public perception was shaped by the miracle stories of high-earning Gojek drivers, the company did not concern itself with the individual welfare of its drivers, nor did it care about flooding the market with an oversupply of drivers. The seeming abundance of 'partner' drivers only fed into the Gojek hype. For company investors, these numbers were an indicator of successful growth, just as the flocks of corporate green motorcyclists increased the public visibility of the platform.

Pricing

Another key difference between the conventional and platform-based service model is related to pricing. In general, *pangkalan* drivers have a fixed pricing scheme for all common destinations, which serves as the base to proportionally estimate fares to less common destinations. These fixed prices, however, do not exist in any written form and are usually reserved for local and regular clients, while one-time customers have to haggle over the fare. In these negotiations, price offers may depend on not only distance, but also weather and traffic conditions, the availability of alternative transport options, and, importantly, the customer's assumed financial capacity. Indonesians who appear to belong to the middle or upper classes and white foreigners (such as myself) have to negotiate hard if they want to pay an amount close to the 'standard' fare, and success is by no means guaranteed, especially when any of the other pricing factors apply. This dual pricing system combines two logics of relationality: a differentiation between familiar people and strangers, and one between those 'people who have' (*orang ada*) and those who do not. Both distinctions are in tension with the liberal ideal of abstract equality, which prescribes pricing as an impersonal process determined by the invisible hand of the market. The relational logic of the *pangkalan*, in contrast, treats pricing as a social practice of balancing inequality (von Vacano, 2019). It is grounded in a morality that recognizes economic inequality and adheres to a processual understanding of fairness. In contrast to the market ethic, where pricing is blind to the conditions of individual economic agents, pricing in the *pangkalan* is oriented precisely towards the different 'abilities and needs' of the transactional partners (see also Graeber, 2014).

Gojek sought to introduce a universal pricing system. This new mode of pricing was strictly impersonal as fares were no longer determined by the drivers, but calculated by the platform's application, based on geographical distance and time of day. However, despite its appeals to tech-powered transparency, the Gojek pricing system was characterized by promotional schemes designed to undermine other providers. These promotional offers were pivotal in attracting customers to the digital service model. They undercut *pangkalan* fares – often significantly – and formed the basis of a fierce price war between platform rivals (see Schor and Attwood-Charles, 2017).

This strategy required vast amounts of initial capital investment as the gap between (extremely) low customer prices and (initially high) drivers' fares had to be compensated. For example, in the six months between October 2015 and March 2016 alone, Gojek was reported to have spent US$73 million on keeping its business model afloat (Al Azhari et al, 2016). Huge amounts of cash were spent in the scramble for market leadership. This dynamic was fuelled and sustained by a constant flow of venture capital from large global players like Google, Temasek and DiDi Chuxing (Wright, 2017). Following the logic of venture capital, these investors were prepared to put 'growth before profits' (Srnicek, 2017, 119), even for a couple of years, as they bid on the eventual prospect of spectacular profits once the platform had reached a position of marked monopoly (Langley and Leyshon, 2017, 25).

Within this financialized business model, prices were completely detached from the actual costs of labour, undermining the ability of conventional drivers – without overseas investors – to compete. The platforms' subsidized expansion became a great concern to *pangkalan* drivers, who accused the platforms of unfair competition and condemned their promotional offers as a practice of unsustainable pricing. This argument stood in clear contrast to Gojek's stated objective to empower the drivers. And yet, it barely found its way into the public *ojek* debate, which focused on the territorial aspect of the conflict, framing it as a 'turf war' (Gokkon, 2015). Conventional drivers were often accused of possessing a 'lack of competitive spirit' and of being jealous of the professionalism of Gojek (reader comments, Jakarta Post, 2015).

With prices declining and economic pressure mounting, a growing number of conventional *ojek* drivers felt forced to join the platforms. This allowed the remaining *pangkalan* drivers to adjust to the new situation and scale down their membership size. By the end of 2016, after more than one and a half years of confrontations and controversy, most of the *pangkalan* drivers had admitted defeat and taken down their protest banners. Jakarta's *ojek* industry transitioned into a new phase of coexistence, in which remaining conventional drivers continued to operate under the *pangkalan* code, while it was recognized that Gojek were working under their own set of rules, as set by the algorithmic code of the platform.

Appropriating platform labour: the drivers fight back

As the conflict between conventional and digital *ojek* drivers subsided, a new antagonism rose to the surface, as Grab and Gojek drivers began to defy their status as 'partners' and confront their respective platforms with labour demands. Mobilization among platform drivers began as early as November 2015, when Gojek management cut the drivers' rates from IDR4,000 to IDR3,000 per kilometre, that is from 30 to 23 US cents. This was just the beginning of a series of deteriorations in the platform's remuneration scheme, as bonuses continued to be cut and rates reduced to IDR1,500 (11 US cents) in July 2016 – less than half of the original rate. Following the international script of platform capitalism (see Schor and Attwood-Charles, 2017, 9), as soon as large numbers of drivers had been enticed to join Gojek, they became a target of the platform's cost saving efforts, since cutting the costs of their labour was the only way Gojek could afford to maintain its subsidized promotion schemes. But with each fee cut, the level of organized protest among digital drivers seemed to grow. Every now and then, these protests chalked up minor victories regarding the details of the platform's performance evaluation and incentive schemes. However, it took Gojek drivers two years to pressure their platform to raise the rate to IDR2,220 (16 US cents) – three months after Grab drivers had achieved similar success.

This tactic of direct negotiations with pseudo-employers was complemented by demands for legal protection. Digital *ojek* drivers were given hope by the Indonesian legislature's efforts to regulate the four-wheeled ride-hailing industry. They demanded the full legal recognition of motorbike taxis as a mode of public transportation. A group of Gojek drivers even managed to force a Supreme Court hearing on this matter, though the court ultimately rejected their case, citing a lack of safety in motorbike passenger transportation. However, by this time, drivers' associations had succeeded in generating sufficient political pressure to attract the interest of legislators in the Transportation Ministry. Invoking 'public interest', the ministry issued a regulation on the 'protection and safety for motorcycle users' (No. 12/2019). The regulation stipulated standardized fares, provisions for customer safety, and transparent procedures for the hiring and suspension of drivers. As a supplement to this framework, Ministerial Decree No. 348/2019 determined regionally specific floor and ceiling prices, from IDR2,000 to IDR2,500 per km for the Jakarta Metropolitan Area.

These price caps fell far short of the drivers' demands, and much of the regulation was difficult to enforce in practice. However, the mobilization of digital motorbike drivers constituted a notable success insofar as it defied the structural fragmentation of the platform drivers (Ford and Honan, 2019). Initially, the process of self-organization was not directed towards the platforms but driven by the need of digital drivers to protect themselves from the wrath of local *pangkalan* members (see, for example, Frey, 2020, 44). However, over time, these coalitions stabilized into local grassroots communities which began to emulate the *pangkalan* system of organizing around a physical meeting place (Ford and Honan, 2019, 529), albeit without fulfilling any of its regulative functions. These local groups were coordinated through digital forms of communication, the most generic way of organizing among platform labourers (Johnston, 2020). In online forums and chat groups, drivers shared the latest information on the changing service guidelines and remuneration schemes of their respective platforms (Ford and Honan, 2019, 539–540). These digital grassroots networks further served as a safety net for emergency assistance, for example, if members were injured in a road accident (Ford and Honan, 2019, 539). However, more centralized and hierarchical structures of organization were required – including affiliation with established labour unions – in order to mobilize larger numbers of drivers and force the platforms and government to the negotiating table (Ford and Honan, 2019). Unlike the *pangkalan*-inspired grassroots communities, these larger organizational structures were created and maintained by a subset of new drivers with a history of employment in the industrial sector, who brought their experiences of formal labour organization to the *ojek* industry.

Conclusion

In this chapter I have investigated the changing and contested modes of work in the Indonesian motorbike taxi industry. Through a deconstructive reading of the in/formality paradigm, I have analysed the different social and economic forms of organization and the different values these modes of work enact. My ethnographic analysis has shown how the platform model of transport work in Jakarta standardized and impersonalized the localized, socially thick system of *ojek* drivers. In contrast to the decentralized *pangkalan* system, Gojek principally operates in the sphere of state governance – as a tax-paying, registered enterprise, which, at least until 2019, managed to exploit the regulative loopholes of Indonesian transportation law. Gojek introduced a 'more structured employment relationship' (Ford and Honan, 2017, 287) into the Indonesian motorbike taxi industry; it generated a new and ambivalent position of dependent self-employment, which was met with a principled refusal to work for someone else's profit (a position upheld by many of the remaining *pangkalan* drivers) and by an attempt to translate the new dependency into a discourse of labour demands (a response driven by a new group of wage labourers joining Gojek).

My comparison has presented Gojek as a prime example of the platform capitalism which prophesizes the values of individual entrepreneurship, 'free' market-based competition, and meritocracy, while pursuing an aggressive expansion strategy driven by the 'growth at all costs' imperative of venture capital. I have further shown how the bureaucratic qualities of the platform, underpinned by a series of liberal-democratic values, are deployed to legitimize this business model, merging the promises of social and technological 'modernization'. Unconcerned by the livelihoods or welfare of drivers in the present, this financialized business model is driven by a detached logic of future accumulation, which aims to generate fabulous profits, once the platform has secured a market monopoly, thus suspending the necessity for economic viability (see Srnicek, 2017, 120–121). However, I have argued that this system did not generate the profit-maximizing entrepreneurial subject it promoted. Instead, Gojek drivers continued to enact relational and cooperative visions of work, recreating the social structure of the *pangkalan* in order to embed the platform within the social and political fabric of the city.

In place of shareholder profits, the *pangkalan* system is driven by the existential immediacy of workers' needs, and the complementary values of distributing and protecting livelihood opportunities. I have shown that the cooperative structure of *ojek* ranks is entrenched in a communal, rather than a liberal sense of (economic) fairness. It produces its own mechanisms of inclusion and exclusion that prioritize relationships rooted in place, including kinship and neighbourhood. Its relational pricing strategy represents a pragmatic approach to negotiating the real-life inequalities which undermine liberal appeals to impersonal equality.

The '*ojek* vs. Gojek' story thus challenges binary understandings of work as formal/informal and stable/precarious, pointing instead to the mundane and constitutive quality of work as the everyday practice of livelihood and 'doing economy'. Furthermore, it illustrates the ways in which the logics and forms of platform capitalism are interpreted and domesticated by workers on Jakartan street corners, complicating accounts of the future of work based on 'simplistic assumptions of convergence' (see the Introduction to this volume).

Acknowledgements

I would like to thank the German Academic Exchange Service (DAAD) for funding my Jakarta fieldwork between October 2014 and September 2015, and the editors of this volume for their dedicated feedback.

Notes

[1] This protective purpose relates to the vernacular notion of wind (*anging*) as a cause of sickness.

[2] Comparable data on Grab's fleet size is hard to find since the company has made it a policy not to release any country-specific numbers on its fleet size.

[3] This vision statement has been modified over the years. The 2016 version is quoted in my own translation from the company's website: www.go-jek.com/ (accessed 17 July 2016).

⁴ Freischlad (2015) reports an age limit of 55 years, whereas Ford and Honan (2017, 282) quote a maximum age of 50 years. The most recent age range is quoted from the company's webpage: www.go-jek.com/faq/mitra/bergabung-menjadi-mitra-kami/#bergabung-menjadi-mitra-go-ride (accessed 18 July 2019).

References

Agbiboa, D.E. (2019) 'State law as a means of resistance: Okada riders versus the Lagos State government', in Agbiboa, D.E. (ed) *Transport, Transgression and Politics in African Cities: The Rhythm of Chaos*. Cities and Society, Abingdon, New York, NY: Routledge, pp 147–171.

Al Azhari, M., Diela, T. and Siniwi, R.M. (2016) 'Go-Jek Burns Cash on Hefty Subsidies, While Grab Gains Traction', *Jakarta Globe*, 18 July, http://jakartaglobe.id/business/go-jek-burns-cash-hefty-subsidies-grab-gains-traction/

Breman, J. (1976 'A dualistic labour system? A critique of the "informal sector" concept: I: the informal sector', *Economic and Political Weekly*, 11(48): 1870–1876.

Breman, J. and van der Linden, M. (2014) 'Informalizing the economy: The return of the social question at a global level', *Development and Change*, 45(5): 920–940.

Budiari, I. (2015) 'Ojek drivers struggle to survive amid rapid urban change', *Jakarta Post*, 15 July, https://www.thejakartapost.com/news/2015/07/15/ojek-drivers-struggle-survive-amid-rapid-urban-change.html

Burchardt, H.-J., Peters, S. and Weinmann, N. (2013) 'Prekarität und Informalität – eine Annäherung in globaler Perspektive', in Burchardt, H.-J., Peters, S. and Weinmann, N. (eds) *Arbeit in globaler Perspektive: Facetten informeller Beschäftigung*, Frankfurt a. Main, New York, NY: Campus, pp 9–28.

Cervero, R. and Golubb, A. (2007) 'Informal transport: A global perspective', *Transport Policy*, 14(6): 445–457.

Cities Development Initiative for Asia (CDIA) (2011) 'Informal public transportation networks in three Indonesian cities, Manila', https://cdia.asia/publication/informal-public-transportation-networks-in-three-indonesian-cities/

Davies, A.R., Donald, B., Gray, M. and Knox-Hayes, J. (2017) 'Sharing economies: moving beyond binaries in a digital age', *Cambridge Journal of Regions, Economy and Society*, 10(2): 209–230.

Doherty, J. (2017) 'Life (and limb) in the fast-lane: Disposable people as infrastructure in Kampala's boda boda industry', *Critical African Studies* 9(2): 192–209.

Ford, M. and Honan, V. (2017) 'The Go-Jek effect', in Jurriëns, W. (ed) *Digital Indonesia: Connectivity and divergence*, Singapore: ISEAS, pp 275–288.

Ford, M. and Honan, V. (2019) 'The limits of mutual aid: Emerging forms of collectivity among app-based transport workers in Indonesia', *Journal of Industrial Relations*, 61(4): 528–548.

Freischlad, N. (2015) 'Why motorcycle taxi drivers are ganging up against on-demand ride apps in Indonesia', *Tech in Asia*, 15 July, https://www.techinasia.com/startups-in-indonesia-indonesia-motorcycle-hailing-taxi-apps-jakarta-gojek

Frey, B. (2020) 'Platform labor and in/formality. Organization among motorcycle taxi drivers in Bandung, Indonesia', *Anthropology of Work Review*, 41(1): 36–49.

Gokkon, B. (2015) 'Go-Jek Navigates "Turf Wars" Amid Industry Shake-Up', *Jakarta Globe*, 2 July, https://jakartaglobe.id/news/go-jek-navigates-turf-wars-amid-industry-shake/

Graeber, D. (2014) 'On the moral grounds of economic relations: A Maussian approach', *Journal of Classical Sociology*, 14(1): 65–77.

Hart, K. (1973) 'Informal income opportunities and urban employment in Ghana', *Journal of Modern African Studies*, 11(1): 61–89.

Hart, K. (2006) 'Bureaucratic form and the informal economy', in Guha-Khasnobis, B., Kanbur, R. and Ostrom, E. (eds) *Linking the Formal and Informal Economy*, Oxford: Oxford University Press, pp 21–35.

Ibrahim, B. and Bize, A. (2018) 'Waiting together: The motorcycle taxi stand as Nairobi infrastructure', *Africa Today*, 65(2): 73–91.

International Labour Office (ILO) (1972) *Employment, incomes and equality: A strategy for increasing productive employment in Kenya*, Geneva.

International Labour Office (ILO) (2002) *Women and men in the informal economy: A statistical picture*, Geneva.

International Labour Organization (ILO) (2019) *ILOSTAT* [data base], https://ilostat.ilo.org/ (accessed August 14, 2019).

Jakarta Post readers' comments (2015) 'Go-Jek fearing violence from traditional ojek, *Jakarta Post*, 18 June.

Johnston, H. (2020) 'Labour geographies of the platform economy: Understanding collective organizing strategies in the context of digitally mediated work', *International Labour Review*, 159(1): 25–45.

Kenney, M. and Zysman, J. (2016) 'The rise of the platform economy', *Issues in Science and Technology*, 32(3): 61–69.

Langley, P. and Leyshon, A. (2017) 'Platform capitalism: The intermediation and capitalisation of digital economic circulation', *Finance and Society*, 3(1): 11–31.

Lee, D. (2018) 'How Ojek Became Go-Jek: Disruptive Technologies and the Infrastructure of Urban Citizenship in Indonesia', *International Journal of Urban and Regional Research*, https://www.ijurr.org/spotlight-on/disruptive-urban-technologies/how-ojek-became-go-jek-disruptive-technologies-and-the-infrastructure-of-urban-citizenship-in-indonesia/

Meagher, K. (2010) *Identity Economics: Social Networks and the Informal Economy in Nigeria*, Woodbridge: Boydell and Brewer.

Pollio, A. (2019) 'Forefronts of the sharing economy: Uber in Cape Town', *International Journal of Urban and Regional Research*, 43(4): 760–775.

Portes, A. (2010) *Economic Sociology*, Princeton, NJ: Princeton University Press.

Pratama, A.H. (2016) 'Go-Jek: A unicorn's journey', *Tech in Asia*, 13 August, https://www.techinasia.com/how-go-jek-became-unicorn

Sassen, S. (1994) 'The informal economy: Between new developments and old regulations', *Yale Law Journal*, 103: 2289–2304.

Schor, J.B. and Attwood-Charles, W. (2017) 'The "sharing" economy: Labor, inequality, and social connection on for-profit platforms', *Sociology Compass*, 11(8): e12493.

Sopranzetti, C. (2017) *Owners of the map. Motorcycle Taxi Drivers, mobility, and politics in Bangkok*, Berkeley, CA: University of California Press.

Srnicek, N. (2017) *Platform capitalism*, Cambridge, Malden, MA: Polity.

Suryarandika, R. (2016) 'Nadiem Makarim, Pendiri dan CEO Gojek Indonesia: Membangkitkan Gairah Usaha Tukang Ojek', *Republika*, 16 March, https://www.republika.co.id/berita/koran/halaman-1/16/03/16/o44e4715-nadiem-makarim-pendiri-dan-ceo-gojek-indonesia-membangkitkan-gairah-usaha-tukang-ojek

von Vacano, M. (2017) '"Sharing economy" versus "informal sector": Jakarta's motorbike taxi industry in turmoil', *ANUAC*, 2(2): 97–101.

von Vacano, M. (2019) 'Reciprocity reconsidered: Toward a research ethic of economic participation', in Stodulka, T., Dinkelaker, S. and Thajib, F. (eds) *Affective Dimensions of Fieldwork and Ethnography*, Cham: Springer, pp 123–134.

Wilson, I.D. (2011) 'Reconfiguring rackets: Racket regimes, protection and the state in post-New Order Jakarta', in Aspinall, E. and van Klinken, G. (eds) *The State and Illegality in Indonesia*, Leiden: KITLV, pp 239–259.

Wright, C. (2017) 'Grab, AirAsia and Go-Jek lead Asean corporate charge into payments', *Euromoney*, 1 June, https://link.gale.com/apps/doc/A534788525/ITOF?u=fub&sid=ITOF&xid=f1f77c03

Yusuf, H.A. (2015) 'Pengemudi Go-Jek dipukul oleh tukang ojek', *Koran Tempo*, 27 July, https://koran.tempo.co/read/378360/pengemudi-go-jek-dipukul-tukang-ojek

10

"I Voted Bolsonaro for President": Street Vending and the Crisis of Labour Representation in Belo Horizonte, Brazil

Mara Nogueira

On Sunday 1 July 2019 I arrived in the town of Prados in Minas Gerais on a coach with 30 street vendors. We arrived in the middle of the night in order for vendors to claim the best spots for their stalls. The vendors sold a wide range of products – from fruits to electronic tweezers – to Catholic pilgrims attending a religious celebration. Ana, who had been a *camelô*[1] for over 40 years, travelled in the coach with her son David. I had spent a long time chatting with her when we eventually approached the topic of politics. I asked her who she had voted for in the last elections. "I voted for Bolsonaro for president," she replied. I asked what had motivated her choice. "Because I hate Pimentel." Fernando Pimentel is a politician and member of Brazil's most traditional left wing party, the Workers' Party (PT), and served as the mayor of Belo Horizonte between 2001 and 2009. During his premiership, the *camelôs* were displaced from public areas as part of a 'revitalization' exercise. While some *camelôs* were relocated to popular shopping malls, street vending became criminalized by law and a zero-tolerance policy was applied to those who attempted to remain on the streets.

Ana described the trauma she had experienced during this period; several of her colleagues got sick and some even committed suicide. "It's very sad when someone works with something for their entire lives and all of a sudden they are not allowed to do it anymore." She emphasized that many who support PT are drug users and that their government had been great for drug dealers like her nephew, "But for the *camelôs* the PT never did a thing. Not even Lula."[2] I had heard similar responses from other street vendors in Minas Gerais. Ana's support for Bolsonaro was rooted in a rejection of the PT. The trauma of the displacement suffered under the PT's local administration was still being felt. A number of vendors emphasized that the PT did not improve their lives and failed to represent the interests of street vendors on the national scale.

The fractured relationship between street vendors and the PT is indicative of a wider crisis of traditional labour organization. Across the world, political parties founded on the idea of the 'worker' are struggling to mobilize voters' support using traditional working class narratives. In Brazil, the symbolic notion of the 'worker' represented in the PT's constitution continues to invoke a nostalgic idea of the male, waged industrial worker of the Fordist era – an idea that is increasingly disconnected from the experiences and aspirations of *camelôs* such as Ana. In this chapter, I demonstrate how the *camelôs*' rejection of the PT in the 2018 national elections must be understood in relation to a broader crisis of labour and its repercussions in the urban environment. Following Sharma and Gupta (2009, 4), I argue that '[t]he emergent transnational economic order is not only reshaping the global labour map, but also transforming the relationship between citizenship, national identity, and the state' at multiple scales.

The flexibilization of labour relations since the 1980s has increased the precariousness of workers across the world, narrowing the gap between experiences of work in the global North and South. However, the political response to this crisis has taken different forms in different regions of the world. For example, the notion of a rising 'global precariat' (Standing, 2014) is rooted in the experiences of workers in post-industrial societies of the global North, concealing the politics and histories of workers in other regions of the world where formal wage employment has never been the norm (Munck, 2013; Breman and Linden, 2014; Ferguson and Li, 2018). In such contexts, the role and significance of traditional working class organizations must be critically examined rather than assumed. Trade unions have played a significant role in the political history of Brazil, most notably during the struggles for democracy in the 1980s. However, they have always been associated with an industrial working class 'elite' (Tyler, 1982), excluding the large proportion of workers that operate outside of labour protection laws. The Brazilian Institute of Geography and Statistics (IBGE, 2019) estimates that 41.1 per cent of the total labour force (38 million people) are employed in the informal economy. This trend is visible in the streets of the country, where many disadvantaged workers strive to make a living as street vendors, facing increasing competition as opportunities in the formal wage workforce continue to shrink.

In 2018, 57.5 million Brazilian citizens surprised the world by electing Jair Bolsonaro as president. Bolsonaro is a far-right Conservative politician, mostly known for his violent rhetoric and extreme views. He is openly homophobic and misogynistic, embraces gun ownership as an anti-violence policy and supports the devastation of Brazil's rainforest. The election results were a resounding defeat for Brazil's traditional left wing PT, which held the presidency from 2002 until Dilma Roussef's impeachment in 2016. Once associated with 'morality and administrative experience' (Samuels, 2004, 1000), the PT was rejected by many voters as a corrupt organization dominated by criminals (Richmond, 2018). Over the course of his campaign, Bolsonaro went from being a fringe candidate supported by a handful of ultra-conservative Brazilians to being the choice of a significant proportion of low-income non-white citizens (Richmond, 2018).

This chapter interrogates the relationship between Bolsonaro's victory and the crisis of wage labour and labour politics in Brazil. I make two key arguments. First, I argue that the decline of the PT must be understood in relation to Brazil's peripheral position in global capitalism, and more specifically, the historical exclusion of non-waged workers and their interests from the trade union movement (Breman and van der Linden, 2014; Chun and Agarwala, 2016). Secondly, I argue that this decline was accentuated at the local level by the PT's resurrection of 'hygienist policies' (Garmany and Richmond, 2020) designed to reproduce the idea of the disciplined, uniformed, documented, 'ordered' wage worker of the world-class city to the detriment of *camelôs* such as Ana.

The rest of the chapter is organized in five sections. The following section traces the emergence of the new trade unionism movement in Brazil and the birth of the PT in the 1980s. It offers a critique of the symbolic idea of the 'worker' implicit in the party's foundation and the forms of exclusion it encoded. I then examine the trajectory of the PT in the city of Belo Horizonte, before considering the ways in which its urban policy displaced and disenfranchised street vendors whose political discourses are shaped by those experiences. The chapter draws upon qualitative data collected during four months of fieldwork between 2018 and 2019, complemented by an analysis of group chat conversations with street vendors during the electoral campaign.

The rise and fall of the Workers' Party in Brazil

Trade unionism in dependent capitalism

Late industrialization emerged in Latin America as a result of fundamental changes at the international level in the context of the Cold War, including the attempts of advanced capitalist countries in the global North to disseminate their model of 'development' to other regions of the world (Hart, 2010). A number of countries in Latin America, particularly Brazil, benefited from the relocation of industries and investment. Commenting on this process, Silver (2003, 5–6) emphasizes that while the emigration of productive capital from industrialized countries has weakened traditional labour movements, it also engendered the emergence of 'powerful new labour movements rooted in expanding mass production industries' in other regions of the world. Not only were those movements 'successful in improving wages and working conditions; they were also key "subjects" behind the spread of democracy in the late twentieth century' (Silver, 2003, 5–6).

Labour movements in Brazil were severely repressed during the dictatorship (1964–1985). This period was also characterized by fast-paced economic growth, culminating in the so-called 'Brazilian miracle', in which the economy grew by 10 per cent between 1969 and 1973. This expansion was led by state-driven industrialization, which relied heavily on the presence of multinationals and engendered the creation of a new industrial proletariat. Industrial growth was geographically concentrated in the ABC region of São Paulo[3] where the automotive and metallurgical belt developed (Antunes and Santana, 2014). While economic growth and rising standards of living provided legitimacy to the authoritarian military government, the economic downturn and accelerated inflation that followed the 1973 oil crisis eroded support for the regime. Facing growing dissatisfaction, the military began to promote reforms that enabled the growth of an opposition within the state-controlled corporatist union movement (Tyler, 1982).

Luis Inácio da Silva was elected to the board of the metalworkers' union in 1978 with a mandate to campaign actively for better working conditions and wages in the context of inflation (Antunes and Santana,

2014). Workers in Saab-Scania decided to go on strike on 12 May 1978. The movement quickly spread to other factories in the region until 45,000 workers in the ABC region went on strike (Humphrey, 1979). These events fostered a new unionism that began to actively oppose the military regime. As Tyler (1982, 316) argues:

> The 1978 strike was fought on a wages issue by workers who, after all, constitute an industrial elite: they are paid about three times the statutory minimum wage or more if they are employed by a big multinational company. But behind the wages issue lie deeper political concerns. The new representatives of the shop floor refuse to accept passively the unequal distribution of Brazil's economic wealth.

Union membership was thus limited to a fairly restricted proportion of Brazil's labour force: industrialized waged workers. These workers were covered by labour laws created in the 1930s during Getúlio Vargas's administration, and able to mobilize through collective bargaining via unions. These laws effectively expanded social rights uniquely to formalized waged workers, deepening previously existing racialized, gendered and class-based inequalities and reinforcing a system of differentiated citizenship (Holston, 2008). Barchiesi (2011, 7) describes a similar situation in post-apartheid South Africa, arguing that 'earning a wage decides here the boundary between inclusion and exclusion, privilege and marginality, prosperity and poverty. Social citizenship appears as a clear-cut line separating the regularly employed from the underemployed and the jobless'. In Brazil, this state-sponsored system of social citizenship excluded huge masses of urban workers, notably in the tertiary sector, such as *pedreiros* (builders), *engraxates* (shoe shiners) and *camelôs e ambulantes* (street vendors) (Holston, 2008). Rather than being a 'surplus population' irrelevant to capital accumulation (Ferguson and Li, 2018), these workers played a critical role on the periphery of capitalism by providing low-cost services to the industrialized proletariat (Oliveira, 2003).

This organized industrial urban proletariat inspired the symbolic notion of 'worker' inherent in the foundation of the PT in 1980. The party became an influential political force, pushing for re-democratization and the reorientation of the country's economic model. Union leaders such as Lula emerged as important players in the national arena. Twelve years after leading the metalworkers' strike, Lula came second in Brazil's presidential campaign of 1989 (Antunes and Santana, 2014, 15).

The emergence of the PT should be understood in relation to the collapse of the authoritarian regime and its import substitution model of industrialization. The global offshoring of industrial production cleared the way for a new era of labour politics – and labour politicians – in Brazil. While the party had a heterogeneous support base, the 'leaders of Brazil's "new unionism" movement of the late 1970s not only formed the nucleus of the PT's founding group but continued to play critical roles as the party evolved' (Samuels, 2004, 1006). However, the union movement in Brazil was – and remains – restricted to a small minority of the working class (Alves, 2000). The unions' continued focus on formal waged workers excluded a large proportion of the working population. As Breman and van der Linden argue (2014, 934):

> The trade unions set up in those [Southern] countries recruited membership mainly from big industry and the public sector. Their fight for labour rights and social security benefits remained restricted to a tiny portion of the total workforce and the formal conditions of employment that this small frontguard came to enjoy were abrogated when the tide of informalization began to swell.

Brazil experienced an economic recession in the early 1990s characterized by increasing unemployment and inflation and decreasing disposable income (Amann and Baer, 2002; Duarte, 2013). Wage employment in the industrial sector began to decline and the share of informal workers in the total labour force increased from 28 per cent in 1991 to 38 per cent at the end of the 1990s (Ulyssea, 2005). Unions from different sectors adapted to the new adverse economic order by attempting to reduce partial sectorial losses through negotiation rather than open confrontation (Boito, 1994; Alves, 2000). Responding to this shifting political landscape, the PT tempered its socialist aspirations with a pragmatic approach, influenced by the party's growing administrative experience in local government (Samuels, 2004; Loureiro and Saad-Filho, 2019). After three defeats in national elections, Lula and the PT sought to become palatable to a majority in order to gain the presidency in 2002. Despite benefiting informal and unwaged workers in indirect ways,[4] I argue that the PT's politics of accommodation overlooked the emerging challenges of a changing world of labour. Policies aimed at waged employees – such as the rise in minimum wages and the strengthening of labour laws – continued to exclude the large proportion of the Brazilian workforce making a living outside the purview of the state. Such workers were fundamental to the successes of industrialization and urbanization but excluded from the benefits of both processes.

Marginalized workers and the right to the city

Urbanizing industrial centres in Brazil have partially been produced by the efforts of marginalized workers who challenged their exclusion by claiming their rights to cities that they were building from scratch (Fischer et al, 2014). Emerging from the peripheries and *favelas* of the large metropolitan centres, this movement of 'insurgent citizens' (Holston, 2008) has opened new avenues for experimentation in participatory democracy (Caldeira and Holston, 2015). The social movements for housing that were also gaining strength during re-democratization constituted yet another support base of the PT. Influenced by housing movements, local administrations of the PT implemented innovative urban policies in the 1980s and 1990s, which were later federalized when the party took the national office (Friendly, 2013). However, despite the progress of Brazil's urban reform, the ascent of neoliberalism has strongly influenced how urban policy evolved in the country (Rolnik, 2013). Moreover, policy innovations have focused mostly on issues around housing and participatory planning, overlooking the increasing relevance of accessing urban space for the livelihoods of unwaged workers such as Ana (Nogueira, 2019).

The production of urban space has become one of the main engines of capital accumulation in contemporary capitalism (Brenner, 2004). Consequently, there is an ongoing 'war of places' (Rolnik, 2015), in which cities are increasingly reliant on property redevelopment and urban revitalization projects for attracting investment and maximizing revenue. Attracted to undervalued areas with potential for valorization, those projects often facilitate the displacement of vulnerable populations, an issue that has been widely debated in gentrification (Lee et al, 2016) and displacement studies (Atkinson, 2015). This literature, however, has tended to focus on the home as the centrepiece of urban belonging, neglecting the ways in which permanence in the city is also a matter of accessing a workspace (Schindler, 2014). Yet workspace displacement often creates similar feelings of loss engendered by the disruption of one's social networks (Nogueira, 2019), impacting the lives of 'marginalised populations who rely on these spaces for their material and symbolic reproduction' (Crossa, 2009, 299).

Despite the continued growth of the informal economy, little has been written about the struggles of informal and unwaged workers to secure access to a workspace (Brown, 2015). Many cities have strict rules prohibiting the activities of street vendors. In order to survive, street vendors are thus often forced into temporary arrangements with the local authorities that do not guarantee any kind of social protection or secure access to space (Itikawa, 2016). They also possess a capacity to resist, challenge and subvert neoliberal entrepreneurial strategies aimed at prohibiting their presence in the urban environment (Crossa, 2009). However, these capacities have not been translated into social protection, which remains mediated by formal wage employment in Brazil. For street vendors such as Ana, the right to work is indistinguishable from the right to workspace in the city, a right that neoliberal urban reforms often undermine.

In the next section, I discuss the case of street vendors in Belo Horizonte, where the PT implemented innovative urban policies after winning the local elections in 1993 (Bedê and de Moura Costa, 2006). I argue that despite advancements in the housing sector, local urban policy has continuously restricted street vendors' rights to space and thus to work. In doing so, I demonstrate the connection between the global crisis of labour and the local crisis of urban governance in Brazilian cities.

A short history of street vending in Belo Horizonte

The *camelôs* represent a historical type of street vendor in Brazilian urban centres involved in the retail of products of small commercial value (food, candies, cigarettes, and so on) for domestic consumption. In Belo Horizonte, *camelôs* and other types of street vendors had been present in the city since its inauguration in 1897. The first planned city in Brazil, Belo Horizonte was built to be the new capital of Minas Gerais and, in the early years, suffered from recurrent shortages of supply. Street vendors then provided a crucial link in the economy as suppliers of subsistence products, while peddlers sold manufactured goods door to door. However, the latter were seen to represent unfair competition to local formal businesses by the local authorities. This conflict led to the creation of a tax for licensed peddlers and a fine for non-licensed vendors in 1908 (Jayme and Neves, 2010). Historically present on the outskirts of the city, street vendors became common in the city centre through a process of 'popularization' in the 1960s that was deepened in the subsequent decades. Despite years of relative economic and demographic decline, the centre has remained a vital space, catering mostly for the working classes from the peripheries, who either work in the centre or travel through it as part of their daily commute (Vilela, 2006).

The unemployment crisis of the 1990s facilitated a rise in the number of street vendors operating in the city centre. Traditional *camelôs* were then joined by a new type of street 'merchant' constituted of unemployed industrial workers who invested redundancy payments in high-quality goods (such as electronics) to sell on the street (Sandoval, 2007). Stimulated by the effects of trade liberalization that made imported goods cheaper, this new group of *camelôs* became a common presence on the streets of all big cities in Brazil, representing a new form of competition for local retail shops. Retail business associations and leaders of commercial workers' unions responded by demanding government regulation of informal street vending. The occupation of public spaces by street vendors brought them into frequent conflict with shop keepers and everyday users of urban space, engendering a difficult situation for the municipal administration (Zambelli, 2006). After a frustrated attempt to promote the registration of a limited number of vendors in the 1990s, the local administration decided to invest in a 'definitive' solution with the creation of popular shopping malls for the relocation of licensed *camelôs*.

In 2003 the local government created a new municipal law for the regulation of urban spaces, described by then mayor Fernando Pimentel (PT) as an 'urban life statute', aimed at 'regulating the coexistence' of different people within the city (Vilela, 2006). Enacted in 2004, the Code of Placements prohibited the use of public space for commercial purposes in the absence of an appropriate licence. In the same year, a programme for the 'revitalization' of the city centre (*Centro Vivo*) was launched. The goal of these policies was to 'clean' the streets of the 'disorder' caused by street vendors, while promoting their 'formalization' and displacement to newly constructed shopping malls. The discourse of 'informality' was strategically deployed by the local government to legitimize the displacement of workers (Crossa, 2016). Supported by local media campaigns that portrayed street vendors as troublemakers, such initiatives aimed to discipline unwaged workers and transform them into formal shopkeepers, while forging new entrepreneurial subjectivities (Carrieri and Murta, 2011; Kopper, 2015). These new entrepreneurs in the popular shopping malls were expected to pay rent and utility bills. Many of them were unable to meet these new financial commitments and went back to the streets, where they found a much more hostile environment (Zambelli, 2006). For the vendors, the main goal of the municipal authority was to clear the streets. After concluding the relocation, the authority abandoned the everyday management of the malls.

The Brazilian economy benefited from favourable external conditions and entered a new cycle of growth in the years that followed. From 2003 onwards, the PT federal government implemented social policies that, combined with economic growth, generated decreasing unemployment, inequality and poverty (de Andrade Baltar et al, 2010). Brazil's 2000s 'success story' was, however, the result of a pragmatic strategy, only viable under a series of conditions (Loureiro and Saad-Filho, 2019). When the favourable landscape was altered, gains were rapidly lost, dissolving the support for the party, which was also entangled in several corruption scandals. As Machado and Scalco (2020) argue, aspirations of social mobility among marginalized workers disintegrated, fostering a sense of betrayal. In the face of deteriorating living standards and the constant threat of criminalization, voters lost trust in the PT – a party they perceived to be incompetent and morally corrupt. In 2013, as the effects of the latest economic crisis became visible, more and more people took to the streets in order to make a living as street vendors. This 'quiet [re]encroachment' (Bayat, 2000) of Belo Horizonte's centre led to the resurgence of conflicts over the use of urban space and to a new round of 'urban revitalisation' in 2017. In the next section, I explore how this policy further exacerbated vendors' opposition to the PT, opening the door for the far-right congressman Jair Bolsonaro.

Street vending and the politics of urban space

"He works when he thinks he should"

In 2017 a new mayor was appointed in Belo Horizonte with a mandate to bring a solution to the issue of 'irregular' trade in the city centre. The Action Plan for Belo Horizonte's Hyper-centre, which sought to relocate street vendors operating in public spaces to popular shopping malls, was sanctioned by municipal law, and a large number of inspection agents were hired to control the use of public spaces. As Elena, a street vendor and social activist noted, "Lacerda [the former mayor] also had inspection agents after us but not as much as now. Nowadays the streets are full of inspection agents." Those attempting to stay on the streets suffered increased levels of harassment.

The policy was justified by the municipal authority as an attempt to promote 'the social and productive inclusion of street vendors', offering them small shops with subsidized rents of BRL20 (GBP3.51) for the first three months, with periodical readjustments thereafter.[5] However, for many vendors, this represented a repackaging of old policy that served to confine their activities and leave them in debt to a landlord. The policy disrupted a vibrant popular economy that provided vital livelihoods for unwaged workers. As Elena noted, "Those who are used to work on the streets do not want to be stuck inside a mall."

While the mall represented a loss of autonomy and mobility to street vendors, it represented a form of discipline and work ethic to city administrators. I asked Lucio, the planning director at the Urban Regulation Secretary, why he thought that the policy had been opposed by street vendors:

> 'Some of them do not adapt because the mall has rules, it has a schedule, a list of products that they cannot sell – for example, smuggled cigarettes. And this person doesn't have our work ethic … When I say ethics, I'm not talking about right and wrong. I'm talking about the fact that we wake up every day at the same time and work from 9 am to 6 pm. This person doesn't, he works when he thinks he should. When he thinks he shouldn't work, he doesn't! … So he prefers the dynamics of the street over the mall dynamics.'

Lucio's testimony attempts to defend the policy with reference to its enforcement of a 'work ethic' and temporal discipline associated with formal wage employment. As noted by Millar (2018), the routinized rhythms of low-end waged work are often incompatible with the lives of the urban poor and its everyday emergencies. The forms of living of street vendors create spatial and temporal dynamics that are alien to state bureaucrats. This mismatch is illustrated by Ursula's (sub-secretary of urban regulation) point of view: "It's all very complicated because the vendors' claims to public space are very random. The vendors' choices of where to locate on the street (*pontos*) are related to the movement of people, the time of the day, etc. Right?" For Ursula then, the 'random' movements of street vendors disturb the 'spatial order' of the city (Roy, 2012). But these movements were far from random. Instead, they represented highly strategic spatial and temporal responses to the ebbs and flows of the urban economy; moving around the city in ways to locate customers for a particular product at a particular time of day while avoiding harassment at the hands of the inspection agents and balancing caring and reproductive responsibilities. The move to the shopping mall thus rendered street vendors out of sync with the rhythms of the city.

As Isabella Gonçalves, a councilwoman for the opposition Socialism and Liberty Party explained, "Street vending is an urban question, it is a question of the struggle for rights on urban space, class struggle on urban space." She had worked closely with street vendors to articulate new forms of engagement with the government. In response to my question of whether street vendors felt included in the category of 'worker' associated with the PT, she responded:

'The street vendors have been historically excluded from the category of "worker" [trabalhadoras/es]. We are fighting for them to be approached [by the state] from a rights perspective, of labour rights, and not from a criminal law perspective. It may be the inspection agency, but it's still a punishing perspective. So, neither the state recognizes them as workers, nor the labour law and not even the unions.'

Critically, Isabella connected the question of urban space to that of the legitimate 'worker' discussed earlier. For her, the exclusion of street vendors from national understandings of the 'worker' had left them vulnerable to criminalization and displacement in a context where ideas of work and citizenship – and thus state protection – are deeply entangled. Indeed, one of the main arguments made by vendors complaining about state harassment was that they are workers (trabalhadoras/es) struggling to make a living and feed their families. In this context, the question of what counts as 'work' and who counts as a 'worker' is not academic – it is a question that has life-or-death implications for those making a living on the margins of the urban economy.

In his seminal work on machinists in Chicago, Burawoy (1982) demonstrates how the shop floor manufactures the consent necessary for the well-functioning of capitalist mass production. His account provides an empirical understanding of how labour is a process that produces particular forms of subjectivity. In her recent book, Millar (2018) explores the subjectivity forged under very different conditions, describing the 'forms of living' of waste pickers making a living on a Rio de Janeiro rubbish dump. She builds on recent critiques of the concept of informality, emphasizing its redundancy in contexts where the bureaucratic form created by the Fordist factory is the exception rather than the norm. Building on Millar's work, I argue that the political subjectivity of the street vendor in Belo Horizonte differs from that of the unionized worker that constituted the popular base of the PT. Critically, this subjectivity was repeatedly misunderstood by the municipality in its repeated attempts to formalize groups of workers for whom formalization often represented a loss of autonomy and mobility.

Ana, the *camelô* introduced at the outset of the chapter, told me that although she successfully trained as a nurse, she never looked for a formal waged job. Instead, she had become accustomed to life as a street vendor and enjoyed the sense of mobility and travel it provided. For many workers, this relative autonomy is crucial for balancing work with the maintenance of social networks and care for others as well as time needed to access social policies and other public infrastructures. However, such key aspects of their 'forms of living' rubbed up against the political priorities of the municipal government.

"The PT sold the street vendors!"

The Action Plan for Belo Horizonte's Hyper-centre successfully displaced many vendors to popular malls but sales were not enough for workers to pay rent and subsistence costs. In response, vendors on the streets and in the malls started to organize for better working conditions. From June to September 2018, I followed their movement, joining in meetings and protests, and making visits to popular shopping malls. It was during this time that I met Fabio, a politically active fruit vendor working on the streets. He added me to two group chats that vendors use to disseminate information, plan actions and, mostly, just to chat and keep in touch with each other.

When the campaign for the Brazilian national elections started, I was surprised that many of the street vendors were vocal about their support for Bolsonaro. My surprise came from the fact that his campaign was framed around a no-tolerance attitude towards criminality; an agenda that was likely to translate into further repression against unlicensed *camelôs*. Nevertheless, street vendors saw in Bolsonaro a possibility for change. As Lucas, another vendor argued:

> 'There is no point wishing for change coming from the PT government. If it has not worked out during all these years, it won't work out in the next four. That is my opinion. Even if Bolsonaro turns out to be bad, he will still bring some sort of change. ... To elect the PT again will bring no change. It only means accepting the disaster.'

In a context where the status quo is a 'disaster', any form of change appears preferable − even if this change ushers in a dictatorship.

Historically marginalized by PT policies at the local and the national levels, many street vendors felt as though they had nothing left to lose. This situation parallels other recent elections around the world, which have enabled the ascent of right wing populism in various different guises. Much like Ana, Lucas believed that the PT's government had brought little positive change to his life. Instead, its policies were experienced as a form of betrayal: "The PT likes workers so much that it built us a little box to tell everyone that street vendors own shops. The PT sold the street vendors!" His testimony demonstrates the ways in which policies implemented at the local level influence the outcome of national elections. His view of PT was shared by Shanghai, a street vendor who worked as an adviser for the office of Isabella Gonçalves (introduced earlier):

> '[Before becoming a social activist] I couldn't see how politics could do anything good for us [street vendors]. So much so that this process of evicting street vendors from the streets started with the Workers' Party. It was a huge deception for us knowing that those who were supposedly representing the workers were actually severely harming us.'

Shanghai's quote further illustrates the sense of disillusionment among street vendors who had been displaced by a party 'supposedly representing the workers'. It thus challenges the narrow idea of the 'worker' invoked in the party's name and its exclusion of street vendors. Other members traced the roots of the current crisis back to Pimentel's administration in the early 2000s: "Guys, it's easy. [The person] who displaced the street vendors from the city centre was Pimentel, who is from the Workers Party. So, think well on Sunday [election day]."

Pimentel's administration was thus seen as a turning point for street vendors in Belo Horizonte. Although harassment by the authorities had long been part of their everyday lives, the approval of the Code of Placements amounted to a total criminalization of their work and a denial of their livelihood. The latest round of 'revitalisation' and displacement triggered a sense of collective trauma that dated back to Pimentel's administration. I have argued that the source of this trauma – and the resultant decision of many street vendors to support Bolsonaro – can be traced back to the narrow idea of the 'worker' enshrined in the foundation of the PT in 1980.

Conclusion

As in much of the world, informal workers in Brazil have historically been excluded from the trade union movement (Chun and Agarwala, 2016). This exclusion, combined with the growing informalization of the economy (Nitahara, 2019) and the commodification of urban space (Klink and Denaldi, 2016) has had a particularly damaging effect on the working lives of street vendors. Lacking the protections of formal wage workers, street vendors have suffered more acutely the effects of the economic crisis, accentuated by the attempts of local authorities to criminalize their presence in the city in the name of 'revitalizing' urban spaces and attracting investment (Crossa, 2009; Costa and Magalhães, 2011; Itikawa, 2016). While Brazil is praised internationally for possessing a progressive urban policy that recognizes the 'right to the city' as a collective right (Fernandes, 2007) the right of street vendors to earn a living in the city has been mostly ignored (Nogueira, 2019).

I have shown that the 'crisis of labour' is a multiscalar crisis which manifests itself at the intersections of local and national politics. As the restructuring of global markets continues to transform the relationship between the state, national identity and citizenship (Sharma and Gupta, 2009), the city emerges as the main stage on which this crisis is negotiated and contested, engendering constant disputes over the use and access to urban space. The urban is thus both a site of speculation that creates uncertainty and threats to marginalized workers, and a potential arena for its contestation through emerging forms of political organization among those excluded from the trade union movement (Chun and Agarwala, 2016; Ferguson and Li, 2018). In Belo Horizonte, displaced workers recently created the Centro de Apoio ao Trabalhador Ambulante (CATA – Support Centre for Street Vendors), which is currently offering support for vendors in the context of the COVID-19 pandemic.

Around the world, political parties founded on organization of industrial wage workers are struggling to mobilize voters while far-right populism is on the rise. I have argued here that the political discourses of street vendors – long excluded from traditional labour organization – shed some light on the possibilities for more inclusive modes of working class politics. Rather than being forged in the Fordist factories of Brazil in the 1970s and 1980s, the political subjectivities of street vendors have been shaped on the streets of cities such as Belo Horizonte since the 1900s. It is only by paying attention to these subjectivities – the rhythms they produce and the 'forms of living' they enable (Millar, 2018) – that we might arrive at a more inclusive politics that is able to overcome the global crisis of labour.

Acknowledgements

The author would like to thank the local participants who have kindly shared their time and insight, particularly the street vendors and support staff at the Centro de Apoio ao Trabalhador Ambulante (CATA – Support Centre for Street Vendors).

Notes

[1] Vernacular term for a common type of professionalized street vendor who usually uses a stall or a table to sell products in public spaces in Brazil. See Richmond (2020).

[2] Luiz Inacio da Silva, popularly known as Lula, was president of Brazil from 2003 to 2010 and is the PT's most influential politician.

[3] The ABC Region is an industrial region formed by three cities in Greater São Paulo – Santo André, São Bernardo do Campo, and São Caetano do Sul.

[4] One must, however, recognize the direct and indirect effects of policies such as the *Bolsa Família* (BF), a conditional cash-transfer programme for which the PT government became internationally recognized. Despite its positive results, the BF should be understood as a social policy implemented to 'compensate the poor for the asymmetric impact of the economic [neoliberal] reforms' (Saad-Filho, 2015, 1232).

[5] After the initial three-month period, rents were set at BRL36.00 (GBP6.32), increasing each year to BRL56 (GBP9.83), BRL105 (GBP18.44) and BRL208 (GBP36.53). After five years, rents will no longer be subsidized by the government and will be set at market levels.

References

Abers, R. (1996) 'From ideas to practice: The Partido dos Trabalhadores and participatory governance in Brazil', *Latin American Perspectives*, 23(4): 35–53.

Abers, R. (2001) 'Learning democratic practice: Distributing government resources through popular participation in Porto Alegre, Brazil', in Freire, M. and Stren, R. (eds) *The Challenge of Urban government: Policies and Practices*, Washington DC: World Bank Group, 129–143.

Alves, G. (2000) 'Do "novo sindicalismo" à "concertação social": Ascensão (e crise) do sindicalismo no Brasil (1978–1998)', *Revista de Sociologia e Política*, 15: 111–124.

Amann, E. and Baer, W. (2002) 'Neoliberalism and its consequences in Brazil', *Journal of Latin American Studies*, 34: 945–959.

Antunes, R. and Santana, M.A. (2014) 'The dilemmas of the new unionism in Brazil: Breaks and continuities', *Latin American Perspectives*, 41(5): 10–21.

Arantes, P.F. (2009) 'Em busca do urbano: marxistas e a cidade de São Paulo nos anos de 1970', *Novos Estudos CEBRAP*, 83: 103–127.

Atkinson, R. (2015) 'Losing one's place: Narratives of neighbourhood change, market injustice and symbolic displacement', *Housing, Theory and Society*, 32(4): 373–388.

Barchiesi, F. (2011) *Precarious Liberation: Workers, the State, and Contested Social Citizenship in Postapartheid South Africa*, Albany: Suny Press.

Bayat, A. (2000) 'From "dangerous classes" to "quiet rebels": Politics of the urban subaltern in the global south', *International Sociology*, 15(3): 533–557.

Bedê, M.M.C. (2005) 'Trajetória da formulação e implantação da política habitacional de Belo Horizonte na gestão da Frente BH Popular 1993–1996', unpublished Masters dissertation, UFMG Belo Horizonte.

Bedê, M.M.C. and de Moura Costa, H.S. (2006) 'Entre as idéias e o contexto: Uma discussão sobre a política municipal de habitação na gestão da Frente BH Popular (1993–1996)', *Revista Geografias*, 2: 56–73.

Boito, A. (1994) 'De volta para o novo corporativismo: A trajetória política do sindicalismo brasileiro', *São Paulo em Perspectiva*, 8: 23–28.

Breman, J. and Linden, M. (2014) 'Informalizing the economy: The return of the social question at a global level', *Development and Change*, 45(5): 920–940.

Brenner, N. (2004) *New State Spaces: Urban Governance and the Rescaling of Statehood*, Oxford: Oxford University Press.

Bretas, P.R.P. (1996) 'Participative budgeting in Belo Horizonte: Democratization and citizenship', *Environment and Urbanization*, 8(1): 213–222.

Brown, A. (2015) 'Claiming the streets: Property rights and legal empowerment in the urban informal economy', *World Development*, 76: 238–248.

Burawoy, M. (1982) *Manufacturing Consent: Changes in the Labor Process under Monopoly Capitalism*, Chicago, IL: University of Chicago Press.

Caldeira, T. and Holston, J. (2015) 'Participatory urban planning in Brazil', *Urban Studies*, 52(11): 2001–2017.

Cardoso, F.H. and Faletto, E. (1979) *Dependency and Development in Latin America* [*Dependencia y desarrollo en América Latina*], Berkeley, CA: University of California Press.

Carrieri, A.P. and Murta, I.B.D. (2011) 'Cleaning up the city: A study on the removal of street vendors from downtown Belo Horizonte, Brazil', *Canadian Journal of Administrative Sciences/Revue Canadienne des Sciences de l'Administration*, 28(2): 217–225.

Castells, M. (1973) *Imperialismo y urbanización en América Latina*, Barcelona: Editorial Gustavo Gili.

Chun, J.J. and Agarwala, R. (2016) 'Global labour politics in informal and precarious jobs', in Edgell, S., Gottfried, H., & Granter, E. (eds) *SAGE Handbook of the Socioliogy of Work and Employment*, Los Angeles, CA: Sage Publications Ltd, pp 634–650.

Costa, G.M. and Magalhães, F.N. (2011) 'Processos sociospaciais nas metrópoles de países de industrialização periférica', *Revista Brasileira de Estudos Urbanos e Regionais*, 13(1): 9–25.

Crossa, V. (2009) 'Resisting the entrepreneurial city: Street vendors' struggle in Mexico City's historic center', *International Journal of Urban and Regional Research*, 33(1): 43–63.

Crossa, V. (2016) 'Reading for difference on the street: De-homogenising street vending in Mexico City', *Urban Studies*, 53(2): 287–301.

de Andrade Baltar, P.E., dos Santos, A.L., Krein, J.D., Leone, E., Weishaupt Proni, M., Moretto, A., Gori Maia, A. and Salas, C. (2010) 'Moving towards decent work. Labour in the Lula government: reflections on recent Brazilian experience', Global Labour University Working Paper.

de Oliveira, F. (2003) *Crítica à Razão Dualistao/O Ornitorrinco*, São Paulo: Boitempo.

Duarte, P.H.E. (2013) 'Structural unemployment in Brazil in the neoliberal era', *World Review of Political Economy*, 4(2): 192–217.

Erickson, K.P. and Peppe, P.V. (1976) 'Dependent capitalist development, US foreign policy, and repression of the working class in Chile and Brazil', *Latin American Perspectives*, 3(1): 19–44.

Ferguson, J. and Li, T.M. (2018) 'Beyond the "proper job": Political-economic analysis after the century of labouring man' Working Paper No. 51. Cape Town: PLAAS, University of the Western Cape.

Fernandes, E. (2007) 'Implementing the urban reform agenda in Brazil', *Environment and Urbanization*, 19(1): 177–189.

Fischer, B., McCann, B. and Auyero, J. (eds) (2014) *Cities from Scratch: Poverty and Informality in Urban Latin America*, Durham, NC: Duke University Press.

Fox, S. (2014) 'The political economy of slums: Theory and evidence from Sub-Saharan Africa', *World Development*, 54: 191–203.

Friendly, A. (2013) 'The right to the city: Theory and practice in Brazil', *Planning Theory & Practice*, 14(2): 158–179.

Garmany, J. and Richmond, M.A. (2020) 'Hygienisation, gentrification, and urban displacement in Brazil', *Antipode*, 52(1): 124–144.

Goul Andersen, J. and Jensen, P.H. (2002) *Changing Labour Markets, Welfare Policies and Citizenship*, Bristol: Policy Press.

Hart, G. (2010) 'D/developments after the Meltdown', *Antipode*, 41(s1): 117–141.

Holston, J. (2008) *Insurgent Citizenship: Disjunctions of Democracy and Modernity in Brazil*, Princeton, NJ: Princeton University Press.

Humphrey, J. (1979) 'Auto workers and the working class in Brazil', *Latin American Perspectives*, 6(4): 71–89.

IBGE (2019). PNAD Contíntua. *Agência IBGE Notícias.* Available at https://agenciadenoticias.ibge.gov.br/agencia-noticias/2012-agencia-de-noticias/noticias/26741-desemprego-cai-para-11-9-na-media-de-2019-informalidade-e-a-maior-em-4-anos.

Itikawa, L.F. (2016) 'Women on the periphery of urbanism: Subordinate informality, disarticulated autonomy and resistance in São Paulo, Mumbai and Durban', *Revista Brasileira de Estudos Urbanos e Regionais*, 18: 51–70.

Jayme, J.G. and Neves, M.D.A. (2010) 'Cidade e espaço público: política de revitalização urbana em Belo Horizonte', *Caderno CRH*, 23(60): 605–617.

Jenkins, J.C. and Leicht, K. (1997) *Class Analysis and Social Movements: A Critique and Reformulation*, Ithaca, NJ: Cornell University Press.

Klink, J. and Denaldi, R. (2016) 'On urban reform, rights and planning challenges in the Brazilian metropolis', *Planning Theory*, 15(4): 402–417.

Koonings, K. (2004) 'Strengthening citizenship in Brazil's democracy: Local participatory governance in Porto Alegre', *Bulletin of Latin American Research*, 23(1): 79–99.

Kopper, M. (2015) 'DE CAMELÔS A LOJISTAS: a transição do mercado de rua para um shopping em Porto Alegre', *Caderno CRH*, 28(75): 591–605.

Lewis, W.A. (1954) 'Economic development with unlimited supplies of labour', *Manchester School*, 22: 139–191.

Loureiro, P.M. and Saad-Filho, A. (2019) 'The limits of pragmatism: The rise and fall of the Brazilian Workers' Party (2002–2016)', *Latin American Perspectives*, 46(1): 66–84.

Machado, R.P. and Scalco, L.M. (2020) 'From hope to hate: The rise of conservative subjectivity in Brazil', *HAU: Journal of Ethnographic Theory*, 10(1): 21–31.

Maram, S.L. (1977) 'Labor and the Left in Brazil, 1890–1921: A movement aborted', *Hispanic American Historical Review*, 57(2): 254–272.

Maricato, E. (1979) *A produção capitalista da casa (e da cidade) no Brasil industrial*, São Paulo: Editora Alfa-Omega.

Millar, K.M. (2018) *Reclaiming the Discarded: Life and Labor on Rio's Garbage Dump*, Durham, NC: Duke University Press.

Munck, R. (2013) 'The precariat: A view from the South', *Third World Quarterly*, 34(5): 747–762.

Navarro, R.G. and de Lacerda Godinho, M.H. (2002) 'Movimentos sociais (populares), Conselho Municipal e órgão gestor na defi nição e implementação da política habitacional em Belo Horizonte–década de 1990', *Cadernos Metrópole*, 7: 59–74.

Nitahara, A. (2019) 'Informalidade no mercado de trabalho é recorde, aponta IBGE', Agência Brasil, available at https://agenciabrasil.ebc.com.br/ublishe/noticia/2019-10/informalidade-no-mercado-de-trabalho-e-recorde-aponta-ibge.

Nogueira, M. (2019) 'Displacing informality: Rights and legitimacy in Belo Horizonte Brazil', *International Journal of Urban and Regional Research*, 43(3): 517–534.

Nylen, W.R. (2002) 'Testing the empowerment thesis: The participatory budget in Belo Horizonte and Betim, Brazil', *Comparative Politics,* 34(2): 127–145.

Polanyi, K. (1944) *The Great Transformation*, New York, NY: Rinehart.

Reis, E.P. (2000) 'Modernization, citizenship, and stratification: Historical processes and recent changes in Brazil', *Daedalus*, 129: 171–194.

Richmond, M.A. (2018) 'Bolsonaro's conservative revolution, Jacobin, 8 March. Available at https://jacobinmag.com/2018/10/brazil-election-bolsonaro-evangelicals-security

Richmond, M.A. (2020) 'Narratives of crisis in the periphery of São Paulo: Place and political articulation during Brazil's rightward turn', *Journal of Latin American Studies*, 52(2): 241–267.

Rolnik, R. (2013) 'Ten years of the City Statute in Brazil: From the struggle for urban reform to the World Cup cities', *International Journal of Urban Sustainable Development*, 5(1): 54–64.

Rolnik, R. (2019) *Urban Warfare*, London: Verso.

Roy, A. (2012) 'Why the middle class matters: Commentary on Victoria Lawson with Middle Class Poverty Politics Research Group's "Decentring poverty studies: middle class alliances and the social construction of poverty"', *Singapore Journal of Tropical Geography*, 33(1): 25–28.

Saad-Filho, A. (2015) 'Social policy for neoliberalism: The Bolsa Família programme in Brazil', *Development and Change*, 46(6): 1227–1252.

Samuels, D. (2004) 'From socialism to social democracy: Party organization and the transformation of the workers' party in Brazil', *Comparative Political Studies*, 37(9): 999–1024.

Sandoval, S.A. (2007) 'Alternative forms of working-class organization and the mobilization of informal-sector workers in Brazil in the era of neoliberalism', *International Labor and Working-Class History*, 72: 63–89.

Schindler, S. (2014) 'Producing and contesting the formal/informal divide: Regulating street hawking in Delhi, India', *Urban Studies*, 51(12): 2596–2612.

Sharma, A. and Gupta, A. (2009) *The Anthropology of the State: A Reader*, Hoboken, NJ: John Wiley & Sons.

Siegmann, K.A. and Schiphorst, F. (2016) 'Understanding the globalizing precariat: From informal sector to precarious work', *Progress in Development Studies*, 16(2): 111–123.

Silver, B.J. (2003) *Forces of Labor: Workers' Movements and Globalization since 1870*, Cambridge: Cambridge University Press.

Standing, G. (2014) 'Understanding the precariat through labour and work', *Development and Change*, 45(5): 963–980.

Tyler, C. (1982) 'Trade unionism in Brazil', *Third World Quarterly*, 4(2): 312–320.

Ulyssea, G. (2005) 'Informalidade no mercado de trabalho brasileiro: uma resenha da literatura', *Brazilian Journal of Political Economy*, 26(4): 596–618.

Vilela, N.M. (2006) 'Hipercentro de Belo Horizonte: movimentos e transformações espaciais recentes', unpublished PhD thesis, UFMG Belo Horizonte.

Zambelli, P.H.L. (2006) 'O trabalho informal dos Camelôs da Região Central de Belo Horizonte e a transferência para os shoppings populares', unpublished dissertation (Masters in social science) Pontifícia Universidade Católica de Minas Gerais, Belo Horizonte.

PART IV

Possibilities

11

Extra-ordinary: Crisis, Charity and Care in London's World without Work

Dora-Olivia Vicol

Introduction

Marcel lives in a three-bed house on the outskirts of Greater London, with ten other Romanian men. Every day from dawn until dusk, seven of the men labour in a car wash, hosing and scrubbing in 11-hour shifts, in the shadow of the city's skyscrapers. It is backbreaking work; the type of work where you have to steal your lunch break between the taillights of the car departing and the headlights of the one approaching, ready to spring to your feet at any moment. But it is work no less – something Marcel has been doing for four years straight – and others have dipped in and out of between return trips to Romania and attempts to 'make it' elsewhere. Despite its drawbacks, car washing offers a sense of dignity. It provides the normalcy that comes with knowing that the roof above his head can be provided for, and that tomorrow may be a little lighter than today. It is, in many ways, ordinary work.[1]

In March 2020 when the coronavirus pandemic sent London, like so much of the global North, grinding to a halt, this work was abruptly interrupted. Marcel and his colleagues were suddenly let go without notice or any compensation, just the categorical rejection of a business that acted as if it owed them nothing. With minimal savings, and unable to find any other work in a city under lockdown, they found themselves struggling to pay for food, let alone rent. It was at this point that they contacted the Work Rights Centre – a small employment rights charity I have had the privilege to be a part of since 2016 – where a team of caseworkers offer free advice in matters of employment justice.

For Marcel and his colleagues who had been doing casual jobs for years, contacting the charity represented a cry for help. It was the realization that, unlike in previous moments of crisis, when they had relied on their ability to adapt and could always find something else, this time work opportunities were lacking. For advisers at the charity on the other hand, theirs was just the first of many cases which revealed how unevenly the pandemic was experienced, and how much effort would go into managing the extraordinariness of a world without work.

This chapter examines the work of charity in the context of a global crisis; a type of work conducted by and for those outside the wage. Drawing on research conducted during the coronavirus lockdown, supported by four years of collaboration with the Work Rights Centre, I argue that frontline caseworkers have come to fill a void left by government through self-reliance. The pandemic instantiated a crisis which required radical redistribution and protection for the most vulnerable. Yet the UK government's response continued to privilege the wage, restricting the safety net of furlough to the securely employed, while leaving the zero-hours hustlers, the self-employed, and gig economy precariat to navigate the vagaries of an ever-thinning welfare system. In this chapter I argue that in this context the work of charity is simultaneously one of service and of care. It is a professional service dedicated to the translation of entitlements, in a system of tiered redistribution, where every state grant is accessed through a detailed digital application. But it is also a personal service of care, which sets out to rebuild a sense of humanity in spite of precarity, often drawing on tragicomedy to invert dominant relations of power.

I start with a brief review of the lockdown measures, and the ways in which they privileged a wage-centric form of redistribution. I then focus more centrally on the work of charity advisers, documenting the moments of translation, humour and community that continue to arise on the frontline. Small and transient as they may be, I argue, these expressions of care articulate an alternative project of social reproduction on the margins of the wage economy.

Grinding to a halt

Marcel and his colleagues at the car wash belong to one of the most populous migrant communities in the city. Concentrated along the northern and eastern suburbs where rent is cheaper and transnational networks well established, the number of Romanian migrants to London increased from 11,000 at the time of European accession in 2007, to as many as 148,000 in 2018 – the second most common nationality after Britons (APS, 2018). Many Romanian migrants took up jobs in the capital's knowledge economy and enrolled in British universities. Many more, however, found work in London's construction sector, in cleaning, hospitality and delivery – in the secondary tier of jobs servicing the global city (May et al, 2007).

The story of Romanian migration is one episode in London's long history of mobility (Panayi, 2020). Every day, 5 million passengers weave through the metropolis, squeezed in its labyrinthine network of underground trains. Overground, the sight of cranes towering over construction sites is testament to the constant movement of earth, materials, capital and people, who have transformed the city for over a century. Some groups of migrants came in the 1950s from the Caribbean and Indian subcontinent, to help rebuild a city crippled and depopulated by the Second World War. Others fled persecution and sought refuge in the UK, such as the Ugandan Asian refugees who escaped Amin's dictatorship in the 1970s, and the asylum seekers who fled wars in Iraq and Afghanistan in the 2000s (Spencer, 2011). Negotiating racialized border regimes that have historically restricted the entry of populations from the global South while enabling the entry of European migrants like Marcel (Fox et al, 2012), many more came in pursuit of work, study, family and personal ambition. As Steve Vertovec (2007) put it, London is a 'superdiverse' metropolis, where two out of every nine residents are migrants (APS, 2018). Until, that is, it ground to a halt.

On the evening of 23 March 2020 the UK went into lockdown. From a sturdy desk in Number 10 Downing Street, a stern-faced Boris Johnson, the Conservative British Prime Minister, called on businesses to shutter up, and for staff to be sent to their homes. SARS-Cov-2, the pathogen commonly known as the new coronavirus, had already claimed thousands of lives in China, Iran, Italy and Spain. After months of detachment and delay, London finally stopped moving. The police were granted the power to fine anyone who left their home for any reason other than to shop for basic necessities, seek medical care, exercise, or travel to essential work. Employers in 'key sectors' such as energy and food production, transport and the National Health Service, were instructed to adapt their workplaces to manage the pandemic – hand sanitizers, face masks and two-metre foot markers flew off shop shelves. Where possible, workers in the knowledge economy grabbed their laptops and set up camp in improvised offices at home. For the rest, however, the lockdown triggered a real-time crisis, and a stark encounter with the UK's wage-centred politics of redistribution.

An 'unprecedented' government intervention

Three days before the lockdown was officially enforced, the recently appointed Chancellor of the Exchequer, Rishi Sunak, announced that the UK government would pay the wages of employees unable to work due to the government's lockdown measures. Under the Coronavirus Job Retention Scheme (CJRS), the government agreed to foot 80 per cent of the salary of staff who were kept on by their employer, covering up to £2,500 per month, or roughly the UK median wage for 2019. There would be no limits to the support available. The Chancellor announced that the government 'would pay grants to support as many jobs as necessary' (Sunak, 2020).

For a Conservative Executive with a history of austerity (see Strong, this volume), this was an unprecedented move. The Confederation of British Industry, a body representing employers, welcomed it as 'an unparalleled joint effort by enterprise and government to help our country emerge from this crisis with the minimum possible damage' (CBI, 2020). The UK press described it as a 'radical move aimed at protecting people's jobs' (BBC News, 2020), vital for preventing firms from going bust or laying off staff. The chief merit of the scheme, one observer noted, was to stop unemployment from rising to the levels last seen during the financial crisis of 2007–2009 (The Economist, 2020a). And yet, despite high levels of public support, the scheme left a lot to be desired.

Critics on the political right pointed first to the unintended economic consequences of the proposed measures. Under the first set of rules, the CJRS was binary. Employers had a choice between either keeping staff on at pre-crisis rates, or sending them home on furlough, creating a bizarre incentive to stop production altogether, rather than adapting (Standing, 2020).[2] The all-or-nothing approach inherent in the government scheme has also been criticized for constraining labour market mobility. One analysis by *The Economist* (2020a) pointed out that workers sent home on furlough with 80 per cent of their previous salary and at lower risk of infection, with lower travel and child-care costs, would have very little reason to take up work in the sectors which were still hiring.

But there was a deeper and, I would argue, more serious limitation to the scheme. Significantly, it failed to recognize and to care for the growing number of people in the UK whose work does not conform to the standard employment relationship. Beyond the language of extraordinariness, the 'unprecedented' rescue package proposed by the UK government did little more than reproduce well-entrenched divisions between waged and unwaged workers.

The exclusion of informal and casual workers

Despite the public show of magnanimity, furlough was not a right available to all. Critically, the ability to apply for government funding was open to employers, not to workers. Advisers at the Work Rights Centre were inundated with queries as members of the public asked how they could 'apply for furlough'. The reality was that the application for furlough was never an option for them. People who worked for companies which were well resourced enough to apply for the government scheme enjoyed the privilege of 80 per cent pay – in some cases, even a top-up financed by the employer. By 3 May 2020, less than two months after the imposition of the lockdown, as many as 800,000 companies, employing a total of approximately 6.3 million workers, had applied to the furlough scheme, costing the government about as much as the National Health Service every month (The Economist, 2020b). For many others, however, the options were limited.

People like Marcel, who worked cash-in-hand, without any written terms, for a man who paid him barely half of the National Minimum Wage (set at £8.72 from April 2020), were automatically excluded. After a few hours on the phone, caseworkers learned that he and his colleagues had "brought each other" to London over the past few years. They lived together and worked side by side, six days a week. Only one of them featured as a worker on the books of the tax authority, HMRC, where he had been registered as a 'part time' member of staff in a gross understatement of his actual work hours. That an employer like Marcel's would suddenly call HMRC, register his workers, admit to years of tax evasion and ask for a government grant was understood to be out of the question.

But you did not have to experience the drama of mistreatment by an individual employer to fall through the safety net. The wage-centric furlough also eluded entire sectors of the formal but precarious labour market. Employment status in the UK distinguishes between *employees*, who enjoy the highest level of protections, and *workers*, who lack some of the rights associated with long-term stability, including the right to redundancy pay. Almost 1 million people in the UK – 13 per cent of whom are migrants – work on zero-hours contracts (ONS,

2020a). In theory, they too were eligible for furlough. At the level of practice, however, access to this depended solely on their employers' preferences. In the absence of statutory obligation, there is nothing to stop profit-weary businesses from dismissing zero-hours workers. As bearers of an employment status characterized by flexibility, they were always already a disposable labour force.

A similar sense of powerlessness was evident among the self-employed who, in March 2020, included more than 5 million people (ONS, 2020b). It is revealing, first of all, that the type of direct assistance originally granted to wage workers was only extended to the self-employed after the Independent Workers Union of Great Britain threatened the Chancellor with litigation (Booth, 2020). Three days later, on 26 March 2020, the Treasury announced another 'world leading' government intervention (HM Treasury and Right Hon Rishi Sunak MP, 2020). The Self-Employed Income Support Scheme (SEISS) promised to pay sole-trading contractors up to 80 per cent of the average profits they registered over the past three years, with one key caveat. Nested on the government website, under the heading deceptively titled 'how to apply', the small print made it clear that there was no application process. HMRC would call candidates if and when they were deemed eligible. For the first couple of months, the only thing left to do was wait.[3] Things looked even bleaker for the 151,000 people who had only recently become self-employed (ONS, 2020c). Given the fact that the scheme was based on past tax returns, and that tax returns are by definition submitted only after the end of a financial year during a ten-month-long window, anyone who had become self-employed since April 2019 and was yet to file a tax return was excluded from the Support Scheme.

In his volume of *Pascalian Mediations*, Pierre Bourdieu remarked that 'making people wait ... delaying without destroying hope', is integral to the working of domination (Auyero, 2011). The coronavirus lockdown suddenly turned millions of workers into silent spectators of a performance of generosity that was aimed at others. As spectators, they watched the government promise extraordinary relief funded from the public purse, only to realize that they had no means of accessing it. Workers like the seven Romanian car washers were rendered ineligible by an employer who kept them on the black market and by a system which had made fighting this in court an almost impossible battle for the poor.[4] The self-employed were teased with applications they could not make, while zero-hours workers were left at the mercy of businesses who had little to lose from dismissing them. In each case, workers outside of the idealized wage employment were rendered invisible by the government's response to the pandemic and left at the mercy of an ever-thinning welfare system. Introduced by the Conservative government in 2013, Universal Credit had ostensibly been designed to streamline a series of previously discrete benefits, with a view to easing administration and minimizing the chance of fraud (Gov.uk, 2013). In practice, it was a system that pressured applicants to update the government at every change of circumstance, or risk losing their benefits (see also Strong, this volume). Universal Credit penalized non-English speakers and the digitally illiterate, who shied away from the online reporting system, and it entrenched the immobility of the poorest. Unlike the CJRS and SEISS, where the more one earned the more one could qualify for, with Universal Credit the more one earned the less one got, as the amount awarded depended on the difference between earnings and expenditure. Additionally, a bitter irony in the bureaucratic logic meant that the poorest applicants who paid their rent in cash because they could not afford to rent formally were awarded *less* on account of being unable to evidence their expenses. While the government was ready to shoulder wages of up to £2,500 per month for furloughed workers, a person like Marcel, who sublet a home he shared with ten other people, qualified for just £410 a month. Were he married, he would have been eligible to receive £594, and were he a father in a family of four, £1,100 per month.

For the past 30 years, economists and social theorists have emphasized the erosion of employment security and degradation of the welfare state across the global North (Beck, 2014; Standing, 2014). Despite the language of interventionism and the carefully choreographed appeals to unity in crisis, the 'unprecedented' measures adopted by the UK government during the coronavirus lockdown served to reproduce familiar divisions between the security of salaried work and the insecurity of the precariat; the celebration of the wage earner and the denigration of the un- and underemployed. So far, so familiar. However, less attention has been given to the question of how people like Marcel got by during the pandemic, and what possibilities for assistance, solidarity and hope exist beyond the wage-based systems of redistribution that have come to characterize the status quo.

Getting by outside the wage

'If all problems in the world were solved, we'd have eternal peace and no exploitation, cures to all diseases, culture and knowledge, we wouldn't need charities. Or we'd look very differently. But we exist because the world is imperfect.

... a world like ours without charities would be horrible.'
(Raluca Enescu, service provider, Work Rights Centre)

I co-founded the Work Rights Centre in 2016 with a group of young women, mostly university students at the time, who had an interest in, and direct experience of, social (im)mobility. I remember the excitement of the first few months spent meeting in cafes, trying to define the contours of our project. One month led us to a written mission and objectives, another to a charity account. Within a year, the Work Rights Centre was a registered organization with a constitution, a board of trustees, and a handful of staff who were willing to give it a go on a voluntary basis.

We started providing a free employment rights advisory service in Wembley Library in the Borough of Brent. We did not have the funds to rent office space. In fact, our only capital at the time was the £600 donated by one of our founding members. One of our main assets was the arrangement we had with library staff. Every Saturday from 11 am to closing time, two desks in a quiet corner of the library were reserved for our advisers. We started seeing people we knew, people I had met during doctoral fieldwork in London, or passers-by drawn by the charity's bright yellow banner. Most of them were Romanian migrants. Today, the Work Rights Centre has secured sufficient funds to rent an office in London, hire more staff, who work alongside a bright and multi-lingual team of volunteers, and open an additional service in Manchester for people in the north of England. The growth of the Work Rights Centre speaks both to the work and commitment of its staff, and to the injustices and structural deficiencies of the UK's social security system, which impair the lives of so many of the people who come to our clinics.

For more than a millennium, Stephen Bubb (2017) notes in his short history, charities in the UK provided the services which we are now accustomed to seeing as a duty of the state. Under the feudal system of the Middle Ages, where the only social contract was the exchange of land for loyalty, and the largest sector of the population were unfree serfs, support for the poor, the ill, the vagrant and the old came either from kin, or in the form of charity. After the reformation in 1601, the Charitable Uses Act specified anything from the creation of houses of correction, the marriage of 'poor maids' and help for tradesmen, to the repair of bridges and ports. Naturally, much has changed in the ethic and legal structure of charitable organizations. Few charities today would describe their work through the tropes of piety which characterized giving in the Middle Ages. Legislative changes, such as the establishment of the Charity Commission in

1853, also formalized the structure and obligations of charitable organizations. In the nineteenth century bigger and better-funded charities, enabled by the introduction of the Limited Company Act in 1855, were at the forefront of campaigning for legislative changes – such as the ten-hour working day, or the abolition of cruelty to animals and children. For most of their history, however, charities were providers of services which most people today would expect to obtain from the state. The twentieth century marked a brief change. With the introduction of a pension after the First World War and a system of National Insurance after the Second World War, Bubb (2017, 25) notes, the post-war orthodoxy was one of subsidiarity, whereby charitable organizations would focus on advocacy, leaving the provision of welfare to the state. Looking at the Work Rights Centre today, this ambition seems little more than a momentary artefact, in a history of public service.

At the time of writing, the Work Rights Centre has seen over 1,800 cases of Romanians, Bulgarians, Italians, Britons and other people active in precarious manual occupations (Vicol and Enescu, 2020). One in three had no written terms of employment, and one in two lacked a tenancy agreement. Most staff, meanwhile, ran the charity part time, sharing the sense of duty Raluca described earlier, while spending the rest of our time parenting, studying, taking on other gigs and doing unrelated nine-to-five jobs. Most of our funding comes from grants, with a time horizon ranging between three months and two years, covering the charity's annual budget like a patchwork. Every board meeting starts with a reminder of the months of funding left, and a review of reserves and plans for applications, as in a rite of exorcizing the spectre of our own fragility. For most of the charity's short history, we have provided support to people in unwaged work while being unwaged ourselves. When the lockdown was instituted, we found ourselves supporting those outside of work altogether.

Translating the state

For the first few weeks of the pandemic, casework felt like an exercise in interpretation. At first, it concerned the management of novelty and crippling uncertainty that set in. Within a few days, advisers' phones were ringing off the hook. Like Marcel and the car washers, many of the people who contacted us had been dismissed by their employers – and in some cases, dismissed in full knowledge that other colleagues had been kept on. Time and again clients asked our team why other people had been furloughed and not them. Was it a case of discrimination and were bosses trying to settle old vendettas? Or was it simply that they were newer in the job, and easier to fire? Suspicion abounded. In other cases, zero-hours workers who had been told they had been furloughed discovered that the sums they had been awarded, based on a calculation they were never shown, were barely enough to live on. Meanwhile, in other cases, people who had been told to continue working feared that the conditions of their workplace were unsafe, but knew nothing about how, and even whether, they could challenge them.

We found ourselves frantically reading government advice, scrutinizing the vagaries of the job retention and self-employed support schemes in an attempt to anticipate clients' questions before anxiety set in. We built scenarios, publicized the answers in infographics, translated them in every language we could speak, then engaged in a relentless outreach exercise on social media groups of Romanian, Bulgarian, Russian and Spanish speakers, whose languages and movement across borders we shared.

There was a generalized sense that communication was a means of managing uncertainty. We felt that we had a *duty* to know, and to share, even though we were all too aware that government advice might change overnight, and every day the hackneyed Aristotelian maxim rang true: 'the more we knew, the more we realized we didn't know'. The wage-centric politics of redistribution proposed by the government left gaping questions such as: on what grounds could workers refuse to attend workplaces they saw as unsafe? How could they check whether employers had furloughed them? And most of all, how could people support themselves in a world without work?

We attempted to translate their entitlements under UK law and fill in the gaps. But sharing knowledge in extraordinary times was not just an exercise of factual translation. It was also an active search for, and performance of, hope. As Adelina, one of the founders and advisers put it: "Where we grew up, hope dies last. And someone actually said it, a client. Adi, we were born with luck and hope on our heads. If we lose those, that's it. And this was a woman who was crying, who got £300 a month after furlough." We made a conscious decision to find and foreground avenues for action, even when the imbalance of power was striking. There was no denying the disparity between the threat to livelihoods posed by a world without work, and the support offered by Universal Credit. Advisers were all too aware of its limitations, and by the second month of the pandemic they were already looking into how to make opportunities for work in key sectors visible. And yet, however small, slow, and barely liveable,

Universal Credit offered a sense of direction. The hope Adelina and the client referenced was not the hope of political manifestos that call for a radical rejection of work. It was the small, tactical 'hope as method' (Miyazaki, 2006); a reorientation of knowledge in an effort to offer a 'propensity towards something' (Bloch, 1986, 18), and a way of cultivating a sense of future possibility when the present had been plunged into uncertainty. For the people who approached the charity after losing their employment, Universal Credit was not the great equalizer. It was the first step in a relationship which started with entitlements from the state, but developed into a conversation about personal endurance and adaptability.

Translating technologies

Another layer of interpretation consisted of bridging over the precipice between a state intent on digitizing, and communities for whom English skills and digital literacy remained a challenge. There is a long-documented injustice in the fact that bureaucracy, that 'utopia of rules' (Graeber, 2015) which claims to offer a level playing field for all, sides with those who have the privilege of learning how to decode and file the form from an early age. Ever since the turn of the millennium the UK government had been inching towards digitizing citizenship. From the days of the ukonline portal launched in 2001, to its later iteration Directgov and the current gov.uk, the government has widened the range of information and services which can be accessed online, to the point where the physical bureau is almost a thing of the past. For citizens with a modicum of IT literacy and English skills, the fact that welfare, tax payments and applications for citizenship can all be initiated, or even wholly carried out, online is a huge time saver. For the fraction of the population who struggle with these skills, however, the digitization of services raises a significant technological barrier, both in the pragmatic sense of accessing a vital resource, and in the Foucauldian sense of self-making (Foucault, 1988). According to a government publication just over half (54 per cent) of benefit seekers managed to complete the Universal Credit application unassisted (DWP, 2018). More than four in ten (43 per cent) reported needing more support registering their claim, and another three in ten (31 per cent) reported needing ongoing support with their digital account (2018, 3).

Service providers could list countless scenarios where they walked clients through the bureaucratic hoops of form filling. One common trap in the Universal Credit application, for instance, was a question about residence. Asked if they 'live[d] with anyone else', applicants who were renting a room in a house share, unable or unwilling to pay for single occupancy, answered 'yes', only to learn that the platform would interpret that as a sharing of rent costs. The role of the adviser, in that scenario, was to mediate between a bureaucratic imaginary premised on the nuclear family, and the ordinary fact that only 3 per cent of the charity's beneficiaries were sole occupants of their homes; the majority lived in situations similar to that of Marcel and his friends from the car wash. In other cases, caseworkers introduced clients to the everyday use of mobile applications such as Google Maps, or even an email address. Helping people create an email address was common among migrants who had grown up in peasant families, but also among elderly Britons, of whom we saw a lot less.

The work of technological translation was thus one of navigating the thresholds of digital interfaces (Ash et al, 2018), but also of introducing clients to the techniques of digital self-making. The mastery of the digital turn in citizenship is not just a question of owning the hardware, but also of constructing a digital persona – what Giles Deleuze (1992) presciently called a 'dividual'. A poor person can only become a benefit claimant to the extent that she makes her poverty legible on the ledgers of the Department for Work and Pensions – in the same way that an ordinary worker only acquires the protections associated with economic activity to the extent that she becomes a tax payer on the ledgers of HMRC (Vicol, 2020). It is personal auditability, that old technique of self-representation through financial categories, that lies at the core of neoliberal governance (Power, 1997) – and, in the case of the pandemic, that mediated access to welfare.

In her introduction to *Audit Cultures*, anthropologist Marilyn Strathern (2000) observed how accountability, in the moral sense, is increasingly reduced to a question of accountancy inspired by the quantitative language of finance. Binding moral worth within the categories of financial accountancy, Strathern argued, 'audit cultures' (2003, 5) risk crushing the ethic they purport to defend by asking the form filler to squeeze her life into financial categories – while leaving the rigidities of the form unquestioned. In a similar fashion, in contrast to the language of unconditional help that characterized the government's communication, at the level of everyday practice getting by on Universal Credit was, in effect, a test in digital and financial literacy.

A veritable market of 'street-level' (Lipsky, 1980) consultants had come to fill this demand for personal auditability. Like the 'lawyers ... fixers and brokers' of the 'migration industry' (Cohen, 2008, 163), accountancy consultants had made a lucrative business of managing migrants' accounts with the British tax authority – and were quick to respond to the need to manage their accounts for welfare in a world without work. With adverts posted on social media groups or circulated informally via migrant networks, they promised to take care of all matters relating to the state, in exchange for a fee (Vicol, 2020). They catered for the poor, and poorly educated. They straddled the line between business and friendship, as many had in fact shared the experience of migration. What was particularly problematic, however, was that despite the language of help, this form of consultancy was based on a lopsided relation of power, where migrants not only paid a fee, but also entrusted their helpers with valuable personal information.

The work of translating technologies at the charity thus often meant fixing the damage caused erroneously, or maliciously, by helpers past. Over the course of the lockdown the charity encountered several cases where migrants who had entrusted a consultant with their application for Universal Credit, or the SEISS, had their details lost or, in a few instances, stolen. In the simplest cases, advisers would spend hours helping beneficiaries retrieve the credentials of accounts created by someone else and coaching them into the practice of digital record keeping. In the most serious cases, they learned that beneficiaries had been the victims of identity theft, and the details they once shared in confidence had been appropriated by another person. Translating technologies was slow, time-consuming work. It was the work of friction management, of making sure that beneficiaries did not trip on the jargon of digital welfare applications. But it was also the work of self-representation, of thinking of oneself as the holder of data points which carried value – on the market of consultants who made a business of managing other people's accounts; on the black market where rule benders bought and sold National Insurance numbers; but also in the relation to the state, where claiming any form of aid first meant making oneself legible.

Refashioning selves

> 'The first day of the lockdown when I was working from home I got a lot of calls. Old clients, new clients, everyone was calling at that time, who had lost their job – in cleaning, construction, restaurants, wherever, everywhere. It was a very depressing day, it was awful … I knew that whole sectors were just down, they're closed. And they can't just go back and find another job, say, in the construction sector. They have to change the

whole sector they've been used to for ten or fifteen years …
We started looking at their CVs, at a cover letter, and say,
"maybe you can work for the supermarket". But sometimes
they don't want to hear it, they want to think it's temporary
… It's a shock.' (Lora Tabakova, Service provider, London)

The shock of a world without work that hit so many of the charity's
beneficiaries during lockdown was amplified by the fact that, ever
since their accession to the European Union, Eastern European
migrants had been framed through the lens of economic agency. At
the 2004 accession of Poland and the A8, the New Labour government
welcomed migrants from the East as a source of accessible, enduring
labour, that could support the UK's then growing economy while
requiring minimal investments in social reproduction (Spencer, 2011).
Like generations of Commonwealth migrants before them, the figures
of the Polish builder and later the Romanian fruit picker emerged as
caricatures of industriousness – sought by employers (MacKenzie and
Forde, 2009; Anderson and Ruhs, 2012), singled out in analyses of
fiscal contribution for paying in more than they take out (Dustmann
et al, 2010), and simultaneously resented by segments of the public
for taking 'British jobs' (Vicol and Allen, 2014).

A vast body of literature has unpacked this framing of Eastern
European migrants through tropes of hard work. Anderson and Rush
(2012) deconstructed the ways in which caricatural antagonisms between
the 'hard-working migrant' and 'lazy Briton' enabled employers to justify
low wages and antisocial work conditions. Indeed, several publications
document the everyday precarity of working hard (Jayaweera and
Anderson, 2008; MacKenzie and Forde, 2009). Other scholars have
unpacked the ways in which hard work is deployed to normalize the
exclusion of migrants from the global South, and implicitly to racialize
immigration politics (Fox et al, 2012). And yet, what remains less
explored in the literature is that 'hard work' is not just an artefact of
immigration debates. It is also developed from within, by migrants who
mobilize the ability to work hard to demonstrate their agentful potential.

In a previous series of interviews with the Romanian Roma, a group
long stigmatized in countries of origin and destination, I listened to
the impassionate ways in which my informants drew on their everyday
work to challenge tropes of otherness, and claim their status as 'normal
people' (Anderson et al, 2018, 20). Work in this case was a political
act – a means of affirming a right to belong in a polity premised on
self-sufficiency, and of challenging the otherness constituted along
axes of class and race. It was also a moral resource. At the time I was

conducting fieldwork with Romanian migrants, where I traced their journeys into precarious employment. There was hardly an interview where my informants did not take pride in their ability to 'work hard' *in spite* of the poor conditions. Often towards the end of our conversations, after histories that included episodes of non-payment, deceit and betrayal by friends who had turned into patrons, one's ability to "work hard and always look ahead", or "make the sign of the cross and never despair" crept up like an old mentor. To work was to master oneself. It was to affirm one's power to carry on and entertain a hope for the future, despite the shortcomings of the present. As one of the Roma informants noted, work was agency – or, in his words, an ability to "do something with [one]self", which was most evident in contrast to the idleness and self-abandon he located in the figure of the beggar. "At least if you steal something," my interviewee continued, "you do something, you make an effort, you risk something! But they [the beggars] do nothing at all whatsoever" (Anderson et al, 2018, 20).

The conceptions of work I encountered in my research and time at the Work Rights Centre reminded me of Hannah Arendt's thesis on the *vita activa*. In the *Human Condition*, Arendt (2013) described action, or the ability to do 'something', as the defining feature of humanity. Unlike the 'labour' of staying alive, and what she calls the 'work' of reproducing human societies, 'action' is the means of expressing individual freedom to create, and to be recognized as a creator. In a similar vein, other contributors to this volume document the yearning for a work filled with meaning, such as in Bäumer Escobar's account of the Catalonian cooperative, or the respect for work which seems little more than exploitative on the outside, as in Strauss's account of the fissured workplace.

COVID-19 and the lockdown that followed generated a dark, unexpected natural experiment into the contours of a world without work – or, at least, a world with fewer opportunities for paid work. For the first few weeks there had been instances where beneficiaries who called to speak to advisers broke down in tears or, as Lora described, could not bring themselves to accept the reality of the lockdown. Doing casework then was not only a matter of providing a service of mediation, it was also emotional labour, the 'management of hearts' (Hochschild, 2012), where the adviser simultaneously became a source of knowledge, hope, care and, wherever possible, humour: "You know what it's like with the teacher and the village priest," Raluca noted, "these were the people you turn to for advice. And I feel like I am a bit like that now. It's like someone said, I'm the village witch."

In his thesis on the Carnivalesque, Mikhail Bakhtin (1984) described the symbolic politics inherent in carnival – the figure of the buffoon playing king for a day, the caricature of a world turned upside down, which reveals the injustices of the present through a display of irreverent imagination. In a similar way, staff at the Work Rights Centre found small comfort in the 'haz de necaz' (literally translated from Romanian as 'fun of misfortune'). We found ourselves savouring the small moments of tragicomedy when, for instance, the group of Romanian car washers found out that not only had they been let go, but a couple of them had also had their identity documents stolen by someone who was using them to work in construction. A tragic sequence of events, by all accounts. But Marcel and his caseworker struggled to hold back the laughter when he remarked, in a nonchalant matter of fact way: "Who knew. I've been working at the car wash, but it turns out I'm an engineer!"

Humour does not reconfigure redistribution. It does not fix the injustices of a wage-centric grant package that penalized workers at the periphery, and it does not address the obscenity of a welfare system that gave the most precarious applicants *less*, on account of their inability to evidence their poverty. But it does create a small space for humanity, care and the imagination, at a time when not only livelihoods, but people's whole sense of self was thrust into uncertainty by the implosion of work. To laugh at oneself was a small act of resistance; an attempt to retake ownership of one's place in the world – even if only in the imagination. To laugh with another, similarly, was a means of building togetherness; an attempt to find a sense of ethical community – an intimacy born out of shared experience, as migrants and workers outside of the wage – parallel to the faceless figure of the digitized state.

Conclusion

At the time of writing, London is inching its way out of paralysis. Marcel has found a job at the supermarket, and charity advisers at the Work Rights Centre have helped his other colleagues apply for, and receive, the minimal sum they were entitled to through Universal Credit. A couple of them returned to the car wash as soon as it was open again.

The extraordinary months of lockdown resulting from the coronavirus pandemic opened a window into the possibilities and harms of a world without work. Taking the lens of the Work Rights Centre, this chapter has drawn attention to the labour of service and care deployed by advisers in order to enable people to get by in London's world without work. I have unpacked the process of translation of the state, and the sinousities of making migrants legible to the digital ledger. I then reflected on the emotional labour of recapturing a sense of self, when work had played a crucial role in migrants' sense of dignity, belonging and self-mastery.

In concluding, I do not want to romanticize the extraordinariness of either living, or supporting those, outside of the wage. There is little justice in the fact that charities are called upon to fill the gaps in state welfare systems, and in the fact that many do so from a position of precarity. In spite of the small comfort of the tragicomic, there is no denying that managing emotions takes its toll. Some advisers make a rite of offloading the emotional charge of the week, in management meetings and to each other. Others admit to taking a strategic emotional distance and are firm about the boundaries they set. I turn to writing.

If there is one thing to consider, and continue theorizing, it is the value of small acts of care – taking one's time to listen, to joke, to provide emotional and pastoral support, and not merely to problem solve. Some activists and social theorists call for a radical end of work, and a new politics of universal redistribution. The inequalities between welfare and wage-centric grants I reviewed here lend support to at least the second part of this proposition. Until that day, however, it is the everyday work of service providers like Lora and Raluca that make the present more liveable.

Acknowledgements

I am deeply indebted to all colleagues at the Work Rights Centre. It is their tireless work and comradeship that have enabled the charity to grow, and their insights that made this chapter possible. Any imperfections are my own.

Notes

[1] A more detailed account of Marcel and the car washers features in a case study I co-wrote with Ana-Maria Cirstea and published on the Work Rights Centre website (Cirstea and Vicol, 2020).

[2] This was updated from August 2020, to allow employers to split staff's time between work and furlough.

[3] This changed on 13 May, when self-employed individuals could actively make an application for government support.

[4] After the previous Conservative government cut legal aid for employment cases, cases brought to the employment tribunal plummeted.

References

Anderson, B. and Ruhs, M. (2012) 'Reliance on migrant labour: Inevitability or policy choice?' *Journal of Poverty and Social Justice*, 20: 23–30.

Anderson, B., Vicol, D.-O., Dupont, P.-L. and Morris, J. (2018) *Political representation and experienced recognition among Roma in the UK*, ETHOS – Towards a European Theory of Justice, University of Bristol. Available at https://www.ethos-europe.eu/sites/default/files/5.3_uk_replacement_for_d5.2.pdf

APS (2018) Population by Country of Birth. London Datastore, https://data.london.gov.uk/dataset/country-of-birth (accessed 6 September 2020).

Arendt, H. (2013) *The Human Condition*, Chicago, IL: University of Chicago Press.

Ash, J., Anderson, B., Gordon, R. and Langley, P. (2018) 'Digital interface design and power: Friction, threshold, transition', *Environment and Planning D: Society and Space*, 36: 1136–1153.

Auyero, J. (2011) 'Patients of the state: An ethnographic account of poor people's waiting', *Latin American Research Review*, 46: 5–29.

Bakhtin, M. (1984) *Rabelais and His World*, Bloomington, IN: Indiana University Press.

BBC News (2020) 'UK to pay wages for workers facing job losses', BBC News, available at https://www.bbc.com/news/ business-51982005, accessed 25 May 2020.

Beck, U. (2014) *The Brave New World of Work*, Cambridge: Polity.

Bloch, E. (1986) *The Principle of Hope* vol.1. Cambridge, MA: The MIT Press.

Booth, R. (2020) 'Rishi Sunak faces legal action from gig economy workers', The Guardian, available at https://www.theguardian.com/politics/2020/mar/22/rishi-sunak-under-pressure-to-bail-out-self-employed, accessed 14 June 2020.

Bubb, S. (2017) *The History of British Charity* (Lecture), Oxford: Charity Futures.

CBI (2020) *CBI responds to the Chancellor's latest support measures.* CBI, available at https://www.cbi.org.uk/media-centre/articles/cbi-responds-to-the-chancellors-latest-support-measures/, accessed 14 June 2020.

Cirstea, A.M. and Vicol, D.-O. (2020) 'The Carwashers'. Work Rights Centre, available at https://www.workrightscentre.org/case-studies/the-carwashers, accessed 25 June 2020.

Cohen, R. (2008) *Global Diasporas: An Introduction*, London: Routledge.

Deleuze, G. (1992) 'Postscript on the Societies of Control', *October*, 59: 3–7.

Dustmann, C., Frattini, T. and Halls, C. (2010) 'Assessing the fiscal costs and benefits of A8 migration to the UK', *Fiscal Studies*, 31: 1–41.

DWP (2018) *Universal credit full service survey*, Department for Work and Pensions.

Foucault, M. (1988) *Technologies of the Self: A Seminar with Michel Foucault*, Amherst, CA: University of Massachusetts Press.

Fox, J., Morosanu, L. and Szilassy, E. (2012) 'The racialization of the new European migration to the UK', *Sociology*, 46: 680–695.

Garapich, M. (2008) 'The migration industry and civil society: Polish immigrants in the United Kingdom before and after EU enlargement', *Journal of Ethnic and Migration Studies*, 34: 735–752.

Gov.uk (2013) 'An introduction to Universal Credit' [WWW Document], available at https://assets.publishing.service.gov.uk/government/uploads/system/uploads/attachment_data/file/263960/universal-credit-an-introduction.pdf

Graeber, D. (2015) *The Utopia of rules: On Technology, Stupidity, and the Secret Joys of Bureaucracy*, Brooklyn, NY: Melville House.

HM Treasury, Right Hon Rishi Sunak MP (2020) 'Chancellor gives support to millions of self-employed individuals', available at https://www.gov. uk/government/news/chancellor-gives-support-to-millions-of-self-employed-individuals

Hochschild, A.R. (2012) *The Managed Heart: Commercialization of Human Feeling*, Berkeley, CA: University of California Press.

Jayaweera, H. and Anderson, B. (2008) 'Migrant workers and vulnerable employment: A review of existing data', Centre on Migration, Policy and Society, Oxford University.

Lipsky, M. (1980) *Street Level Bureaucracy. Dilemmas of the Individual in Public Services*, New York, NY: Russell Sage Foundation.

MacKenzie, R. and Forde, C. (2009) 'The rhetoric of the "good worker" versus the realities of employers' use and the experiences of migrant workers', *Work, Employment & Society*, 23: 142–159.

May, J., Wills, J., Datta, K., Evans, Y., Herbert, J. and McIlwaine, C. (2007) 'Keeping London working: Global cities, the British state and London's new migrant division of labour', *Transactions of the Institute of British Geographers*, 32: 151–167.

Miyazaki, H. (2006) *The Method of Hope: Anthropology, Philosophy, and Fijian Knowledge*, Stanford, CA: Stanford University Press.

ONS (2020a) 'EMP17: People in employment on zero hours contracts – Office for National Statistics, available at https://www.ons.gov.uk/employmentandlabourmarket/peopleinwork/employmentandemployeetypes/datasets/emp17peopleinemploymentonzerohourscontracts

ONS (2020b) 'Employment in the UK – Office for National Statistics, available at https://www.ons.gov.uk/employmentandlabourmarket/peopleinwork/employmentandemployeetypes/bulletins/employmentintheuk/march2020.

ONS (2020c) 'Coronavirus and self-employment in the UK', Office for National Statistics, available at https://www.ons. gov.uk/employmentandlabourmarket/peopleinwork/ employmentandemployeetypes/articles/coronavirusandselfemploy mentintheuk/2020-04-24

Panayi, P. (2020) *Migrant City: A New History of London*, New Haven, CT: Yale University Press.

Power, M. (1997) *The Audit Society: Rituals of Verification*, Oxford: Oxford University Press.

Spencer, S. (2011) *The Migration Debate*, Bristol: Policy Press.

Standing, G. (2014) *A Precariat Charter: From Denizens to Citizens*, London: Bloomsbury.

Standing, G. (2020) 'Why the UK's job retention scheme makes no sense', *Financial Times*, available at http://ftalphaville. ft.com/2020/04/16/1587025923000/Why-the-UK-s-job-retention-scheme-makes-no-sense/

Strathern, M. (2000) 'Introduction: New accountabilities: Anthropological studies in audit, ethics and the academy', in *Audit Cultures*, London: Routledge, pp 1–19.

Sunak, R. (2020) 'The Chancellor Rishi Sunak provides an updated statement on coronavirus', available at https://www.gov.uk/ government/speeches/the-chancellor-rishi-sunak-provides-an-updated-statement-on-coronavirus

The Economist (2020a) 'Labour market – The jobs retention scheme's unintended consequences', 26 March, The Economist, available at https://www.economist.com/britain/2020/03/26/ the-jobs-retention-schemes-unintended-consequences

The Economist (2020b) 'Who bears risk – people or government?' The Economist, available at https://www.economist.com/ britain/2020/06/11/who-bears-risk-people-or-government, accessed 14 June 2020.

Vertovec, S. (2007) 'Super-diversity and its implications', *Ethnic and Racial Studies*, 30: 1024–1054.

Vicol, D.-O. (2020) 'Into and out of Citizenship, through personal tax payments: Romanian migrants' leveraging of British self-employment', *Social Analysis*, 64: 101–119.

Vicol, D.-O. and Allen, W. (2014) 'Bulgarians and Romanians in the British national press', The Migration Observatory, University of Oxford.

Vicol, D.-O. and Enescu, R. (2020) 'Our work in numbers Q3 2016–Q1 2020', Work Rights Centre, London.

12

Defending the Wage: Visions of Work and Distribution in Namibia

E. Fouksman

The idea of giving people money – with no strings attached, simply to ensure a minimum standard of living – is enjoying a global moment. Over the last decade, the UN and the International Labour Organization (ILO) have been promoting the idea of universal social protection floors. Rather than the old-fashioned social safety net, which was there to catch those who fell, a social protection floor is a baseline to build on, typically in the form of cash to those who need it (often along with other public goods such as health care) (ILO, 2012). The 2016 Swiss referendum on instituting a universal basic income guarantee (a sum of money unconditionally and regularly disbursed to every resident – also known as a basic income grant, a negative income tax or a social dividend) garnered a huge amount of press attention around the world, despite the proposal being rejected by 77 per cent of Swiss voters. Finland, the Netherlands, Scotland, Kenya and the US are all sites of recent, ongoing or planned universal basic income experiments – some funded by national governments, some by municipalities or provinces, others by private philanthropy.

Meanwhile, conditional and unconditional cash transfers – both policy cousins of basic income – have become fashionable interventions in the world of international development. Cash transfers have moved from NGO and university-run experiments, to government welfare programmes,[1] and have garnered the support of large mainstream development institutions. In 2015 World Bank president Jim Yong Kim and ILO director general Guy Ryder co-authored a joint mission and plan of action to promote universal social protection – to provide '*income security* and support *to all people* ... Anyone who needs social protection should be able to access it' (ILO and World Bank, 2015, my emphasis).

At the root of these proposals lies the possibility of something novel and radical: a partial decommodification of labour, a separation between basic livelihood and wage work. As an increasing number of people around the globe are transformed into 'surplus populations' no longer needed by labour markets, nor able to access land in order to provide for their own subsistence (Li, 2010, 2013), wage work has begun to look untenable as the sole source of income security.

The surge of policy interest in universalizing social protection in both the global North and South has been greeted with excitement by a number of academics – James Ferguson has referred to it as the dawn of a 'new politics of distribution' (2015, 80) while Hanlon et al (2010) call it a quiet 'revolution from the South'. Yet just how new are such proposals? Basic income of one form or another has been a policy proposal for at least 220 years, since Thomas Paine's land-tax-funded proposal for a universal inheritance in *Agrarian Justice* (Paine, 1796; Birnbaum, 2016). There have been other historical moments in which universal redistribution stood at the brink of reality, for instance, in the UK in the years leading up to World War II, in the US in the 1970s, and in southern Africa in the early 2000s (Widerquist, 2017). In all these cases, universal systems of redistribution were ultimately rejected by policy makers, often in favour of either welfare schemes that only benefit those physically unable to engage in wage labour (children, the elderly, the disabled) or public work programmes. Why?

The obvious answer is elite interests. Economic and policy elites underscore the existences of the undeserving poor (see Strong, this volume), who misuse their welfare pay-outs. Politicians insist that money must come from work and worry about the lazy poor. In the words of Hein Marais, welfare and social protection systems everywhere tend to pivot on the idea that 'waged work and entrepreneurial zest will provide a secure basis for well-being for the majority of society' (2018, 84). The assumption is that such ideas and systems are the product of policy makers and politically influential elites.

But what about the attitudes of those who stand to benefit the most from universal income guarantees? This population represents a less obvious, more counter-intuitive source of resistance to universalizing social protection. Based on interviews in two rural sites in Namibia, this chapter proposes that it is not only politicians, economic elites or even the middle classes who are reluctant to divorce income from wage labour, and who cling on to the idea that 'employment is available to those who seek it and that waged work ensures well-being' (Marais, 2018, 86). Instead, my research suggests that such attachment to wage labour as the key legitimate source of resources is often held by the very people to whom waged work is *un*available or is insufficient to ward off poverty and hardship. Rather than being imposed from above, this attachment is often held by the very people who are failed by the current workfarist system.

This chapter examines grassroots resistance to universal social protection policies, with a particular focus on poor unemployed and underemployed populations. Based on interviews with the long-term unemployed in Namibia (with some reference to more recent periods of fieldwork in urban South Africa), I highlight the existence of a deeply held resistance to receiving income from (or through) the state without labour – even among those that only survive thanks to social grants and other government transfers. I argue that the logic behind this resistance is rooted in three forms of attachment to wage labour: a *moral* attachment to wage labour as a source of worth and deservingness; a *psychological and physiological* categorization of wage labour as a source of mental and physical well-being; and a *social* attachment to wage labour as a source of community and social relationships.

The logics behind such broadly held attachment to wage labour must be understood and challenged if a new politics of distribution is to be realized. While governments and economists have claimed that universalizing social protection is neither fiscally feasible nor socially desirable (Barchiesi, 2011), scholars have focused on taking apart the dependency arguments against universal income security (Ferguson, 2013, 2015). In this chapter, I propose that it is moral, social and cultural logics and intuitions around the links between wage labour and income that lie at the root of broad-based resistance to the separation of employment and livelihood.

Grants, unemployment and poverty in Namibia

Namibia is an ideal lens through which to explore attachments to wage work. Like many other countries in sub-Saharan Africa, wage labour and work discipline in Namibia was inflicted through both coercive and ideological means by first German and then White South African colonial rule (Seekings and Nattrass, 2005; Nattrass and Seekings, 2011; Wallace, 2011; Cooper, 2018).[2] First Christian missionaries and then colonial administrators insisted upon the value of what they referred to as the 'work ethic' in transforming 'lazy natives' into hard-working labourers (Wallace, 2011). This ideology was enforced through centuries of land and water dispossession and the imposition of hut and land taxes which forced people into the cash economy, and thus into various forms of forced and bonded labour. These violent interventions produced a migrant labour system in which Namibians were compelled to work in mines (long a major source of national wealth in Namibia) and on White-owned farms for six-month to two-year periods, before returning to their communities and grazing lands. Forged in the colonial era, this system has left a lasting mark on Namibian culture, politics and society.

Under late nineteenth-century German rule, short-term contract labour in the diamond mines and on the road and railway crews was a way for young Black men to acquire material wealth and social status, as well as to 'define new meanings of modernity in their behaviour, dress and language' (Wallace, 2011, 95). And under twentieth-century apartheid South African rule – which reproduced the migrant contract labour system while deepening race-based dispossession and segregation – wage labour (and in particular labour unions) became the site of nationalist anti-apartheid organizing and resistance, often through contact with South African protest politics (Barchiesi, 2011; Wallace, 2011; Lawhon et al, 2018).

For much of Namibia's colonial history, labour was a scarce resource. First German and then South African administrations attempted to coercively (and often violently) extract labour by depriving native people of land and mobility. These policies were backed by an ideological commitment to 'prevent[ing] vagrancy and idleness' (The Native Labour Commission, 1920, cited in Wallace, 2011, 219). Yet by the late 1970s, Namibia had shifted from a labour-scarce to a labour-surplus economy. A time of drought and recession, this period also saw the rise of organized labour resistance and mass strikes against the contract system in Namibia. The trade union movement expanded rapidly in the 1980s, along with labour militancy, which increasingly became a tactic against the apartheid South African regime (Wallace, 2011). Much as in South Africa and other parts of the continent, by the time Namibian independence was won in the 1990s, national liberation parties valorized the organized working class and the unionized worker as the site of resistance to not only economic, but also political oppression (Cooper, 2005; Barchiesi, 2011; Lawhon et al, 2018). In short, the history of wage labour and the capitalist productivist work ethic is a complicated one in Namibia, as it is in southern Africa more broadly. Wage work has long been resisted as a site of racialized exploitation and coercion (Comaroff and Comaroff, 1987; Makhulu, 2012), yet simultaneously valorized and desired as a vehicle of urbanization and modernity, a symbol of socio-economic status, and a source of political action and citizenship.

These contradictions continue in contemporary Namibia, where endemic unemployment has persisted from the late 1970s. Namibia is classed as an upper middle-income country with high levels of poverty, unemployment (33 per cent overall, and 46 per cent for youth in 2018 (Namibia Statistics Agency, 2019)), and inequality (by some metrics Namibia is the second most unequal major country in the world, after South Africa) (World Bank, 2020). In response to these challenges Namibia operates a welfare grant system that is similar to, though less extensive, than South Africa's. These grants support the elderly through a pension scheme dating back to the 1960s, as well as disabled people and children in foster care via direct cash transfers. It is significant that these transfers go to those physically unable to work – indeed, unlike in South Africa, even children in poor households do not receive monetary support from the state, unless they are orphaned or in foster care. As Ferguson argues (2015, 156), the list of those requiring 'social' intervention continues to trace 'a kind of photographic negative of the figure of the wage-earning man'.

A coalition of churches, NGOs, labour unions and activists began to advocate for a basic income grant in Namibia in the 2000s. The feather in the Basic Income Grant Coalition's cap is a basic income pilot, which ran for two years (2008–9) in the small village of Otjivero and was financed by German church groups and NGOs. The results of the pilot were compelling: though only giving out 100 Namibian dollars (about US$9) per month to each recipient, crime fell by 42 per cent, food poverty fell from 76 per cent to 16 per cent, school dropout rates went from 40 per cent to zero, and engagement in economic activities went up from 44 per cent to 55 per cent (Haarmann et al, 2009).

However, despite these apparent successes, then-President Pohamba rejected the proposal out of hand, emphasizing that 'we can't dish out money for free to people who do nothing' (Haarmann and Haarmann, 2012, 8). The labour unions followed his lead, leaving the Basic Income Grant (BIG) Coalition. Basic income activists thus waited in hope for a change in government policy following the election of President Geingob in 2015. Not only had Geingob paid for a family's basic income during the Otjivero pilot, but once in office he appointed the former head of the Coalition, Bishop Zephania Kameeta, as the head of the new Ministry of Poverty Eradication. Many activists around the world saw this as a possible return of basic income to Namibia's main policy agenda. However, these hopes were dampened in 2016, when Geingob released the Harambee Prosperity Plan, which explicitly stated that basic income was *not* part of the plan. Instead it proposed instituting food banks and infrastructure-oriented youth work programmes (Republic of Namibia, 2016). This turn away from the enthusiasm around universal basic income seemed confirmed by Namibia's Fifth National Development Plan (2017–22), which makes no mention of basic income. The Ministry of Poverty Eradication's 2018 Strategic Plan and its 2018 Blueprint only mention basic income in passing and do not suggest implementing the policy (Ministry of Poverty Eradication and Social Welfare, 2018a, 2018b; Republic of Namibia, 2017).

But there are some recent signs of revival. The list of those eligible to receive social payments has been expanded to include unemployed adults who do not receive another form of grant in light of the COVID-19 pandemic (though this is only a one-off payment). Furthermore, President Geingob recently mentioned 'investigating the feasibility' of shifting from foodbanks to what he termed 'a modified basic income grant' in his State of the Nation address in June 2020 (The Presidency, 2020).

In this context of inequality, high unemployment and policy debates around universal forms of income security, how do Namibia's poor and unemployed think about the decoupling of income and work?

Income and labour in Namibia: a rooted attachment

Many of the long-term unemployed poor that I spoke with in Namibia had heard of basic income – though most did not recognize the term 'basic income grant'. The 2008–9 pilot project in Namibia may have spread the idea of universal basic income in ways that public policy discussions and advocacy campaigns simply cannot. Indeed, the Basic Income Grant Coalition had capitalized on the outreach possibilities of the pilot by sending pilot participants to speak about their experiences in other towns and cities (Herbert Jauch, personal communication, 8 April 2016).

I spent time interviewing some of those in the village of Otjivero who had taken part in the basic income pilot. Everyone I spoke with – the young and old, male and female – supported the proposal and spoke highly of their experience during the pilot. All wanted the basic income grant to resume, and insisted that even with its small size (NAM$100 or what was then USD$12 per month) the grant had made a real difference in their lives. One young woman told me that the grant enabled her to leave the village to go to search for work in Windhoek (Namibia's capital, an hour's drive in a pricy shared taxi). Another noted that she opened a hair salon during the pilot and her customer base swelled, illustrating the knock-on effects of income transfer programmes in promoting local growth and entrepreneurship. Others told me that the grant provided them with food security so that they did not have to worry about feeding their children or grandchildren during that time. Many used the grant to buy food and travel to look for work, but also to buy phones and TVs, making them feel "connected to the world", in the words of the village's former school principal. Everyone expressed disappointment that the grant ended, though most were optimistic that the current president, who seemed to be widely liked, would do something similar to a basic income, even if it was not called such in name.

But some key nuances began to emerge when I asked people whether they would prefer the government to provide a basic income grant or a public work programme of some kind. Even when I proposed that the amount of money paid out would be same in both the grant and the work programme, and left the type of work and the hours in the work programme quite vague, many of my respondents told me that they would prefer the work programme. A middle-aged woman with ten dependents (children and grandchildren) who was enthusiastic in her initial support of the basic income pilot insisted that a work programme would suit her better than a grant because she is "at home doing nothing all day, and she wants to get out, to be active". When I asked what jobs would be ideal, she proposed sewing or ironing, which surprised me as this type of work is done inside, without much movement. When I pushed and asked why she did not simply choose to receive the grant and then look for work, or spend her time pursuing enjoyable but unpaid outdoor activities, she insisted "There is nothing to do here, the village is too small." In fact, her ideal state intervention would be for the government to build a factory near the village (in part because she thought the pay would be higher than any government grant).

Others in Otjivero echoed this preference for a work programme rather than cash transfers, even when the amount of money to be gained from each was the same. A young woman[3] I spoke with in the village told me that while she thought a basic income grant was a good idea, she preferred a work programme because she wanted to "keep busy, not just stay at home." Similarly, two young men I spoke with told me that the basic income was a "good programme", that they would want the government to implement it, and when prompted even said they would be willing to participate in a demonstration or protest in Windhoek in support of a basic income grant. Yet they both told me that they would prefer a work programme that paid the same amount because "there is nothing to do, and [we] need something to do." Wage work, by contrast, "gives health, it's not good to do nothing." Boredom and physicality are key motifs in all of these responses. Work for my interlocutors represented a source of purpose, diversion and physical well-being.

However, not everyone in Otjivero shared this liking for work programmes. Several young women told me that they would prefer a grant over an employment programme because they would use the money to run a hair and beauty salon. One of these young women had in fact done exactly this during the basic income pilot, and the others were her sisters and friends. Inspired by her success during that time, they intended to pool together to do the same if a basic income ever reappeared in Otjivero. It is significant that even in these cases, those who preferred a transfer over a work programme had a clear business proposal in mind, which would give them easy access to work that would be facilitated by a grant. Work for payment (in this case for profit rather than wage) nevertheless remained the preferred choice.

This emphasis on the role of work in providing 'busyness' and relief from boredom was echoed by many of the people I spoke with in Otjivero, throwing new light on attachment to work among the unemployed and underemployed. Unlike my findings from comparative research in South Africa, where the long-term unemployed were apprehensive that giving money 'for nothing' to able-bodied adults might lead to idleness or misuse (Fouksman, 2020), the residents of Otjivero were not deeply bound up in moral concerns with the laziness of grant recipients. Instead, wage labour was understood to play a psychological and physiological, almost a medicinal role in people's lives. My interlocutors seemed to value busyness as an end in itself (Weeks, 2011; Bellezza et al, 2017) – watching TV or talking with friends was not sufficient as a way to pass time, nor was there anything else to take wage work's place. Work also seems to be needed as external motivation to activity, to action – and perhaps thus to meaning. When I asked whether such busyness could be gained outside of wage labour, the suggestion was quickly dismissed. André Gorz's category of 'non-commodity activities', including 'work for self' (work that is necessary but not bought and sold, such as housework or child rearing) and 'autonomous activity' (activities for mastery and pleasure, such as creative or social activities like singing in a church choir), was not on the table, or even in the conversation in Namibia (Gorz, 1989).[4]

The preference for wage work over transfers was repeated in Spitzkoppe village in western Namibia. This small village is far from Otjivero, and most of the people I spoke with there had not heard of the pilot or the English term 'basic income', though many had heard about the idea of a universal grant. As in Otjivero, many of the people I spoke with thought the idea of a universal grant was a good one – though some did hold moral concerns regarding grants leading to laziness and misuse (Fouksman, 2020). And yet, as in Otjivero, almost everyone I spoke with said that they would prefer a public work programme over a grant, even if they paid the same amount.

There was of course variation in these responses. One young woman I spoke with wavered between a preference for a food-for-work programme – because she would not worry about others misspending grant money – and a cash for work programme – because she needed to buy her children clothing, not just feed them. Her concern with misspending echoed the moral concerns I heard in my fieldwork in South Africa, where many long-term underemployed people worried about the potential misuse of more universally accessible social grants on alcohol and drugs (Fouksman, 2020). Crucially, both of her suggestions were for work programmes, not cash transfers. When I asked about this preference, she repeated again and again that "one must work for money." She saw no need for further explanation – it seemed to her to be something obvious, beyond explaining.

A group of men I spoke with in the village – one in his thirties, two middle aged and one the oldest man in the village at 90 years old – also expressed some difference of opinion overlying a uniform desire for wage labour. One of them, an artist who painted t-shirts, spoke the liturgy of entrepreneurship. He told me that rather than giving grants, the government should give everyone start-up loans so that they could grow businesses; that everyone should be a businessman. One of the middle-aged men agreed; he thought livestock was the way to go, and that the government should start everyone off with some chickens. They all initially thought a universal grant was a good idea (all agreed that they would be willing to go to the capital and agitate for it from the government), but one of the middle-aged men was concerned that it might make people 'lazy', even though he himself would invest it in a business. But as the conversation evolved all four men waivered in their assessment, and at times thought that it was better to work for money, that "money for free is bad" – once more, a definitive moral judgement, a moral grammar that seemed obvious to everyone. Another of the men was convinced that the government would eventually stop a basic income grant because of the "the lazy people" that would take advantage of the grant, echoing the workerist discourses of both colonial and some present-day governing elites.

When I asked why a work programme was better than a grant that pays the same amount, one of the answers that emerged was that a work programme was likely to benefit the local community. My interlocutors suggested that it might help clean up the village or achieve essential public works. Indeed, although there was a broad agreement that it is "better to work for money, and money for free is bad", the social and personal meaning of the work was as important as the moral. For example, when I asked if the men would be willing to dig a ditch and then fill it in over and over again in return for wages, all said absolutely not – they wanted their work to be helpful, to have purpose. The 90-year-old man added that cash grants were appropriate for the elderly, who had already worked their whole life, but a young person "mustn't wait for money, must work", and if the young "sit around and do nothing" they will remain like that "for their whole life" (a close echo of the discourse around the chronic nature of welfare dependency in the US and UK). After much probing, one of the middle-aged men agreed that a basic income could enable the community to self-organize and improve itself. But this took much discussion – and the other men remained doubtful that this would actually happen.

Reframing redistribution

What was missing from these discussions – in contrast to academic debates on basic income – was any mention of the moral imperative of redistribution, that the rich should be giving some of their wealth to the poor. I proposed this directly in Spitzkoppe, and the men agreed that the government should make the rich give up some of their money to the poor, but only after considerable prompting. Ferguson (2015) has argued that the increasing popularity of cash transfers and debates around basic income might be tied to a growing sense that such grants are a 'rightful share' of national wealth. However, this connection was not obvious to many of the people I spoke with. Despite appeals to distributory justice in the academic literature, most of the men and women I interviewed in Namibia did not see social grants in this light.

Yet when I reframed basic income as a matter of distribution, people enthusiastically supported the idea. Indeed, even those who were initially reluctant to support a basic income grant became enthusiastic when I described it as not a government 'grant' but a 'dividend' or a rightful share of the country's wealth. This became clear when I conducted comparative fieldwork in South Africa, where I heard largely the same sentiments as held by my interlocutors in Namibia. Initially, many expressed a preference for wage work over other forms of resource distribution and called on the state to provide jobs rather than to directly distribute cash grants (Fouksman, 2020). But I added new questions at the end of the interviews, asking what people thought of a universal natural resource dividend, a share of natural resource wealth that would be distributed to all citizens on a monthly basis. To my surprise, even the people who thought 'getting money for nothing' was categorically bad or would lead to laziness or misuse of the funds were in support of this proposal. Take, for instance, Mthokozisi, a 19-year-old who lived in an abandoned warehouse in inner-city Johannesburg, South Africa. When I first brought up the idea of a basic income grant, he insisted that this was a bad idea because "if you give people a grant, [people] will waste it, [they will] just sit around." However, when I reframed the idea of a basic income grant as instead a share of South Africa's natural resource wealth that could be given out to every citizen, he enthusiastically supported the idea, and his concern with laziness appeared to fade away. When I asked him the difference between receiving such a share and a grant, he told me, "We must benefit from our economy ... a social grant comes from the government, not the mine – that's the difference." The psychic space between grant and share, charity and right, seems to be vast for my interlocutors.

In order to understand why wage labour remains central to accessing income, even in a place of such high systemic unemployment and inequality as in Namibia, we must pay attention to the nuances of the way ordinary people think about distribution, and the deeply rooted links between cash, work ethic and deservingness. As I have argued elsewhere (see Dawson and Fouksman, 2020; Fouksman, 2020), my interlocutors were not resistant to all forms of redistribution; nor did they think that the state has no role to play in distributory justice. Indeed, many of them were dependent on networks of distribution between family members, romantic partners and patrons, wherein distribution becomes a social as well as an economic activity (Ferguson, 2013, 2015). They emphasized that the state *should* provide them with education, health, housing, land and services such as sewage, electricity and water, as well as income-generating jobs. And as Mthokozisi's comments show, they did not oppose the distribution of what is seen as collective wealth, such as land or natural resources. Indeed, as noted as the start of this chapter, a more just redistribution of land and natural resources formed a key focal point of anti-colonial struggles in Namibia. Yet it is worth noting that the idea of a natural resource dividend did not come up spontaneously in my interviews, but only emerged when introduced by me. While for my interlocutors land seemed a natural place to claim a share of collective resource, cash – and in particular livelihood and social protection – still seemed to be associated with wage labour.

Many theorists of post-work take as a given that shortening working hours, guaranteeing income security to all regardless of wage labour, and decommoditizing work to allow more 'autonomous activity' (Gorz, 1989) would be popular among 'ordinary' people (Frayne, 2015, 119). For instance, while acknowledging the ongoing centrality of the capitalist work ethic, Gorz (1999) argues that people prefer to engage in meaningful 'multi-activity' that is not bought and sold for a wage or a profit. But the evidence for these assumptions is almost exclusively based on the opinions of well-educated middle class or upper middle class workers in the global North, who are either employed or have the option to be employed in relatively stable, secure, decently paid white-collar jobs. This group critiques wage labour for being unfulfilling, full of 'bullshit' tasks with no real value, or too all-consuming in the face of other forms of necessary and meaningful activity (Gorz, 1999; Frayne, 2015; Graeber, 2018). Yet the empirical research presented in this chapter calls into question how much can be generalized from such a group. It might seem intuitive to assume that if people with relatively privileged positions in the global labour market are dissatisfied with the centrality of wage labour and the productivist work ethic in their everyday lives, then those most disadvantaged by this system – such as those quoted in this chapter – would be even more critical. Yet my research suggests the opposite. My interlocutors expressed deep nostalgia for a mid-twentieth-century Fordist vision of social membership and citizenship via universally available wage work. This 'post-Fordist affect' (Muehlebach and Shoshan, 2012) has been shaped by Namibia's history of national liberation and the political centrality of wage workers during the colonial and apartheid period, as well as the pervasive normalization of inequality through the rhetoric of hard work, meritocracy and deservingness.

Conclusion: towards new post-work imaginaries

In the words of Frederick Cooper, 'imaginative projects have material consequences' (1996, 457). Despite a context of wide-ranging structural unemployment and high inequality, my interlocutors do not all believe that income security should be unconditionally guaranteed. Their resistance to the idea of redistribution via universal *cash grants* (when framed as welfare or social protection) seems to stem from three types of attachment to wage work: moral, psychological and social. The first is concerned with ways in which social payments might produce 'laziness' and misuse of money by absolving recipients of their obligation to engage in paid employment. The second is based on a longing for the structure, activeness and busyness that work is seen to bring. And the last is concerned with the ways in which paid work provides collective goods and builds social relationships. All three of these attachments are ultimately linked to *time use* – how, where, and with whom our time is spent, and what this says about us, our moral worth, our place in the world.

The testimonies presented here thus invite us – as workers and as researchers – to reflect on our own ideas of the right and wrong ways to spend time. It is these assumptions that must be 'made strange' if universalist redistributory systems and the decommodification of labour could ever become widely accepted and demanded. Current debates on automation and a post-work future (Coote et al, 2010; Srnicek and Williams, 2015) must then be tied to new political and social imaginaries around both resource distribution and time use that go *beyond* the idea that basic income provides compensation for the unemployment caused by automation. We need to try to imagine what meaningful activity and the just distribution of time and resources could look like in such a future.

There are two possible utopian approaches here: one political, one academic, but both integral to the other. The first approach is to connect current interest in social protection floors and universal basic income to the campaign for shorter working hours. This approach would distribute available opportunities for wage work in an era of wage work attachment while destabilizing the moral assertion that 'hard work' is the key to deserving income and wealth. Alongside this, we must reframe proposals for universal income security not as a form of welfare or poverty alleviation, but rather as a way of justly distributing shares of collective wealth that is already rightfully ours.

The second approach is to reimagine social, cultural and political institutions that are able to replace the meaning-making and relational dimensions of work (Standing, 2009). This terrain is largely missing from the public imagination and would include the resurgence of voluntary associations, the defence of public and community space, the reform of education systems, and the rise of 'leisure unions' alongside labour unions. We must take seriously current moral, social and psychological attachments to wage labour, not to defend such attachments but rather to reimagine how they could be fulfilled outside of labour markets. This will require empirical work that unpicks what people think and desire – and to what extent these desires are a response to the normalization of wealth accumulation and inequality. Only with such 'thick' understanding can we really begin to reimagine new categories and structures to challenge and replace the current attachment to wage employment.

In order to realize a new politics of distribution, we first need to engage in the long-term political work of reclaiming livelihood, identity and community from the confines of wage labour. We need interventions that are sensitive to the social, psychological and moral as well as the economic role that wage labour plays in people's lives, and the way this is varied and differentiated across geography and class. We need to understand the broader social role of wage labour in mediating facets of our social experience – particularly the imposition of structure, value, order and hierarchy. People chose to engage in wage labour not simply for income, but to be embedded in capitalist relationships of dependence (Ferguson, 2013) and discipline. In a world in which the promise of stable, full-time wage employment has become a form of 'cruel optimism' (Berlant, 2006), we must create a new social imaginary in which our livelihoods, identities and communities are built upon mechanisms beyond the wage.

Acknowledgements

This work has been made possible by the funding support from the Ford Foundation and the Leverhulme Trust. It has also benefited from the support and feedback of members of the Society, Work and Politics Institute (SWOP), where the chapter was first workshopped, the African Studies Centre at the University of Oxford, and participants in the Post-Wage Economy Workshop at Queen Mary University London. My sincere thanks to all of them, as well as the editors of this volume, for their time, engagement and insight.

Notes

[1]   The most well-known large-scale cash transfer programmes include Mexico's Oportunidades (more recently called Prospera) and Brazil's Bolsa Família (both government run, conditional and targeted at low-income families), as well as the NGO GiveDirectly's unconditional (but targeted) cash transfer programme in East Africa. Universal basic income grants have been piloted in Namibia and India, and now are about to be experimented with in East Africa (by GiveDirectly), Europe, Canada and the US. All of these are small-scale pilots. For a recent meta-review of cash transfers see Bastagli et al (2016).

[2]   While Namibia officially became a German colony in 1884, and was then ruled by South Africa from 1920 to 1990, the colonial encounter in Namibia dates back

to 1485, intensified from the early nineteenty century, and included not only the Germans, but also the Portuguese, British and Dutch.

3   This interview subject had not received the grant during the pilot because she was working outside the area at the time, but her sisters had been recipients.

4   It is beyond this chapter and even this project to hypothesize in detail the reasons and histories behind these attachments, though potential explanations could range from the history of capitalism in southern Africa to contemporary education to socialization to a cultural and public world that is built around the idea of full-time work for all. 'Work for self' and 'autonomous activity' might require teachers, equipment, space and places of interaction, as well as a society that no longer valorizes wage work – all of which are missing in a place like Otjivero.

References

Barchiesi, F. (2011) *Precarious Liberation: Workers, the State, and Contested Social Citizenship in Postapartheid South Africa*, Albany, NY: SUNY Press.

Bastagli, F., Hagen-Zanker, J., Harman, L., Barca, V., Sturge, G., Schmidt, T. and Pellerano, L. (2016) *Cash Transfers: What Does the Evidence Say?* London: Overseas Development Institute.

Bellezza, S., Paharia, N. and Keinan, A. (2017) 'Conspicuous consumption of time: When busyness and lack of leisure time become a status symbol', *Journal of Consumer Research*, 44: 118–138.

Berlant, L. (2006) 'Cruel Optimism', *Differences: A Journal of Feminist Cultural Studies*, 17(5): 20–36.

Birnbaum, S. (2016) 'Basic Income', *Oxford Research Encyclopedia of Politics* (Nov 2016): 1–29.

Comaroff, J.L. and Comaroff, J. (1987) 'The Madman and the Migrant: Work and Labor in the Historical Consciousness of a South African People', *American Ethnologist*, 14(2): 191–209.

Cooper, F. (1996) *Decolonization and African Society: The Labor Question in French and British Africa*, Cambridge: Cambridge University Press.

Cooper, F. (2005) *Colonialism in Question: Theory, Knowledge, History*, Berkeley, CA: University of California Press.

Cooper, F. (2018) 'From Enslavement to Precarity? The Labour Question in African History', in Adebanwi, W. (ed) *The Political Economy of Everyday Life in Africa*, pp 135–156.

Coote, A., Franklin, J. and Simms, A. (2010) *21 Hours: Why a Shorter Working Week Can Help Us All to Flourish in the 21st Century*, London: The New Economic Foundation.

Dawson, H. and Fouksman, E. (2020) 'Labour, laziness and distribution: Work imaginaries among the South African unemployed', *Africa*, 90(2): 229–251.

Ferguson, J. (2013) 'Declarations of dependence: Labour, personhood, and welfare in Southern Africa', *Journal of the Royal Anthropological Institute*, 19(2): 223–242.

Ferguson, J. (2015) *Give a Man a Fish: Reflections on the New Politics of Distribution*, Durham, NC and London: Duke University Press.

Fouksman, E. (2020) 'The moral economy of work: Demanding jobs and deserving money in South Africa', *Economy and Society*, 49(2): 287–311.

Frayne, D. (2015) *The Refusal of Work: The Theory and Practice of Resistance to Work*, London: Zed Books.

Gorz, A. (1989) *Critique of Economic Reason*, New York, NY: Verso.

Gorz, A. (1999) *Reclaiming Work: Beyond the Wage-Based Society*, Cambridge: Polity.

Graeber, D. (2018) *Bullshit Jobs: A Theory*, London: Allen Lane.

Haarmann, C. and Haarmann, D. (2012) 'Piloting basic income in Namibia – Critical reflections on the process and possible lessons', in *Pathways to a Basic Income: 14th Congress of the Basic Income Earth Network (BIEN)*, Munich.

Haarmann, C., Haarmann, D., Jauch, H., Shindondola-Mote, H., Nattrass, N., van Niekerk, I. and Samson, M. (2009) *Making the Difference! The BIG in Namibia: Basic Income Grant Assessment Report, April 2009*.

Hanlon, J., Barrientos, A. and Hulme, D. (2010) *Just Give Money to the Poor: The Development Revolution from the Global South*, Sterling, VA: Kumarian Press.

International Labour Office (2012) *Social Security for All: Building Social Protection Floors and Comprehensive Social Security Systems. The Strategy of the International Labour Organization*.

International Labour Organization and the World Bank Group (2015) 'Joint Statement by World Bank Group President Jim Yong Kim and ILO Director General Guy Ryder', available at http://www.ilo.org/wcmsp5/groups/public/---dgreports/---dcomm/documents/statement/wcms_378989.pdf

Lawhon, M., Millington, N. and Stokes, K. (2018) 'A labour question for the 21st century: Perpetuating the work ethic in the absence of jobs in South Africa's waste sector', *Journal of Southern African Studies*, 44(6): 1115–1131.

Li, T.M. (2010) 'To Make Live or Let Die? Rural Dispossession and the Protection of Surplus Populations', *Antipode*, 41(1): 66–93.

Li, T.M. (2013) 'Jobless growth and relative surplus populations', *Anthropology Today*, 29(3): 1–2.

Makhulu, A.M. (2012) 'The conditions for after work: Financialization and informalization in posttransition South Africa', *Pmla*, 127(4): 782–799.

Marais, H. (2018) 'The employment crisis, just transition and the universal basic income grant', in V. Satgar (ed), *The Climate Crisis: South African and Global Democratic Eco-Socialist Alternatives*, Johannesburg: Wits University Press, pp 70–106.

Ministry of Poverty Eradication and Social Welfare (2018a) 'Blueprint on Wealth Redistribution and Poverty Eradication', Windhoek.

Ministry of Poverty Eradication and Social Welfare (2018b) 'Strategic Plan 2017/2018–2021/2022', Windhoek.

Muehlebach, A. and Shoshan, N. (2012) 'Introduction', *Anthropological Quarterly*, 85(2): 317–343.

Namibia Statistics Agency (2019) *The Namibia Labour Force Survey 2018 Report*, Windhoek.

Nattrass, N. and Seekings, J. (2011) 'The Economy and poverty in the twentieth century', in Hamilton, C., Mbenga, B. and Ross, R. (eds) *The Cambridge history of South Africa, Vol. 2*, Cambridge: Cambridge University Press, pp 518–572.

Paine, T. (1796) *Agrarian Justice*, digital edn, available at www.grundskyld.dk

Republic of Namibia (2016) 'Harambee prosperity plan, 2016/17–2019/20: Namibian government's action plan towards prosperity for all', Windhoek.

Republic of Namibia (2017) 'Namibia's Fifth National Development Plan', Windhoek: Government of Namibia.

Seekings, J. and Nattrass, N. (2005) *Class, Race, and Inequality in South Africa*, New Haven, CT: Yale University Press.

Srnicek, N. and Williams, A. (2015) *Inventing the Future: Postcapitalism and the World without Work*, London: Verso.

Standing, G. (2009) *Work After Globalization: Building Occupational Citizenship*. Cheltenham, UK and Northampton, MA: Edward Elgar Publishing.

The Presidency (2020) 'State of the Nation Address by His Excellency Dr Hage G. Geingob, President of the Republic of Namibia', Windhoek.

Wallace, M. (2011) *A History of Namibia: From the Beginning to 1990*, New York, NY: Columbia University Press.

Weeks, K. (2011) *Problem with Work: Feminism, Marxism, Antiwork Politics, and Postwork Imaginaries*, Durham, NC and London: Duke University Press.

Widerquist, K. (2017) 'Basic income's third wave', *Open Democracy*, 18 October.

World Bank (2020) 'GINI Index (World Bank Estimate)', available at http://data.worldbank.org/indicator/SI.POV.GINI/, accessed 7 June 2020.

Index